my **revision** notes

OCR GCSE (9–1)

HISTORY A

EXPLAINING THE MODERN WORLD

Aly Boniface
Catherine Flaherty
Lizzy James
Harriet Salkeld
Martin Spafford

HODDER EDUCATION
AN HACHETTE UK COMPANY

The Publishers would like to thank the following for permission to reproduce copyright material.

Photo credits: p35 Heritage Image Partnership Ltd/Alamy Stock Photo; **p43*l*** Chronicle/Alamy Stock Photo; **p43*r*** INTERFOTO/Alamy Stock Photo; **p49** Pictorial Press Ltd/Alamy Stock Photo; **p53** McCutcheon, John T. Artist, A Wise Economist Asks a Question. C, 1931/Library of Congress LC-USZC4-13012; **p57*l*** National Museum of American History, Kenneth E. Behring Center; **p57*r*** Library of Congress, LC-DIG-fsac-1a35337; **p139** Pictorial Press Ltd/Alamy Stock Photo; **p145** FALKENSTEINFOTO/Alamy Stock Photo; **p151** World History Archive/Alamy Stock Photo.

Acknowledgement: Palgrave Macmillan for an extract from *Chamberlain and Appeasement: British Policy and the Coming of the Second World War* by Robert Parker, 1993.

Every effort has been made to trace all copyright holders, but if any have been inadvertently overlooked, the Publishers will be pleased to make the necessary arrangements at the first opportunity.

Orders: please contact Bookpoint Ltd, 130 Milton Park, Abingdon, Oxon OX14 4SE. Telephone: +44 (0)1235 827720. Fax: +44 (0)1235 400454.
Email education@bookpoint.co.uk Lines are open from 9 a.m. to 5 p.m., Monday to Saturday, with a 24-hour message answering service. You can also order through our website: www.hoddereducation.co.uk

ISBN: 978 1 5104 0405 2

First published in 2018 by
Hodder Education,
An Hachette UK Company
Carmelite House
50 Victoria Embankment
London EC4Y 0DZ

www.hoddereducation.co.uk

Impression number	10 9 8 7 6 5 4 3 2
Year	2022 2021 2020 2019 2018

Cover photo © Shutterstock/Militarist
Typeset in Bembo and produced by Gray Publishing, Tunbridge Wells
Printed in Spain

A catalogue record for this title is available from the British Library.

How to get the most out of this book

Features

Each topic from the specification is covered in a double-page spread with the following features.

Progress tracker

Tick this box to track your progress.

- One tick when you have revised and understood the content.
- Two ticks when you have tackled the revision tasks and/or practice questions.

Key term

- Key terms are **highlighted** (sometimes with a definition in brackets).
- These are the terms that you need to understand in order to write clearly about a topic. Precise use of language is very important for top marks.
- All the key terms are gathered together at **www.hoddereducation.co.uk/myrevisionnotes** (along with lots of other helpful support).

Practice question

- All the main question types are practised either as part of revision tasks or practice questions.
- Model answers to the practice questions are available on-line at **www.hoddereducation.co.uk/myrevisionnotes**.

Key point

If you forget everything else, remember this.

Revision point

Instead of headings, the content is divided into revision points. These are worth learning in their own right. They summarise the three to five key points about each topic. Take the revision points together and you have the course covered.

Revision task

These tasks develop your exam skills. Sometimes you write in the book, sometimes you write in your notebook. Our advice is to work through each chapter twice:

- the first time learning the content
- the second time using the revision tasks and practice questions.

Answers to revision tasks, with the exception of Stretch and Challenge, are provided online at **www.hoddereducation.co.uk/myrevisionnotes**.

Bullet points

This is the detailed knowledge you need to back up the revision point. The GCSE course emphasises the use of relevant, precise and detailed knowledge. Think of the revision point as the headline and the bullets the detail you can use in your answer:

- Learn this your own way – make mnemonics, use highlights.
- Mark this up. Use your pen. This should look like your book once you have finished.
- Sometimes we have used tables and charts to make it easier to remember. A good way to revise is to turn a table into bullets or turn the bullets into tables. Whenever you change the format of the knowledge your brain has to process it.

Test yourself

- As you revise the content the first time, use these to check your knowledge and recall.
- Try answering them without looking at the bullets. See how you get on.
- Usually the answers are obvious but in case they are not there are answers at **www.hoddereducation.co.uk/myrevisionnotes**.
- Don't worry about these questions second time through. Focus on the revision tasks instead.
- If you want to revise on the move, there are also self-marking knowledge quizzes on each topic at **www.hoddereducation.co.uk/myrevisionnotes**. These can be viewed on your phone or computer.

Answers online

At **www.hoddereducation.co.uk/myrevisionnotes** we have provided model answers for all tasks and exam-style questions (with the exception of Stretch and Challenge). However, just because you write something different from us it does not mean yours is wrong! Often history does not have right and wrong answers. As long as you can explain your point clearly and support your argument with evidence you can say many different things.

My revision planner

This book covers the most popular options. You will use Chapter 1 (everyone studies the same period study) and one other chapter from each section. But remember that certain thematic studies are paired with certain British depth studies. Make sure that you revise the right one!

- Highlight the chapters you are studying and cross out the ones you are not.
- To track your progress, tick each topic as you complete it. One tick when you have learned the content, another tick when you have tackled all the revision tasks.

CONTENT TASKS

Section 1A Period study

4 **What the period study is about and how it will be examined**

1 International Relations: the changing international order 1918–2001

6 **1.1** The Versailles Peace Settlement
8 **1.2** The League of Nations in the 1920s
10 **1.3** The impact of the Great Depression
12 **1.4** The origins of the Second World War
14 **1.5** Controversy 1: Appeasement
17 **1.6** Emerging superpower rivalry, 1945–49
20 **1.7** The Berlin Wall and the Cuban Missile Crisis
22 **1.8** The Vietnam and Afghan Wars
24 **1.9** Controversy 2: Who was to blame for the Cold War?
26 **1.10** Gorbachev and the end of the Cold War
28 **1.11** After the Cold War: the rise of al-Qaeda

Section 1B Non-British studies

30 **What the non-British depth study is about and how it will be examined**

2 Germany 1925–1955: The People and the State

32 **2.1** The Nazis during the Weimar 'Golden Years' and the Depression
34 **2.2** Nazi consolidation of power, 1933–34
36 **2.3** Nazi control through terror and propaganda
38 **2.4** Nazi economic and social policies
40 **2.5** Opposition towards the Nazis, and Nazi treatment of minorities
42 **2.6** The impact of the war on Germany, 1939–45
44 **2.7** The impact of defeat and occupation of Germany, 1945–55

3 The USA 1919–1948: The People and the State

46 **3.1** The US economy in the 'Roaring Twenties'
48 **3.2** US society in the 1920s
50 **3.3** Prejudice and discrimination in 1920s' society
52 **3.4** The Depression
54 **3.5** The New Deal
56 **3.6** The Second World War and the economy
58 **3.7** Division in the war

4 The USA 1945–1974: The People and the State

60 **4.1** The Red Scare
62 **4.2** McCarthyism
64 **4.3** The position of African Americans in US society
66 **4.4** The civil rights movement, 1960–68
68 **4.5** Other key issues in civil rights
70 **4.6** The fight for equality for other minority groups
72 **4.7** Women's rights, gay rights and poverty in the USA

Section 2 Thematic studies

74 **What the British thematic study is about and how it will be examined**

5 War and British Society c.790 to c.2010

(if you are studying this thematic study you must choose Chapter 8 to go with it)

76 **5.1** Viking raids and the Norman Conquest
78 **5.2** Feudal society
80 **5.3** War and medieval society

CONTENT TASKS

82 **5.4** The war with Spain
84 **5.5** The British civil wars
86 **5.6** The changing relationship with Scotland
88 **5.7** Imperial warfare
90 **5.8** The First and Second World Wars
92 **5.9** War since 1945
94 **5.10** Think thematic!

6 Power: Monarchy and Democracy in Britain c.1000 to 2014
(if you are studying this thematic study you must choose Chapter 9 to go with it)
96 **6.1** Anglo-Saxon England, c.1000–1066
98 **6.2** The Norman Conquest and its impact
100 **6.3** Struggles over power in the medieval period
102 **6.4** Tudor government
104 **6.5** Civil War to Restoration
106 **6.6** The Glorious Revolution
108 **6.7** Parliament and the people, c.1800–1918
110 **6.8** Parliament and the people, c.1914–c.1980
112 **6.9** Challenges to Parliament and democracy, c.1980–2014
114 **6.10** Think thematic!

7 Migration to Britain c.1000 to c.2010
(if you are studying this thematic study you must choose Chapter 10 to go with it)
116 **7.1** The Middle Ages, c.1000–c.1500
118 **7.2** European immigration, c.1500–1730
120 **7.3** African and Asian immigration, c.1500–1730
122 **7.4** African and Asian immigration, c.1730–1900
124 **7.5** European migrants in the industrial age, c.1730–1900
126 **7.6** The era of the First World War, 1900–1920s
128 **7.7** The era of the Second World War, 1920s–1948
130 **7.8** Commonwealth immigration after the Second World War
132 **7.9** Immigration as a political issue, c.1990–c.2010
134 **7.10** Think thematic!

Section 3 British depth studies

136 **What the British depth study is about and how it will be examined**

8 Personal Rule to Restoration 1629–1660
(paired with Chapter 5)
138 **8.1** The end of Charles I's Personal Rule
140 **8.2** Events leading to civil war
142 **8.3** Attempts to reach an agreement between Charles and Parliament, 1646–47
144 **8.4** The execution of Charles I
146 **8.5** The relationship between the Rump Parliament and Cromwell, 1649–53
148 **8.6** The relationship between the Rump Parliament and Cromwell, 1653–58
150 **8.7** Attempts to reach a settlement, September 1658–April 1660, and Restoration

9 The English Reformation c.1520–c.1550
(paired with Chapter 6)
152 **9.1** The role and importance of the Church in the sixteenth century
154 **9.2** Critics of the Church
156 **9.3** Henry VIII breaks with Rome
158 **9.4** The suppression of the monasteries
160 **9.5** Responses to the Dissolution of the Monasteries
162 **9.6** Reforming the churches
164 **9.7** Reaction of the people to the Reformation

10 The Impact of Empire on Britain 1688–c.1730
(paired with Chapter 7)
166 **10.1** Ireland, 1688–c.1730
168 **10.2** Scotland
170 **10.3** Emigration, 1688–c.1730
172 **10.4** The Atlantic trade
174 **10.5** The role of the East India Company
176 **10.6** The British economy
178 **10.7** The social and political impact of empire
180 Indicative mark scheme

Section 1A Period study

What the period study is about and how it will be examined

Overview of the period study

The period study examines international relations during the years 1918–2001, covering how events unfolded from the end of the First World War to the War on Terror. More importantly, it also includes the study of **interpretations**, which examine how two major events in this period have been viewed differently by different historians at different times.

The period study requires you to have a clear understanding of the narrative of events across this whole period, including understanding the interpretations.

- You will need to have a good overview understanding of each part of the period.
- You will need to be able to explain specific events.
- There are two **historical controversies** which you need to understand:
  - Appeasement
  - blame for the Cold War.
- You must understand the following things about each controversy:
  - The narrative of what took place at the time.
  - What each of the major groups of historians thinks about the issue.
  - How these views have changed over time.
  - What affected the views of each set of historians (what was happening in the period they were writing to make them think what they thought?).

Key skills needed for the period study

'Second-order concepts' are thought processes that allow us to study the past. They do so by providing us with a way to organise 'big ideas' in history.

Below, you will find guidance on the second-order concepts **most** relevant to the period study.

THE PERIOD STUDY

Cause – Why did this happen? There are **always** a variety of reasons for events taking place, and your job is to explain these reasons. Some questions will ask you to explain which **factors** were most important, and the best answers will explore how this selection of factors links together, and the relationship between them. For example, was Hitler the most important factor in the outbreak of the Second World War? He probably was, but what **else** also contributed? Useful words: 'created', 'produced', 'prompted'

Similarity and difference – this concept is about how far experiences are shared in the same place and at the same time: in other words, did **every** individual have the same experience? Therefore, you will be looking at the diversity of people's experiences in a given historical situation. For example, everyone present at the Paris Peace Conference experienced the same conference, but every nation had a very different agenda and the Germans were not represented at all

Main question types in the period study

This is Paper 1. It is worth 105 marks in total. You will be asked the following types of question:

1 **Outline ...** *(5 marks)*

This question is more straightforward than it seems. It will generally be asking for an overview of a given period, usually five to ten years, and you must demonstrate your understanding of that period.

There is no need for a huge amount of depth, but you must look for the overall **trend** in the given period, and why that was taking place.

2 **Explain/evaluate ...** *(10 marks)*

This question is designed to test your understanding of specific events. It might be phrased in a number of different ways, such as: 'Explain'; 'How successful' or 'How far'.

The key to answering this question is to ensure that you show your overall understanding of the **causation** of the events, and then show the role of factors.

Interpretation questions

Two questions about how views of **Appeasement** and **Cold War blame** have changed, and why.

The period study requires you to revise in a slightly different way to the rest of your courses as it needs you to have deep understanding of the interpretations.

3 **How fair is ...** *(25 marks)*

This question requires that you understand that **all** interpretations are reasonable to a degree, although some are fairer than others.

Your answer requires a clear **argument** that focuses on whether the interpretation in the question has made a reasonable judgement. You must make it clear that there are aspects of the interpretation which are fair and others that are not.

The best way to demonstrate this, and thus demonstrate your knowledge, is to talk about where other historians have also agreed/disagreed on that issue. So, for example, if most historians would disagree on a point, it is likely to be unfair, and if most agree then it is likely to be fair.

4 **Explain why some historians disagree ...** *(20 marks + 5 SPaG)*

This question may seem similar to question 3, but it is in fact asking for something quite different. Question 3 focuses on the content of the interpretations, but this question focuses on the historians and their views.

As with question 3, your answer requires a clear **argument**, but in this case you must be clear about why some historians would have held different views, and what was going on at the time of writing which would have led many people to hold an opinion from that school of thought.

You must show clear examples from at least two other viewpoints to get the top level.

How we help you develop your exam skills

The revision tasks help you build understanding and skills step by step. For example:

- **Which is best?** will allow you to consider the demands of exam question types.
- **Support or challenge?** will help you to use content to inform your judgement in an essay question.
- The **practice questions** give you exam-style questions.

Plus:

- There are annotated model answers for every practice question online at **www.hoddereducation.co.uk/myrevisionnotes** or use this QR code to find them instantly.

1 International Relations: the changing international order 1918–2001

1.1 The Versailles Peace Settlement

REVISED

The Treaty of Versailles was an unhappy compromise between the USA, Britain and France

- There were three leaders (the **Big Three**) at the conference that was set up to negotiate peace at the end of the First World War: David Lloyd George (Britain); Georges Clemenceau (France); and Woodrow Wilson (USA).
- The Big Three had very different agendas: Clemenceau wanted to punish Germany severely. Woodrow Wilson wanted a lenient peace that would reduce the likelihood of another war.
- Lloyd George was stuck in the middle, because while the British people wanted revenge (like France), Britain needed Germany's economy to recover.
- Ultimately, the Treaty was a compromise. It stripped Germany of:
  - all of its colonies
  - ten per cent of German land
  - 12.5 per cent of the German population
  - and limited its armed forces to 100,000 men and six small naval vessels.
- Crucially, German had to accept the blame for the war.
- Germany was banned from uniting (***Anschluss***) with Austria.
- The League of Nations was established as an international police force, but Germany was barred from joining.

Key point

The terms of the Versailles Peace Settlement severely punished Germany for the First World War.

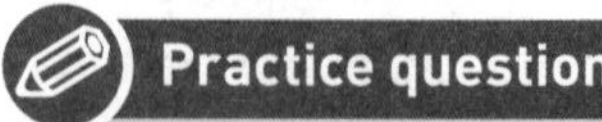

Practice question

Outline the terms of the Treaty of Versailles. (5 marks)

Test yourself

1 Who represented Britain, France and the United States at the Paris Peace Conference?
2 Why did David Lloyd George have a more difficult agenda to achieve than Wilson and Clemenceau?
3 Which clause of the Treaty of Versailles allowed the Allies to punish Germany?

Versailles was wildly unpopular in Germany and many people saw it as a mistake

- The reaction against the Treaty in Germany was immediate and it was heavily criticised in the media.
- Many Germans believed Germany had signed an armistice, but had not lost the war. The Treaty was therefore seen by many as a betrayal.
- The reparations terms were hugely unpopular, and it was felt that **Article 231** – the **War Guilt clause** – was unfair in blaming only Germany.
- The resentment of the Treaty was used by many German politicians, particularly Hitler, to discredit the new German government (see Chapter 2).

The League of Nations was established to maintain peace

- The League of Nations was the idea of President Wilson. It comprised:

- **The Council:** the main decision-making body of the League. Met five times a year or when there was an emergency. The council was established so nations could bring their grievances to be **arbitrated** rather than resorting to war
- **The Assembly:** a parliament which met once a year
- **The Court of International Justice:** helped settle disputes between countries
- A number of committees:
  - **Financial Committee:** promoted trade throughout the world in the belief that countries who were trading with each other were less likely to fight
  - **Refugee and Health Committee:** designed to improve the quality of life and organise people fleeing from zones of warfare or disease
  - **International Labour Organisation:** designed to improve the rights of workers. (This was also designed to limit the spread of Communism from the USSR, which had recently experienced a revolution)

The League of Nations was fundamentally **weakened** by the absence of the USA

- President Wilson wanted the League of Nations to be the organisation which would prevent war and encourage peace and prosperity throughout the world. The rest of the United States did not feel the same way, and so chose not to join the League (see page 9).
- This left the League in the hands of Britain and France. Both countries were recovering financially from the effects of the war. They worked as best they could to lead the League, but they did not have the money or will to make a major impact.

Stretch and challenge

Explain why the absence of the United States made the League so much weaker.

You're the examiner

Below are a sample exam-style question and a paragraph written in answer to this question. Read the paragraph and the mark scheme provided on pages 180–2. First, decide which level you would award the paragraph. Then decide where in the level you would place it. Write the level below, along with a justification for your choice.

Outline the functions of the League of Nations. (5 marks)

The League of Nations was designed to maintain world peace by eliminating the causes of war. Most importantly, all member states could bring their grievances against others before the Council which would then decide fairly and reasonably which side should win. It also aimed to tackle the problems which had been at the heart of conflict in the past: poverty, trade and resources. To this end, the League set up several bodies to address these issues. They set up a Refugee and Health Committee designed to save lives and improve the living conditions of ordinary people. They also attempted to prevent the spread of Communism from the Soviet Union with the International Labour Organisation, which was designed to improve the pay and conditions of workers throughout the League of Nations.

Level: ☐

Reason for choosing this level: ______________________________

____

____

Eliminate irrelevance

Below are a sample exam-style question and a paragraph written in answer to this question. Read the paragraph and identify parts of the paragraph that are not directly relevant to the question. Draw a line through the information that is irrelevant and justify your deletions in the margin.

Why did the absence of the United States weaken the League of Nations? Explain your answer. (10 marks)

Woodrow Wilson was an idealist who wanted to ensure world peace. One of his main aims at the Paris Peace Conference was to ensure this by creating the League of Nations. The League was designed to act as the world's policeman, and it was going to need a lot of money and men to be able to do this. The US Senate decided that it did not want to waste money and lives on conflicts that had nothing to do with the USA, so it voted not to join. This meant that the League had lost the richest country in the world, and the only country that would have had the real desire to lead the League. Instead, Britain and France were left in charge of the League, and both countries were more interested in their own agendas and running their empires rather than ensuring peace.

1.2 The League of Nations in the 1920s

REVISED

The League dealt **successfully** with **minor** international disputes

Early 1920s	1921	1920–29	1922–23
The League co-ordinated efforts to help 400,000 people who had been displaced at the end of the First World War, and helped ensure that a major influenza outbreak was not considerably worse	The first test for the League was between the newly independent Finland and Sweden for control of the Aaland Islands. Despite some vote manipulation by the Finnish, the rules of the League were obeyed and the Council settled the dispute quickly and effectively. There was also the settlement of the division of Upper Silesia between Germany and Poland	The Polish army seized control of Vilna, the capital of Lithuania. Lithuania appealed to the League for help, but since Britain and France wanted Polish help in a potential future war against the Communist Soviet Union, help was not given	Hungary and Austria received financial aid to prevent them from experiencing **anarchy**

The League had two major tests in the 1920s: **Corfu** and **Bulgaria**

- In 1923, the new **dictator** of Italy, Benito Mussolini, wanted a major incident to consolidate his position of power. When an Italian general was killed in Greek territory, he used it as an excuse to capture the Greek island of Corfu. The League condemned his actions.
- However, the British and French could not agree on a course of action and finally judged that the Greeks must apologise and pay compensation to Italy.
- This was a win for Mussolini and a failure for the League.
- In 1925, having been the victims against Italy, the Greeks tried to create an identical incident against the Bulgarians to get compensation. On this occasion, however, the League acted as it was supposed to and thus the Greeks were punished appropriately.
- The Great Powers were in agreement over the issue in Bulgaria and so the League acted successfully.

Key point

The League did not suffer any major failures in the 1920s, but it also did not face many major challenges.

Several **international agreements** were reached **outside** the **League** of Nations

- The League of Nations was meant to attempt to eliminate the large armed forces that had led to the First World War. Only Germany had been forced to disarm as a result of the Treaty of Versailles.
- The League failed in this pursuit. At the **Washington Conference** of 1921, the USA, Japan, Britain and France agreed to limit the size of their navies. This, however, was the only **disarmament** agreement of note in the 1920s, and many countries developed and improved their armed forces.
- There were, however, several international agreements reached during the 1920s, outside the League of Nations – although the League helped to create the spirit of internationalism that they needed:
  - Through the **Dawes Plan** (1924) the USA lent money to Germany to help its industry recover and rebuild.
  - Through the **Young Plan** (1929) the overall reparations burden was reduced.
  - Germany and other Western powers signed the **Locarno Treaties** (1925). Germany agreed to its western borders, but said nothing about its eastern borders with Poland, implying they might change.
  - The **Kellogg–Briand Pact** (1928) was signed by 65 countries as an official agreement to never go to war.

Test yourself

1. Which two countries were involved in the Corfu Crisis?
2. Which islands were disputed by Sweden and Finland?
3. Name the agreement of 1924 that made Germany's reparations burden easier.

The League of Nations was **fundamentally weakened** by a number of factors

- Most of the questions you will be asked about the League will focus on success or failure. It is important to understand that the League only appears to be relatively successful in the 1920s because of the catastrophes of the 1930s.
- By choosing not to join the League, the United States made it very unlikely that it would ever succeed. Though they made some effort to be leaders, neither Britain or France was wealthy, powerful or committed enough to try to make the League a strong force in the 1920s.
- The Corfu crisis was exactly the kind of event the League had been set up to deal with, but it failed to protect this small country against a large aggressor.
- Above all, no major progress was made at international cooperation or disarmament. There were a few successes in improving conditions for workers, but ultimately the League achieved little.

Practice question

Outline the successes of the League of Nations in the 1920s. (5 marks)

Stretch and challenge

Create a small profile of what the USA, Britain and France wanted and achieved throughout the 1920s.

Complete the paragraph

Below are a sample exam-style question and a paragraph written in answer to this question. The paragraph contains a point and specific examples, but lacks a concluding explanatory link back to the question. Complete the paragraph, adding this link in the space provided.

Why was the absence of the United States a major blow to the League of Nations? Explain your answer. **(10 marks)**

It was critically important that the League had serious sanctions available to it that all member states would take seriously. Without American money, the League would not be able to …

____

____

____

____

You're the examiner

Below are a sample exam-style question and a paragraph written in answer to this question. Read the paragraph and the mark scheme provided on pages 180–2. First decide which level you would award the paragraph. Then decide where in the level you would place it. Write the level below, along with a justification for your choice.

Outline the actions of the League in dealing with the Corfu and Bulgarian crises. **(5 marks)**

Both the Corfu and Bulgarian crises were cases of a more powerful country trying to intimidate a less powerful country into cooperating and surrendering land or money. In the case of Italy bullying Greece, the League, notably Britain and France, did not feel powerful enough to deal with Italy's actions appropriately. In contrast, the League was more than powerful enough to intimidate Greece when it attempted to bully Bulgaria in 1925, and so the Greeks backed down.

Level: ☐ Reason for choosing this level: ____________________

____

____

1.3 The impact of the Great Depression

REVISED

America's central role in global finance led to financial collapse

Boom: America had experienced a colossal **technological and economic boom**. The USA lent money to Britain, France and Germany, and encouraged heavy spending in those countries

▼

Crash: the Wall Street Crash in October 1929 caused financial panic. US loans were stopped and recalled. Countries struggling to deal with the Crash then fell into **economic depression**

▼

Depression: Britain and France were forced to cut a great deal of public spending, and recalled their own loans from Germany

▼

Collapse: Germany owed loans to the USA and to Britain and France, all of which were demanding immediate repayment. Germany fell into economic depression and unemployment soared

Key point

The Wall Street Crash caused a global economic disaster which led directly to the rise of Germany, Japan and Italy as major aggressors, and ultimately to the collapse of the League.

Powerful dictatorships emerged because of the Great Depression

- The global financial collapse led many countries to elect more extreme governments, or in some cases (such as Spain and Poland) for democratically elected governments to be removed and replaced with dictatorships:

Germany		Hitler offered radical economic solutions including rearmament, state control of industry and the end of Versailles reparations
Italy		Mussolini, dictator of Italy, tightened his grip on the country by taking over its banks and industries
Japan		Japanese trade was severely affected by the economic downturn, particularly as **tariffs** had been imposed by China and the USA. As people turned against the government, Japan effectively became a military dictatorship

- In each of these countries, the leaders also had military ambitions which threatened to destabilise international peace.

The League of Nations failed to protect Manchuria

- The Japanese decided on **military expansion** to seize resources for their economy. In September 1931, the Japanese used troops disguised as Chinese soldiers to stage an attack on a Japanese railway line, near the Chinese–Korean border.
- The Japanese response to this 'aggression' was to invade and seize Manchuria, the north-eastern region of China. China turned to the League of Nations for help.
- The League sent a delegation to 'investigate' which took a year to report back.
- When it finally rendered judgement, the League merely condemned the Japanese and ordered them to withdraw. The League's members were incapable of matching Japan's military strength and sanctions would have had little effect without the backing of the USA.
- The Japanese instead invaded more of Manchuria, claiming that the area was unstable. In March 1933 Japan resigned from the League.
- The League had shown that if a strong nation took aggressive action, it could and would do nothing.

Practice question

What was the impact of the Great Depression on international relations? Explain your answer.

(10 marks)

The **Abyssinian crisis** effectively **destroyed** the League of Nations

- Mussolini decided to test the League's powers, closer to home.
- In late 1934, an 'incident' took place at Wal-Wal, 50 miles inside Ethiopian territory: a force of Italians was attacked and this was used by Mussolini as an excuse to invade.
- Unlike the Manchurian crisis, Britain and France were ideally placed to offer military assistance to the Abyssinians. They had armed forces in colonies all around Abyssinia, and they controlled the **Suez Canal**, which was the route that Italian forces were taking. They could easily have intervened with little cost to themselves.
- Instead, the British and the French tried to secretly negotiate a scheme (known as the **Hoare–Laval Pact**) wherein Italy would get two-thirds of Abyssinia in exchange for support against Hitler. Details of the plan were leaked in the press. This not only humiliated the British and French, but effectively destroyed the League.
- Immediately after this, Mussolini abandoned Britain and France and signed an alliance with Hitler – the **Rome–Berlin Axis**. Hitler had also used this moment of distraction to remilitarise the Rhineland.

Test yourself

1. What disguise did the Japanese soldiers who blew up the railway at Mukden use?
2. What could the British and French have closed to prevent the Abyssinian Crisis?
3. Name the British and French foreign ministers who tried to give much of Abyssinia to Italy.

Spot the mistake

Below are a sample exam-style question and a paragraph written in answer to this question. Why does this paragraph not get into Level 5? Once you have identified the mistake, rewrite the paragraph so that it displays the qualities of Level 5. The mark scheme on pages 180–2 will help you.

How did the Great Depression lead to the effective collapse of the League? Explain your answer. (10 marks)

Because of the major financial problems caused by the Great Depression, it made Japan and Italy want to take over other countries to get their money and resources. To do this, they both made excuses to invade countries they wanted to conquer. These actions were popular with their people because their people were poor because of the Wall Street Crash.

Developing the detail

Below is a sample exam-style question and a paragraph written in answer to this question. The paragraph contains a limited amount of detail. Annotate the paragraph to add additional detail to the answer.

Outline the failures of the League of Nations between 1930 and 1936. (5 marks)

The League of Nations was led by Britain and France. During the 1930s, they were not prepared to go to war to defend other countries. They did not help China when it was invaded by Japan. They did not make enough of an effort to stop Hitler rearming. The British and the French tried to let Mussolini take over some of Abyssinia, but they were exposed and humiliated.

Stretch and challenge

Once you have been through this whole section (pages 6–29), come back to this topic, and make a note of how you think that Hitler would have reacted to each of the crises of the 1930s, and what he would have learned about the League, and the British and French.

1.4 The origins of the Second World War

REVISED

The 1930s saw the **failure** of **disarmament**

- US President Herbert Hoover called the **Disarmament Conference** in 1932. It recognised that it was unfair that only Germany had been forced to disarm as a result of the Treaty of Versailles, but struggled to find an agreement for disarmament.
- In 1933, Hitler took power in Germany and immediately began rearming in secret.
- In October 1933, Hitler walked out of the conference and in 1935 openly announced **rearmament**.

Key point

Throughout the 1930s, Hitler took increasingly aggressive steps until finally war was declared in September 1939.

- By this time, other nations had suspected German rearmament and had themselves begun to rearm.

Hitler was unchallenged when he bombed **Guernica** and seized control of **Austria**

- In 1936 a **civil war** broke out in Spain between a Republican force supported by Britain, France and Russia, and a Fascist force supported by Germany and Italy. Britain and France refused to intervene militarily.
- On 26 April 1937, the German air force bombed, and effectively destroyed, the Republican city of Guernica in the north of Spain. Hundreds of people were killed.
- This bombing highlighted the military strength of Germany and the inability to act by Britain and France when Hitler was clearly acting against the terms of the Treaty of Versailles.
- Another clause of the Treaty banned Germany from uniting with Austria (*Anschluss*). In March 1938, the Austrian people voted in a **plebiscite** (referendum) to join with Germany and Hitler marched troops into Austria. Nothing was done to stop him.

Chamberlain pursued a policy of **Appeasement** to prevent war

- Later that year, Hitler started a campaign to try to **annex** (take control of) the Sudetenland region of Czechoslovakia. He claimed, as with Austria, that he wanted to bring Germans back into the Fatherland.
- Czechoslovakia had promises from Britain and France that they would protect the country against a German invasion.
- In September 1938, Chamberlain organised a conference in Munich between Britain, France, Italy and Germany. Czechoslovakia was not invited.
- Hitler initially demanded just some of the Sudetenland, then when the British and French agreed, he upped his demand to the whole of the Sudetenland.
- The British and the French gave in and the **Munich Agreement** was signed.
- Chamberlain arrived back in Britain a hero, claiming 'Peace in our time'.

Hitler took one **gamble** too many and **war** was declared

- Despite the agreement, in March 1939, Hitler invaded the rest of Czechoslovakia.
- There were major protests from Britain and France, who promised to declare war on Germany if it invaded Poland.
- Hitler did have his sights set on Poland. He was sure Britain and France would do nothing in response, but he was concerned about the threat of the USSR on the border with Poland.
- The leader of the USSR, Josef Stalin, had grown impatient with the ineffective response of Britain, France and the League in the face of the German threat. In August 1939, after several failed attempts to ally with Britain and France against Hitler, he signed the **Nazi–Soviet Non-Aggression Pact**.
- The Pact secretly divided Poland into two halves.
- Despite last-minute warnings from Britain and France, Hitler invaded Poland on 1 September 1939. Britain and France declared war the following day. The Second World War had begun.

Checklist

Below is a list of events that *may* have taken place in the lead-up to the outbreak of the Second World War. Tick or highlight those events which you know *did* take place.

- Hitler began German rearmament in 1933.
- Britain began arms sales to the Nazis in 1934.
- Saar plebiscite a huge success for the Nazis in 1935.
- Spanish city of Salamanca destroyed by *Luftwaffe*.
- Stalin attempted to create alliance with Britain and France.
- *Anschluss* between Austria and Germany.
- Chamberlain handed over all of Czechoslovakia at the Munich Conference.
- The Nazi–Soviet Pact was signed in 1939.
- Britain and France declared war after Nazi invasion of Poland.

Spot the mistake

Below are a sample exam-style question and a paragraph written in answer to this question. Why does this paragraph not get into Level 5? Once you have identified the mistake, rewrite the paragraph so that it displays the qualities of Level 5. The mark scheme on pages 180–2 will help you.

How did Appeasement help lead to the Second World War? Explain your answer. (10 marks)

Appeasement was a policy of ensuring that Hitler did not get what he wanted, and to contain him within Germany. Because of this, the British and French continually clashed with Hitler, which led to Neville Chamberlain choosing to declare war in September 1939.

Stretch and challenge

You will need to know the details of events in the 1930s to answer questions on Appeasement. Make a timeline of the key events on the road to war from 1933 to 1939.

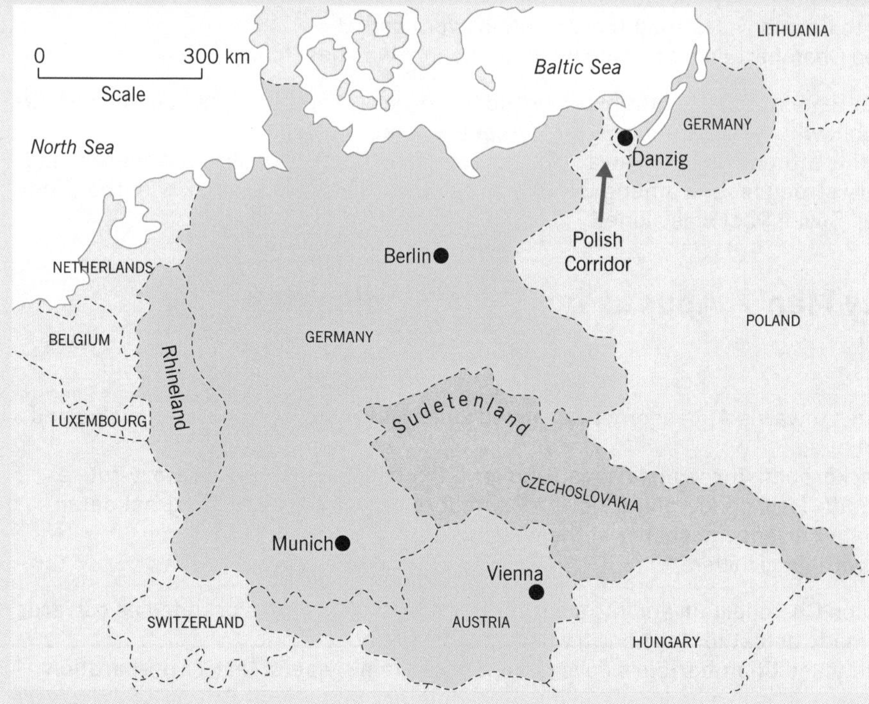

The Sudetenland not only contained a great deal of Czechoslovakia's natural resources, but was also their natural defence against Germany – a line of mountains and fortresses that the Germany army would have found it very hard to break through.

Test yourself

1. Was Hitler ever serious about the disarmament process?
2. Name the region of Czechoslovakia given to Germany at Munich.
3. Molotov and Ribbentrop negotiated which pact?

Practice question

How did Hitler's actions lead to the outbreak of the Second World War? Explain your answer. (10 marks)

1.5 Controversy 1: Appeasement

REVISED

TIP

The two controversies on your Paper 1 are worth 50 marks, which is a quarter of your overall grade. It is worth spending a lot of revision time on this page!

- Whatever question you are asked, you will need to know all five stages of interpretation and reinterpretation to be confident of answering.
- You need to be able to explain how the interpretation changed over time and why.
- For each stage you need to be able to explain how the **Context** created the **Content**, and why this led to **Controversy**.

Key point

Opinions on the strategy of Appeasement have varied widely and have developed in the years following the Second World War.

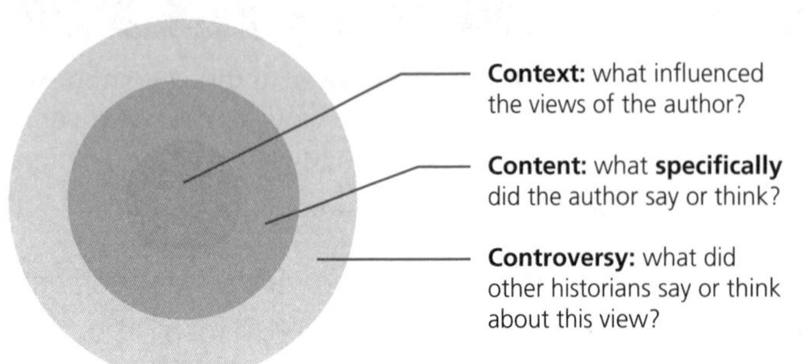
Context: what influenced the views of the author?
Content: what **specifically** did the author say or think?
Controversy: what did other historians say or think about this view?

View 1 (1936–39): pro-Appeasement policy – Chamberlain's actions reflected public opinion

Context	• Many people supported **Appeasement** because they could still remember the horrors of the First World War, and they knew that Britain was not prepared to fight a war
Content	• Appeasement was the policy adopted by Prime Minister Chamberlain in an attempt to prevent war with Germany. He sought conciliation over conflict • People believed Chamberlain was doing what he thought was best to prevent a war
Controversy	• Not everyone in Britain agreed with this view and there were several notable people such as Winston Churchill who were strongly against Appeasement • Furthermore, this attitude dropped away sharply after Czechoslovakia was conquered, and there was a very strong feeling among the British people of the need to work with the USSR before the Nazi–Soviet Pact was signed

View 2 (1940–48): 'Guilty Men' – Appeasement was a disaster and Chamberlain was a fool

Context	• Popular attitudes towards Appeasement changed when Hitler invaded Czechoslovakia and as the war continued • Against this background, three historians, who gave themselves the name **Cato**, wrote a book entitled *Guilty Men*, condemning Neville Chamberlain personally and in great detail • The public also felt a sense of shame at the willingness of the people to support Appeasement without criticism
Content	• A huge assault on Chamberlain and his advisers personally. They were branded as cowards and as having made defeat to Germany a very real possibility • They further attacked Chamberlain's government for Britain's woeful lack of preparation going into the war – massive underspending on the military meant that Britain's forces were simply not ready for the conflict
Controversy	• This view was almost universal at the time, due to the conquest of France and the very real possibility of defeat by Nazi Germany. Views on Chamberlain softened somewhat after he died in 1940. All subsequent views have been more favourable than this

View 3 (1948–1960s): 'orthodox' view – Appeasement was a **mistake** but the leaders had good intentions

Context	• With the defeat of the Nazis in 1945, views about Appeasement softened slightly from *Guilty Men*, if only because the defeat that was looming in 1940 had not happened. He was regarded as a good man who made the wrong decision • The main figure behind this view was Churchill who, after being defeated in the 1945 general election, wrote *The Gathering Storm*, a book about the causes of the Second World War
Content	• The critical difference between this view and *Guilty Men* is that this view does not contain direct attacks on Chamberlain personally • The view makes it clear that Chamberlain was a decent man who had to be reasonably personally brave in order to follow a policy that was at least trying to save lives and prevent war
Controversy	• Some historians have criticised the view, and Churchill personally, for using the book more as a way to make himself look good, rather than to promote a balanced viewpoint • At this time, the Cold War was developing (see Section 2.1, page 32) and Churchill was keen to ensure that the mistakes of Appeasement were not repeated

View 4 (1960s–1990s): **revisionist view** – Chamberlain was in an impossible position and did the **best he could**

Context	• The orthodox view of Appeasement remained well into the 1960s, but gradually altered as historians became more critical of Cold War politics, and as more information became available • In Britain, most government documents are classified top secret, so they cannot be read by the public for 30 years. In the 1960s they became public • This was also a time of radical thinking in other areas of society. The USA's conflict in Vietnam was going badly at that time and some interpreted this as proof that Appeasement may not have been a bad policy
Content	• Historians such as Donald Cameron Watt and Paul Kennedy held this view. When the documents about 1936–39 became available in 1966–69 they revealed that Britain was not prepared for a war before 1939. Britain did not have the money, the military or the technology to take on Germany, leaving Appeasement as the only reasonable choice
Controversy	• This view is the only historian's view that supports the idea that Appeasement was a good policy (View 1, the view from the time, was not a historian's opinion). This is one that is particularly worth revising as it is likely that the given interpretation is likely to disagree with it • The problem with the documents that were used by these historians is that they came from the government at the time, and so reflect what the government thought at the time

View 5 (1990s–present): **counter-revisionist view** – Chamberlain was a fair politician but with an inexplicable (and inexcusable) view on Appeasement

Context	• By the mid-1990s, the view that Chamberlain had no choice in appeasing had started to be challenged, particularly with the release of new documents from the USSR which showed its attempts to work with Britain • The new view of Chamberlain and Appeasement began with historian Robert Parker in 1993. Chamberlain was not attacked, but his ability to deal with Hitler, and his strange refusal to listen to anyone who tried to push him to stand up to Hitler, were questioned
Content	• The biggest criticism of Chamberlain in this view, which is still the view held by most historians, is that Chamberlain betrayed Czechoslovakia. However, most historians now say that apart from his pursuit of Appeasement, Chamberlain was a decent man and a reasonable politician • Like most modern interpretations, there are a variety of criticisms and slight differences within this view. Some historians have used **counter-factual history** to try to work out what would have happened if Chamberlain had gone to war earlier

Review question

The interpretation questions are the most challenging questions in the whole of your History GCSE. It is essential that you know not only what historians have believed about Appeasement, but also what was happening in the world at the time to make them believe this. To help you remember this, complete the timeline below for Appeasement, to show how and why views have changed over time.

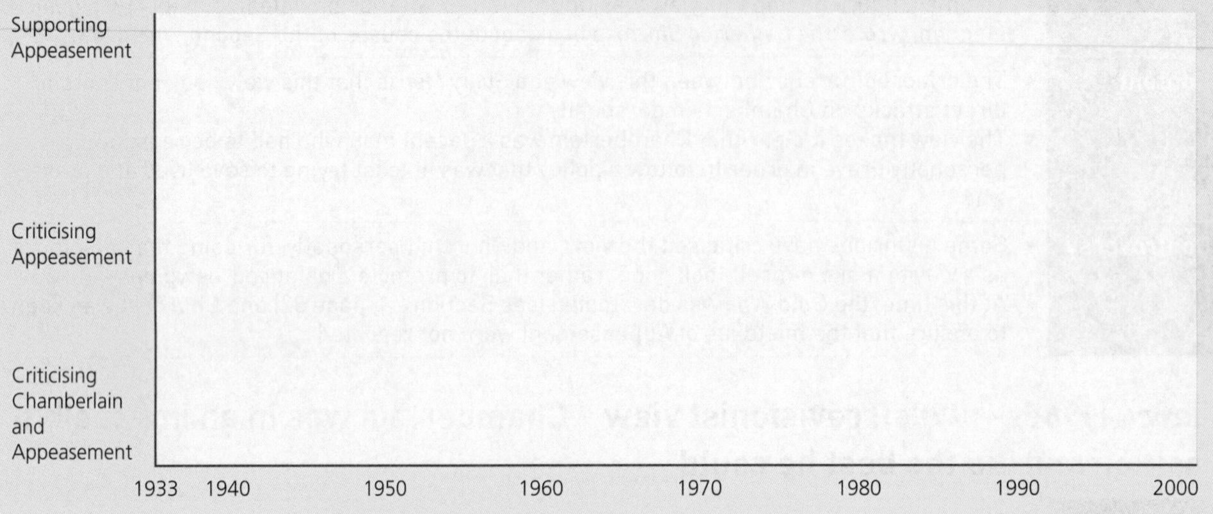

Review summary

Fill in the table below to summarise all the views on Appeasement as clearly as possible.

View	When was this view held	Who held this view	Pro/anti Chamberlain	Pro/anti Appeasement	Who would they disagree with?
Pro-Appeasement					
Guilty Men					
Orthodox					
Revisionist					
Counter-revisionist					

Practice question

Study Interpretation A.

Explain why **not** all historians would agree with Interpretation A. Use other interpretations and your own knowledge to support your answer. (20 marks)

INTERPRETATION A *An extract from* Chamberlain and Appeasement: British Policy and the Coming of the Second World War *by British historian Robert Parker, 1993.*

Chamberlain succumbed to the temptation to believe that actions which were specifically his own were triumphing. Hitler helped. He appealed to Chamberlain's vanity and encouraged Chamberlain to think he had a special influence over him. Sir Neville Henderson, the British Ambassador in Berlin, encouraged Chamberlain even though he lost the confidence of his own colleagues in the Foreign Office. Chamberlain's appeasement was not a feeble policy of surrender. He never pursued 'peace at any price'. But he made big mistakes, especially after Munich. He could have built a strong alliance with France. He could have tried to ally with the USSR but he refused to try in any serious way. Chamberlain refused to listen to alternative views and his powerful personality probably stifled serious chances of preventing the Second World War.

1.6 Emerging superpower rivalry, 1945–49

REVISED

The USA and USSR had fundamental **differences** in **ideology**

- The USA and USSR had successfully worked together during the war in what is known as the **Grand Alliance**, but with the end of the conflict this alliance was short lived. The main reason for this was the different ideology held by each country:

USA	USSR
Capitalist	**Communist**
Democracy	Dictatorship
Believed people should be free from the controls of government	Believed the rights of individuals were less important than the good of society as a whole so the lives of individuals were tightly controlled
Believed other countries should be run in the American way	Believed other countries should be run in the Communist way

Key point

The Cold War began largely because of the fundamental differences in ideology, economy and views on the future of Europe, between the USA and USSR.

The **Potsdam Conference** highlighted the **differences** between the USA and USSR

- With the defeat of Hitler imminent in February 1945, the Big Three (Stalin, Roosevelt and Churchill) met at Yalta in the Crimea. Roosevelt maintained a harmonious relationship between the three.
- At the **Potsdam Conference** in July 1945, relations changed. Roosevelt had died, and was replaced by Harry Truman. The relationship between Truman and Stalin was poor, and the successful American test of the **atomic bomb** worsened tensions.

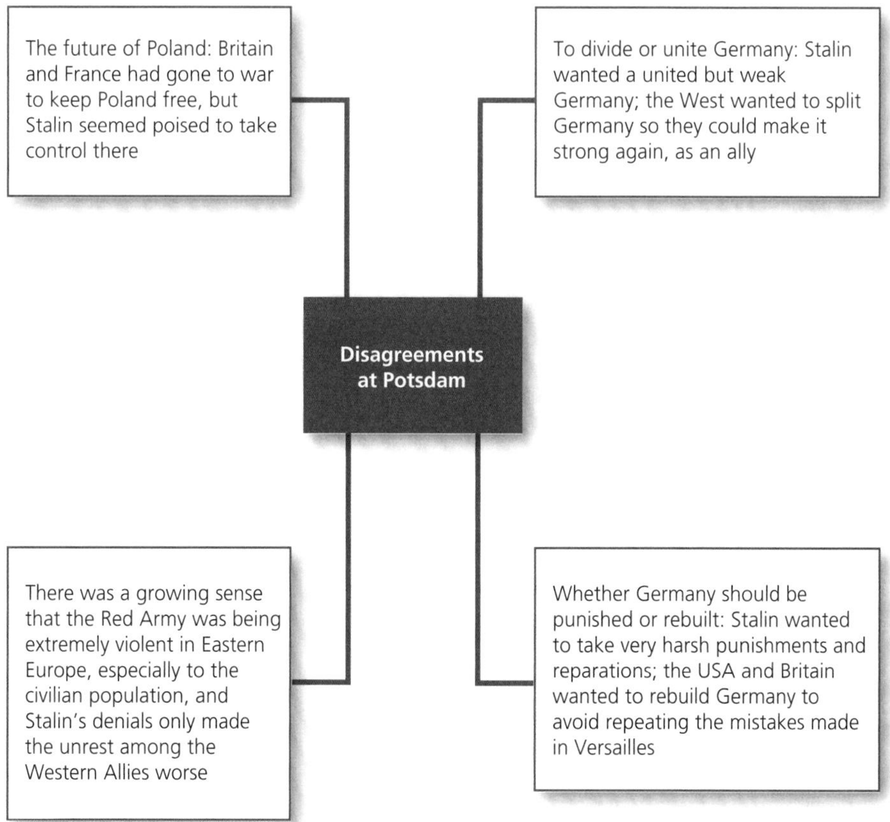

Disagreements at Potsdam
The future of Poland: Britain and France had gone to war to keep Poland free, but Stalin seemed poised to take control there
To divide or unite Germany: Stalin wanted a united but weak Germany; the West wanted to split Germany so they could make it strong again, as an ally
There was a growing sense that the Red Army was being extremely violent in Eastern Europe, especially to the civilian population, and Stalin's denials only made the unrest among the Western Allies worse
Whether Germany should be punished or rebuilt: Stalin wanted to take very harsh punishments and reparations; the USA and Britain wanted to rebuild Germany to avoid repeating the mistakes made in Versailles

The USSR took control in **Eastern Europe**, 1945–48, prompting the **USA** to respond with **aid**

- Stalin was determined to secure the USSR and during this period established Communist governments in many Eastern European countries: East Germany, Czechoslovakia, Poland, Hungary, Romania, Bulgaria, Yugoslavia and Albania.
- Stalin created COMINFORM to protect and oversee these Communist governments.
- The West was suspicious of this expansionism and in response Truman introduced the **Truman Doctrine**. Its purpose was to stop the spread of communism by supporting any country threatened with a Communist takeover, with weapons, money and resources.
- The USA established **Marshall Aid** to provide up to $17 billion to the countries of Europe, again to help prevent communism. It rapidly accelerated recovery in Western Europe.
- Stalin viewed this aid as an economic attack on communism and forbade the countries of Eastern Europe from receiving it.

By 1949 **Germany** was firmly **divided into two nations**

- After the war, Germany was divided into four zones controlled by France, Britain, the USA and the USSR.
- Believing that a stronger Germany would be a better ally, in 1946 the Western powers combined their zones.
- Berlin was also divided into four zones, but lay deep within Soviet territory in East Germany.
- Feeling threatened by the strength of West Germany, Stalin used the Red Army to **blockade** (seal off) West Berlin to prevent people or supplies from reaching the city. Stalin hoped this would force West Berlin to turn to the Communists for help.
- The Allies responded by airlifting all of the resources the city needed over a period of ten months.
- By May 1949, the blockade had failed and as a result Germany was divided into two nations:
  - the Western-controlled zone officially became the Federal Republic of Germany (FRG), known as West Germany
  - the Soviet zone became the **German Democratic Republic (GDR)**, or East Germany.
- In 1949, the Western powers met and agreed to the formation of **NATO**.

Stretch and challenge

Create a list of the factors and elements which caused the breakdown of the Grand Alliance. Once you have done this, use highlighters to colour-code who was to blame for each point: Stalin, the USA or both.

Practice question

Outline the events which caused the breakdown of the relationship between the USA and USSR between 1945 and 1948. (5 marks)

Identify an argument

Below are a series of definitions, a sample exam-style question and two sample conclusions. One of the conclusions achieves a high level because it contains an argument. The other achieves a lower level because it contains only description and assertion. Identify which is which. The mark scheme on pages 180–2 will help you.

- **Description:** a detailed account.
- **Assertion:** a statement of fact or an opinion which is not supported by a reason.
- **Explanation:** a statement which explains or justifies something.
- **Argument:** an assertion justified with a reason.

Why did the relationship between the superpowers deteriorated so rapidly between 1945 and 1949? Explain your answer. (10 marks)

The two sides of the Cold War were Communist and capitalist. They had totally different beliefs, and they disagreed about what to do with Eastern Europe. Stalin wanted a buffer zone which would make it more difficult for the USSR to be invaded again. The USA wanted Europe to recover so that it could trade with it again. Both sides believed the other to be a threat.

The fundamental reason for the deterioration of relations between the two sides was the defeat of Hitler. Without a common enemy, the fact that the USSR and USA were Communist and capitalist was always going to cause conflict as they were actively seeking to stop each other having influence. This was particularly the case in Europe, where Stalin had effectively conquered the countries in the east. The situation was made more serious by the fact that each side was treating their half of Germany very differently, leading to conflict in the Berlin Blockade.

Flow charts

Below is a blank flow diagram into which you must put the five key events that led to the breakdown of the Grand Alliance. For each you should indicate who was responsible for that act, the USA or the USSR. The first one has been completed for you. A list of events that you could have chosen can be found on page 17.

Roosevelt's death				

Test yourself

1 Which came first, the atomic test or Roosevelt's death?
2 How many countries became satellite states?
3 How did the USA and Britain respond to the Berlin Blockade?

1.7 The Berlin Wall and the Cuban Missile Crisis

REVISED

West Berlin remained a problem for the USSR

- Following the division of Germany into East and West, Berlin was also divided. West Berlin increasingly became a problem for the Soviets for a number of reasons:

Strategically	Ideologically	Economically	Intellectually
It was a notable area of territory, controlled by their potential enemy, deep within the Soviet sphere of influence	East Germans were very aware of the higher standard of living, the greater access to resources and to freedom which were being enjoyed in West Berlin	Hundreds of thousands of East Germans were fleeing to West Berlin every year – making a total of 3.5 million by 1961	Educated East Germans were staying in the East long enough to get a free education and then fleeing to high-paying jobs in the West. This was a **brain drain**

- In July 1961, Khrushchev demanded that President John F. Kennedy (the new US president) remove all troops from Berlin. Kennedy refused and instead increased troops there.
- In August 1961, Khrushchev ordered a barbed-wire fence to be erected between the two zones of Berlin. This was soon replaced by a wall. All free movement between the two sides was forbidden.
- The creation of the Berlin Wall did not lead to war, but it remained a symbol of the division between the two superpowers throughout the Cold War.

Key point

The 1950s and early 1960s saw a steady increase in Cold War tension as new weapons technology developed nuclear weapons and the missiles to deliver them.

Cuba became the next hotspot in the Cold War

- In 1959, the anti-Communist dictator of Cuba, Batista, was overthrown by the Communist Fidel Castro. Castro was then supported by funds from the USSR to protect Cuba against the USA.
- President Kennedy attempted to overthrow Castro in 1961, but the **Bay of Pigs** was a disaster and a humiliation for Kennedy.
- On 14 October 1962, a US U-2 spy plane took a series of photographs over Cuba. In doing so, it spotted what was quickly realised to be launch facilities for nuclear weapons.
- The US reaction was swift: Kennedy was informed and he quickly established **ExComm**.
- The solution agreed on was a naval blockade around Cuba. (The Soviets did not have the technology to bring in the equipment by air.)
- On 22 October, Kennedy made a speech on live TV to announce the blockade. The world was on the brink of nuclear war.

Test yourself

1 What was the brain drain?
2 When was the first version of the Berlin Wall erected?
3 In the Cuban Missile Crisis what happened on:
14 October?
22 October?
26 October?

Secret negotiations led to an end to the conflict

- Throughout the crisis, there had been the suggestion that in return for the Soviet withdrawal from Cuba, the USA would remove its **Jupiter IRBMs** from Turkey.
- The USA was already planning to remove these missiles, but it would have been politically disastrous for Kennedy to withdraw the missiles due to Soviet pressure.
- During the middle of the night of 26 October, Kennedy's brother Robert, who was attorney general, met in secret with Soviet ambassador Anatoly Dobrynin. They agreed to the mutual withdrawal, with Robert Kennedy insisting that the US withdrawal from Turkey be kept secret.

The end of the Cuban Missile Crisis led to **improved relations**

- As both sides realised how close they had come to global nuclear war, the period following the crisis saw an improvement in relations.
- A 'hotline' telephone was set up between the White House and the Kremlin and in 1963 the **Nuclear Test Ban Treaty** was agreed.
- The Cuban Missile Crisis was the last direct confrontation between the two countries in the Cold War.

Practice question

How did the Berlin crisis end without resorting to war? Explain your answer. (10 marks)

Event overview grid

Complete a one-sentence summary of the events listed in the grid below.

The Berlin Wall	
The Cuban Revolution	
The Bay of Pigs invasion	
Spy photographs of Cuba	
Quarantine of Cuba	
Meeting of Kennedy and Dobrynin	

Eliminate irrelevance

Below are a sample exam-style question and a paragraph written in answer to this question. Read the paragraph and identify parts of the paragraph that are not directly relevant to the question. Draw a line through the information that is irrelevant and justify your deletions in the margin.

Outline the factors that led to the resolution of the Berlin crisis. (5 marks)

The Berlin crisis was caused by Khrushchev's desire to show strength at the time when he had just seized power. He thought that a good way to show his strength to people in the Communist Party was to solve a problem that Stalin failed to solve with the Berlin Blockade. The various efforts he made, however, were all political and both Eisenhower and Kennedy correctly guessed that he was largely bluffing about his willingness to go to war. Their refusal to act, and Kennedy's willingness to call up extra soldiers and increase defence spending, forced Khrushchev to consider a radical solution. The construction of the Berlin Wall is viewed as a failure for the USSR because it forced them to admit that brain drain was costing them dearly. Around 2.7 million East Germans had fled from the East and into the West during this period to seek a better life. The building of the wall brought this to a sudden end and thus brought the crisis to a swift close.

Stretch and challenge

'One of the most positive things to come out of the Cuban Missile Crisis was a greater willingness for the USA and USSR to work together.'

1 Go back through this section and highlight examples of the USA and USSR cooperating.
2 Predict why the USA and USSR might be more willing to work together as a result of the Cuban Missile Crisis.
3 Use this information to say whether or not you agree with the statement.

1.8 The Vietnam and Afghan Wars

REVISED

Vietnam was **divided** into North and South with USSR and USA involvement

- For nine years following the end of the Second World War, the **Viet Minh**, who controlled the north of Vietnam, fought against the French, who controlled the south, for independence.
- The Viet Minh received funding from the USSR, so the USA gave financial support to the French. However, France pulled out of Vietnam in 1954.
- The Geneva Conference that followed, divided the country into North and South and planned for elections to be held.
- The Americans knew that the Communist leader, Ho Chi Minh, would win a huge victory, so they did not hold the elections, and instead supported dictator Ngo Dinh Diem, who set up the Republic of South Vietnam.

Key point

Events of the Cold War played out in foreign wars which were costly failures for both the USA and USSR.

- Diem's regime was corrupt and unpleasant: despite a huge amount of US support, he began losing control of the countryside to the **Viet Cong**, who were a mixture of North Vietnamese Army soldiers and people from the South who wanted to fight against Diem's regime.
- The USA sent advisers to train the **South Vietnamese Army (ARVN)**. Diem was so unpopular that he was overthrown by his own generals, but even this did not help and the South looked in danger of turning Communist.

The USA was unable to defeat the **tactics** used by the Viet Cong

- The USA decided to intervene directly, starting at the Battle of Ia Drang in November 1965. The USA had far greater resources to fight against the Viet Cong, but Ho Chi Minh's tactics were superior. He:
  - used **guerrilla** warfare
  - had the support of the people
  - used the Ho Chi Minh trail to supply the Viet Cong from Laos and Cambodia
  - had committed and resilient fighters.
- The Americans' frustration with these tactics led them to use unpleasant tactics:
  - **bombing**: the USA dropped more bombs on Vietnam than were dropped on Germany during the Second World War
  - **search and destroy**: villages were destroyed and people killed as soldiers searched for Viet Cong
  - **chemical weapons**: **napalm** and **Agent Orange** were used against people and villages.

Changing **attitudes** in America led to a US **withdrawal**

- Several factors led to a change in the support for the war in the USA:
  - **the Tet Offensive**: Viet Cong fighters took the US by surprise by attacking over 100 cities and other military targets
  - **the media**: after the Tet Offensive the media became more critical of the US position in Vietnam
  - **the My Lai massacre**: US forces killed 300–400 civilians in an atrocity in the village of My Lai. Americans began to question whether the USA was fighting on the right side.
- The change in support ultimately led to an end to the conflict as the peace movement gained strength.
- President Richard Nixon worked to end US involvement in the war and in January 1973 a peace agreement was signed.
- Within two years South Vietnam had fallen to the Communists.

Test yourself

1 Name the corrupt leader of South Vietnam.
2 What tactics did the Viet Cong use?
3 In what year did the Soviets withdraw from Afghanistan?

Practice question

Outline the reasons for the US entry into the Vietnam War. (5 marks)

The USA and USSR both became **involved** in events in Afghanistan

- Afghanistan borders the USSR. In 1978, pro-Soviet army officers led by Nur Mohammad Taraki overthrew the existing government and set up a new Communist state.
- The new government wanted to modernise Afghanistan. It made changes to land ownership and brought in social reforms. These policies were accepted in the city, but not in rural parts of the country. Warlords reacted against the reforms and the government opposed them violently.
- The USA began funding the warlords who were fighting against the Afghani government.
- The USSR became increasingly concerned when Islamic leader Ayatollah Khomeini took over Iran, on the border with Afghanistan.
- In March 1979, the Communist government asked the USSR for help.
- Brezhnev knew that there was a danger of facing the same problems as the USA had in Vietnam, but he was afraid that if he did not intervene, Afghanistan could well become either a militant Islamic state, or a pro-US ally.

The **Cold War** was played out further in the Afghan War

- Intervention came in the form of an invasion of Soviet troops. President Carter responded with anger.
- Carter introduced trade sanctions. He stopped all nuclear arms negotiations. He called for a boycott of the 1980 Moscow Olympics and set up alternative games in Philadelphia.
- Carter authorised the CIA (Central Intelligence Agency) to begin funnelling weapons to the **mujahidin** (Afghan warlords) through its ally Pakistan. This was done secretly to avoid war with the USSR.
- The Afghan War was the USSR's Vietnam – a costly war fought on unknown territory, and with thousands of lives lost on both sides. Soviet forces were eventually withdrawn in 1988.

Spot the mistake

Below is a sample exam-style question and a paragraph written in answer to this question. Why does this paragraph not get into Level 5? Once you have identified the mistake, rewrite the paragraph so that it displays the qualities of Level 5. The mark scheme on pages 180–2 will help you.

How did Viet Cong tactics force the withdrawal of American forces from Vietnam in 1973? Explain your answer. **(10 marks)**

The Viet Cong used a variety of tactics to fight the US forces in Vietnam. It used a combination of guerrilla tactics to sneak attack and surprise US forces on the ground, and the tactic of destroying the jungle with weapons like napalm and Agent Orange.

Event overview grid

Complete a one-sentence summary of the events listed in the grid below.

The Geneva Conference	
US support for Ngo Dinh Diem	
Viet Cong tactics	
US tactics	
US public opinion	
Taraki's new Afghan government	
Soviet intervention in Afghanistan	
Carter's response to Soviet intervention in Afghanistan	

1.9 Controversy 2: Who was to blame for the Cold War?

REVISED

View 1 (late 1940s–early 1960s): US **orthodox view**

Context	• The orthodox interpretation developed this view, laying the blame for the Cold War solely on the aggression and dishonesty of the Soviet Union. Certainly it is true to say that the USSR acted with aggression throughout the conflict • Historians such as Herbert Feis and George Kennan were leading academics who held this view. Both of these men had previously worked with the US government and had seen a lot of evidence about the actions of the USSR in Eastern Europe • The **Red Scare** was the fear among many Americans that communism was seeking to destroy the USA from within. This led historians to publish only extremely pro-USA/anti-Soviet books. If they did not, they risked being sacked, or worse, investigated by the government
Content	• There was an idea established in America that the Allied victory in the Second World War was down to the USA. The public therefore believed that the USA could do no wrong. In this view, the Soviet Union was seeking to destroy the United States and would do so with any means necessary
Controversy	• This view may seem similar to the modern view which does place a lot of blame on the USSR, but the key difference is that this suggests that the whole of the blame should be put on the USSR because they were Communists

Key point

Views on the origins of the Cold War conflict have varied and developed from the 1940s, with both sides of the argument widely supported.

View 2 (mid-1960s–early 1970s): US **revisionist view**

Context	• In the 1960s, American public opinion about the government started to change dramatically. Events during the Cuban Missile Crisis (page 20) and the Vietnam War (page 22) led many people to blame the United States for poor foreign policy decisions
Content	• The Allies failed to offer the Soviet Union sufficient help in the Second World War • Marshall Aid was simply an attempt by the USA to achieve economic and political dominance over Europe • That these actions then forced the USSR to react defensively
Controversy	• Even though this view is the opposite of the orthodox view, it also has strong elements of truth – the US certainly was trying to achieve economic dominance, but critically it leaves out the fact that the Soviet Union had already mostly achieved dominance over Eastern Europe before Marshall Aid • This was probably the most provocative of all the views put forward in either of the controversies, as it directly challenged, and some ways personally attacked, the previous view. The best way to see it is as a stepping stone to what came next: the post-revisionist view

View 3 (early 1970s–1989): post-revisionist view

Context	• Many factors led to a notable improvement in how historians viewed America from the early 1970s onwards: withdrawal from Vietnam; the Moon landings; vastly improved relations with the USSR and with China • This last factor led to historians such as John Lewis Gaddis advocating the post-revisionist view
Content	• It was essentially a hybrid of orthodox and revisionist views. It did place marginally more blame on the USSR and Stalin's aggressive actions, but also placed a good deal of blame on the USA continually over-reacting to Soviet actions and perceived intentions
Controversy	• It was also around this time that history as a subject was changing. Historians tried to interpret and re-examine history in new and innovative ways, and on this subject a more balanced view was aimed for • The biggest criticism of this view is that it is trying too hard to be neutral and balanced, and thus is not a deep as it might be. It was, however, widely accepted from the early 1970s right until the end of the Cold War in 1989

View 4 (1989 onwards): new Cold War historians

Context	• With the end of the Cold War, it was possible for Western historians to visit former Soviet archives in Moscow
Content	• Strangely, even though they now had access to all the documents, and there was no Cold War pressure to hold a given view, historians still do not agree
Controversy	• This can be somewhat challenging in terms of the exam, as you want to learn just a nice simple argument. One of the issues was that even with the end of the Cold War bringing a level of cooperation not seen since the Second World War, there was some discomfort around how President Ronald Reagan had briefly sparked a Second Cold War (see Section 3.1, page 46) • Historians now have a wide range of opinions. John Lewis Gaddis, for example, used the records in Moscow to advance the view that his previous judgement had been wrong, and that it was in fact the Soviet Union and Stalin who were largely to blame • In contrast, Michael Cox and Caroline Kennedy-Pipe have found evidence that suggests that it was the establishment of Marshall Aid that forced the Soviet Union to form its own political and economic bloc in self-defence

Practice question

Study Interpretation B.

Explain why not all historians would agree with Interpretation B. Use other interpretations and your knowledge to support your answer. (25 marks)

INTERPRETATION B *British historians Michael Cox and Caroline Kennedy-Pipe, writing in 2005.*

It was Stalin who eventually sealed the fate of Eastern Europe. However, the way that US aid was originally conceived under the Marshall Plan ... propelled the Soviet Union into a more antagonistic and hostile stance, including the establishment of its own economic and political bloc. We do not assume Soviet ... innocence ... Nevertheless, we would still insist ... that Soviet foreign policy was not just driven by ideology, but a series of responses and reactions that were just as likely to be shaped by the way others acted toward the Soviet Union as by Stalin's own outlook.

Stretch and challenge

Arrange all of the views on a line (or 'continuum') from most pro-US to most pro-Soviet. Summarise each view along the line, in your own words.

1.10 Gorbachev and the end of the Cold War

REVISED

Ronald Reagan began a **Second Cold War** by massively increasing military **spending**

Key point

By 1991, communism had disappeared from Eastern Europe and the Soviet Union had collapsed.

- Ronald Reagan had been an actor for several decades, but he came to national prominence in large part by attacking Jimmy Carter for being too soft on the Soviet Union. The Soviet invasion of Afghanistan reinforced this argument, and Reagan comfortably beat Carter in the 1980 election.
- As soon as he was in office, Reagan massively increased military spending, telling an adviser, 'I don't consider defence a budget item'. He authorised development of new weapons like the **stealth bomber**, and ordered an increase in the size of the army.
- Most significantly, he ordered the development of the **Strategic Defence Initiative (SDI)**. Nicknamed 'Star Wars', this was a plan to protect the USA from nuclear attack by creating a huge network of satellites armed with lasers which could shoot down incoming missiles.
- This was all part of what became known at the Second Cold War, as Reagan denounced the USSR as an 'Evil Empire'. Most historians now agree that this aggression was not as militaristic as it might seem, but was an attempt to force the Soviets into an arms race they could not afford.

Gorbachev's programme of **reform** led to a new relationship with the USA

- The Soviet Union was in a difficult state by the early 1980s. Brezhnev and the **Politburo** had been unwilling to consider any reform since the early 1960s and as a result the economy had stagnated and technology had fallen far behind the West.
- There were several leaders in a short time: Brezhnev, Andropov and Chernenko were all old-fashioned **hard-line** Communists who pushed the war in Afghanistan and made little attempt to improve the economy. When Chernenko died, he was replaced by the progressive Mikhail Gorbachev.
- While initially sceptical of Reagan, the **Chernobyl disaster** forced Gorbachev to move forward with a controversial series of reforms known as **Glasnost** and **Perestroika**.
- With these reforms underway, Reagan and Gorbachev began to improve their relationship with a series of meetings designed to end the Cold War.

A series of **negotiations** between Reagan and Gorbachev ended the Cold War

- The first meeting took place in Geneva in November 1985, and was very cordial. Both sides wanted to negotiate to reduce their stockpiles of nuclear weapons, which stood at over 12,000 each and were costing both sides a fortune to build and maintain.
- The first milestone was the **INF Treaty**. This was an agreement to remove intermediate-range missiles from Eastern and Western Europe.
- This treaty was followed by the **Strategic Arms Reduction Treaty (START)**, which began a programme of reducing the size of nuclear arsenals. The USA also provided billions of dollars in aid to help the Soviet Union dismantle its nuclear arsenal.
- At the same time, Gorbachev informed all the members of the **Warsaw Pact** that the Red Army would no longer be supporting them, and withdrew it over the course of 1987–89.

The **end** of communism in Eastern Europe was followed by the **collapse** of the Soviet Union

- The withdrawal of Soviet forces from Eastern Europe was followed by a surge in anti-government activity across the region. In every instance, the Communist regimes were aware that they could no longer remain in control by force alone.
- Beginning in Poland, the demonstrations forced governments to offer open elections. In most cases this process was peaceful, though in Romania, dictator Nicolae Ceausescu was killed along with his wife as he attempted to flee the country after years of brutal dictatorship.
- In East Germany, the hard-line government came to an end after the accidental opening of the Berlin Wall in November 1989. This triggered a process of **reunification** where East Germany was absorbed into the government of West Germany to create a single united nation with its capital in Berlin.
- Although these events made Gorbachev very popular in the West, they deeply angered the Politburo who attempted to overthrow him in August 1991. Although the attempt failed, thanks to Boris Yeltsin (President of Russia, 1991–99), it led to a series of demands from the Soviet republics (such as Ukraine and Estonia) for independence.
- Unable to hold the country together, Gorbachev dissolved the Soviet Union on 25 December 1991.

Test yourself

1. What was the official name for the 'Star Wars' programme?
2. What was the first treaty signed between Reagan and Gorbachev?
3. When did the USSR cease to exist?

Practice question

Why did the Cold War come to an end in 1991? Explain your answer. (10 marks)

Developing the detail

Below is a sample exam-style question and a paragraph written in answer to this question. The paragraph contains a limited amount of detail. Annotate the paragraph to add additional detail to the answer.

Outline the events that led to the end of communism in Eastern Europe. (5 marks)

Once the Soviet leader Gorbachev had taken power, he realised the USSR could no longer afford to maintain its competition with the United States. After he had realised this, he told the leaders of the Communist countries in Eastern Europe that he would no longer be keeping the army in their countries. This meant that when many countries began to experience protests against communism in the later 1980s, they did not have the strength of the USSR to keep them in power. Most Communist governments were forced to agree to elections where they were voted out of power.

Delete as applicable

Below is a paragraph written in answer to this question.

'The Cold War came to an end because of the willingness of Gorbachev to compromise and give in to what Reagan and Bush asked for in negotiations.' How far do you agree with this statement? (18 marks)

Read the paragraph and decide which of the possible options in bold is most appropriate. Delete the least appropriate options and, on a separate piece of paper, complete the paragraph by justifying your selection.

I agree to a great/fair/limited extent that it was Gorbachev who ended the Cold War. Gorbachev showed willingness to completely change the stance on the Soviet Union over matching the USA in weapons capabilities. His willingness to let the countries of Eastern Europe be free from the Red Army showed his general reformist attitude, as did Glasnost and Perestroika. Additionally, he worked well with Reagan when …

1.11 After the Cold War: the rise of al-Qaeda

REVISED

The end of the Cold War saw a period of great **global unrest**

- The end of the Cold War briefly seemed likely to herald the end of **global conflict**, but this dream was short lived. Throughout the 1990s there was conflict and warfare across the globe:

Iraq	Yugoslavia	Rwanda
The first **Gulf War** broke out in 1990 after Iraq invaded the oil-rich state of Kuwait. A UN force expelled the Iraqi army within days, but did not pursue the invaders back into Iraq	The collapse of Communist Yugoslavia began a series of civil wars between the various ethnicities and religions of the Balkans, leading to hundreds of thousands of casualties	In 1994, Rwanda in central Africa became the scene of one of the worst **genocides** in history as the majority Hutu people massacred nearly 1 million Tutsi people in just three months before order was restored

Al-Qaeda emerged in response to anger among individuals like **Osama bin Laden**

- In Afghanistan, within the mujahidin, there emerged a movement that believed Islam (or at least, their form of **fundamentalist** Islam) was under severe threat, both from the West, and even from Islamic groups and states that did not hold the same strict beliefs. This movement was called **al-Qaeda**.
- Osama bin Laden emerged as the most significant leader of this movement. He was the son of a Saudi Arabian billionaire. When Saudi Arabia was threatened by Iraq during the invasion of Kuwait, bin Laden offered the services of al-Qaeda to defend the country.
- The Saudi King, Fahd, refused and took the help of the USA and its allies instead. Bin Laden openly criticised the king and was in turn forced into **exile** (forced to leave his own country).
- From here, bin Laden turned al-Qaeda into an extremely efficient and well-trained terrorist organisation. It gave support to the **Taliban**, which was attempting to take control of Afghanistan, and it began to attack Western and Israeli targets.

Key point

New challenges to international peace and security have arisen following the end of the Cold War.

Al-Qaeda developed into a notable and increasingly violent, force

- Al-Qaeda's success can be explained by a number of factors:

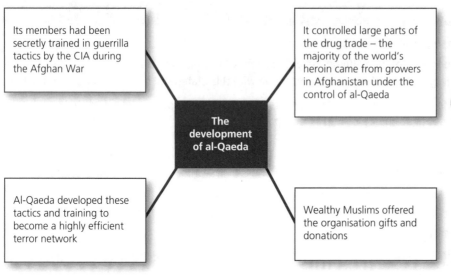

The development of al-Qaeda

- Its members had been secretly trained in guerrilla tactics by the CIA during the Afghan War
- It controlled large parts of the drug trade – the majority of the world's heroin came from growers in Afghanistan under the control of al-Qaeda
- Al-Qaeda developed these tactics and training to become a highly efficient terror network
- Wealthy Muslims offered the organisation gifts and donations

Test yourself

1. What nationality was Osama bin Laden?
2. Where did Osama bin Laden seek refuge when he was exiled?
3. How long did it take allied forces to seize Afghanistan?

- As the 1990s continued, al-Qaeda became more extreme in its actions:
  - 1998 – a large truck filled with explosives was left outside the US Embassy in Nairobi, the capital of Kenya. 213 people were killed and 4600 injured.
  - 2000 – US naval destroyer USS *Cole* was attacked by suicide bombers and seventeen sailors were killed.
  - 11 September 2001 – two hijacked airliners crashed into and destroyed the twin towers of New York's **World Trade Center**, killing 2606 people. A third plane crashed into the **Pentagon** (US military headquarters), killing 125 people. A fourth plane crashed into woods in Pennsylvania. 265 people were killed on the four planes. The events are known as **9/11**.

The USA responded with the **'War on Terror'**, which led to the **invasion** of Afghanistan

- The response from the USA was swift and brutal. Very soon after the attack, al-Qaeda claimed responsibility. US President George W. Bush demanded that the Afghan leader, Mullah Omar, hand over bin Laden. Omar refused.
- In response, the United States built a coalition and attacked Afghanistan beginning in October 2001, less than three weeks later. Initially, there was a huge aerial assault using **cruise missiles**. This assault lasted for three weeks and destroyed Afghanistan's ability to fight by attacking bases, communications, roads and airports.
- This was followed by a land invasion by US, British and allied forces which crushed all opposition and captured the capital Kabul in less than two weeks. The final stronghold of Tora-Bora, a cave network in Afghanistan's eastern mountains, was captured by mid-December.
- The critical thing for the allies now was to learn from Afghanistan and win the '**hearts and minds**' of the Afghan people. To do this, the allies set about building schools, hospitals and other infrastructure to greatly improve the quality of life for the Afghan people. While this has proved effective in some urban areas, it has caused violence, tension and terror in much of the country.

Practice question

Explain why al-Qaeda attacked the USA on 11 September 2001.
(10 marks)

Stretch and challenge

Make a list of the mistakes that the United States made in the Vietnam War (refer to Section 1.8, pages 22–3). Then, beside this list, write down ways in which the USA tried to act differently in the War on Terror.

Checklist

Below is a list of events that may have taken place following the end of the Cold War. Tick or highlight those events which you know **did** take place.

- War broke out when Saddam Hussein invaded Kuwait.
- There was a civil war in Czechoslovakia.
- A genocide took place in Rwanda in 1994.
- The mujahidin had been supplied by weapons by the USA.
- Osama bin Laden was the son of an Afghan farmer.
- Al-Qaeda was formed to defend Islam against threats from all over the world.
- The 9/11 attacks were all successful.
- The American President, Bill Clinton, demanded that Afghanistan turn over bin Laden.

Spot the mistake

Below are a sample exam-style question and a paragraph written in answer to this question. Why does this paragraph not get into Level 5? Once you have identified the mistake, rewrite the paragraph so that it displays the qualities of Level 5. The mark scheme on pages 180–2 will help you.

Outline the events of the War on Terror that followed 9/11. (5 marks)

The American response to 9/11 was swift and severe. The invasion of Afghanistan was soon after 9/11, and victory was quick. Once they had secured control of the country, Afghanistan experienced a long period of peace.

Section 1B Non-British studies

What the non-British depth study is about and how it will be examined

Overview of the non-British depth study

The non-British depth study is a study of a short time period. The focus here is on the complexity of a society or historical situation.

Depth studies require you to:

- Demonstrate an understanding of the relationship between the people and the state; this includes knowledge of the policies of the state.
- Engage with how different groups of people were affected by state policies.
- Consider the reasons for, and nature of, support and/or opposition to the state from different groups.
- Consider the influence of international affairs on a domestic situation (this connects it to the period study).
- Engage with primary source material.

Key skills needed for the non-British depth study

Second-order concepts are thought processes that allow us to study the past. They do so by providing us with a way to organise 'big ideas' in history.

Below you will find guidance on the second-order concepts **most** relevant to the thematic studies. It important to acknowledge that some of the points below are **generalisations**; there are exceptions to all.

THE NON-BRITISH DEPTH STUDY

Cause – Why things happened. There is always a **variety** of reasons for events taking place. Your job will be to **explain** these reasons. The 18-mark question may involve you explaining which **factors** were most **important**; the best answers may explore how factors **link** together and the **relationship** between them. Useful words: 'created', 'produced', 'prompted'

Similarity and difference – This concept is about **how far** experiences are shared in the same place and at the same time: in other words, did **everyone** experience something in the same way? The answer to this question is never going to be a straightforward 'yes' and therefore you will be looking at the **diversity** of people's experiences in a given historical situation. Useful words: 'stereotype', 'typical', 'common'

Consequence – You may be asked to consider the impact of an action or event, and who and what was **affected** by it. You may also want to consider whether some consequences were more **significant** than others. Useful words: 'resulted', 'ensued', 'arose'

Evidence – You will be asked to compare sources and explain their usefulness of sources for an enquiry

Main question types in the non-British depth study

This is Section B of Paper 1. It is worth 40 marks in total. You will be asked the following types of question:

1 **Describe one example of ...** *(2 marks)*

This is a basic describe question. One mark will be awarded for an example and another for development/description (as 2 marks are available you will only be expected to do this once).

You do not need to go into a huge amount of depth here – the development/ description just need to add depth to the example that has been identified.

2 **Explain how/why ...** *(10 marks)*

This question will come from a different key issue than that focused on in the previous question.

A full-mark answer would explain more than one feature in relation to the question with a good amount of supporting detail.

The focus is not on the number of examples explained. You should concentrate on producing an explanation which is focused on the second-order concept identified by the question (for example, cause, consequence, change): this type of response would reveal a detailed understanding of the issue.

The source-based part of the paper will either be:

A single 10-mark question that asks you to make some sort of comparison of the sources. For example: 'Which of the two sources is the most useful for telling us about ...'

Two separate 5-mark questions that test your source skills (the same types of source skills will be addressed as by the 10-mark questions). For example: Explain how this source is useful to a historian studying ...'

A variety of sources will be found in this part of the paper.

There is no pattern as to whether you will have two 5-mark questions or one 10-mark question.

For both types of question source analysis should be the driving force of your answer. Own knowledge will only be credited when directly linked to source analysis.

You should consider and make use of source features to answer any type of source question, for example, provenance, purpose or context.

3 **How far do you agree (with a statement)?** *(18 marks)*

Arguments in response to this question should pick up on the second-order concept(s) being addressed in the statement.

For a full-mark answer you should consider both sides of the argument, make sure that your response is fully supported with examples that are entirely relevant to the question, and produce a substantiated conclusion.

How we help you develop your exam skills

The revision tasks help you to build understanding and skills step by step. For example:

- **Flow chart** will help you to check your understanding of a sequence of events, and to consider why something happened.
- **Delete as applicable** will allow you to check the relevance of information.
- **Considering usefulness** will allow you to consider the utility of a source.
- **Support or challenge?** will help you to use content to inform your judgement in an essay question.
- The **practice questions** give you exam-style questions.

Plus:

- There are annotated model answers for every practice question online at **www.hoddereducation.co.uk/myrevisionnotes** or use this QR code to find them instantly.

2 Germany 1925–1955: The People and the State

2.1 The Nazis during the Weimar 'Golden Years' and the Depression

REVISED

The years **1924–29** were regarded as the **'Golden Years'** of Weimar

- 1919–23 were traumatic years for Germany, with a series of economic and political crises.
- Gustav Stresemann became chancellor in August 1923. Under his leadership the Weimar Republic was more stable, although there were still problems.

Key point

Support for the Nazi Party grew following the Depression and the failure of Weimar democracy.

	Positive aspects, 1924–29	Negative aspects, 1924–29
Economic	• Dawes Plan, 1924. The USA agreed to lend Germany £40 million. It stabilised the economy • In 1928, levels of industrial production reached the same levels as before the First World War • Germany regained its status as the world's second greatest industrial power	• US loans could be called in at any time • Economic growth was uneven, favouring big business and landowners • Peasant farmers and sections of the middle classes did not benefit from economic gains
Cultural	• Free expression of ideas was allowed • There were new artists, architecture and international film stars • Berlin became known for its night-life and by 1927 there were 900 dance bands	• Some felt this represented a moral decline, especially those living in villages • The Wandervogel movement wanted a return to simple country values and help for those in the countryside
Political	• The Locarno Treaties, 1925. Germany's borders with France and Belgium wouldn't be changed • As a result, in 1926 Germany was permitted to join the League of Nations • By 1929, Stresemann had also negotiated the Young Plan, which further reduced reparations payments	• The Weimar Republic was a coalition government • Around 30 per cent of votes in elections went to extremist parties • Paul von Hindenburg was appointed president in 1926. He was opposed to democracy • Stresemann was criticised for agreeing the Locarno Treaties and joining the League – these actions showed he accepted the Treaty of Versailles

The Nazis became **well known**, but were **not successful** in elections

- In 1919, Anton Drexler founded the German Workers' Party. By 1921 Hitler was its leader.
- The 'Twenty-Five Point Programme' set out the policies of the party, stressing the superiority of the German people and promoting **anti-Semitism**.
- Hitler tried to seize power in November 1923, through the Munich Putsch. This failed and Hitler was sent to prison.
- Hitler wrote ***Mein Kampf*** (*My Struggle*) while in prison. This set out his beliefs, such as ***lebensraum*** (living space) and that **Aryans** (white Europeans) were the 'master-race'.
- He also realised that the tactics of the Nazis had to change and rather than seize power by force, they would have to come to power democratically.
- But the Nazis still failed to win popular support, gaining only twelve seats in the Reichstag in the 1928 elections. Their anti-Semitic policies did appeal to some, but they failed to win over the majority of workers.

The **Wall Street Crash** in the USA led to a **Depression** in Germany

- Following the Wall Street Crash, US banks called in their loans from Germany. Businesses went bankrupt, and industrial production declined.
- Many people lost their savings, as the banks failed and German money lost its value. The middle classes and pensioners were hit hard.
- Unemployment rose. In October 1929, there were 1.6 million people out of work. By February 1932, this had risen to over 6 million. More than half of young Germans aged 16–30 were unemployed in 1933.

The economic depression led to a **political crisis** in the Weimar Republic

- The Weimar politicians seemed unable or unwilling to deal with the economic problems.
- Heinrich Brüning, chancellor from March 1930, cut salaries and social benefits, and raised taxes.
- This was unpopular with the Reichstag. Brüning had to use **Article 48**, allowing Hindenburg to make decisions without parliamentary support.
- Germany was no longer functioning as a democracy. Germans turned to more extremist parties.
- Between 1928 and 1932, the Nazi Party grew in popularity, reflected in election results of the period. By November 1932, it was the largest party in the Reichstag.
- In the 1928 elections, the Nazi Party won three per cent of the vote. By November 1932, this had risen to 33 per cent of the vote.

Test yourself

1 Give three positive aspects and three negative aspects of the Weimar Republic between 1924 and 1929.

2 How did the Depression impact Germans?

3 How did the political crisis aid the Nazis?

Practice question

Describe **one** example of an achievement of the Weimar Republic in the 1920s. (2 marks)

Stretch and challenge

Would the Nazis have succeeded in their rise to power without the events of the Great Depression? Summarise your view in three sentences.

The Nazi Party **appealed** to **voters** in Germany for many reasons

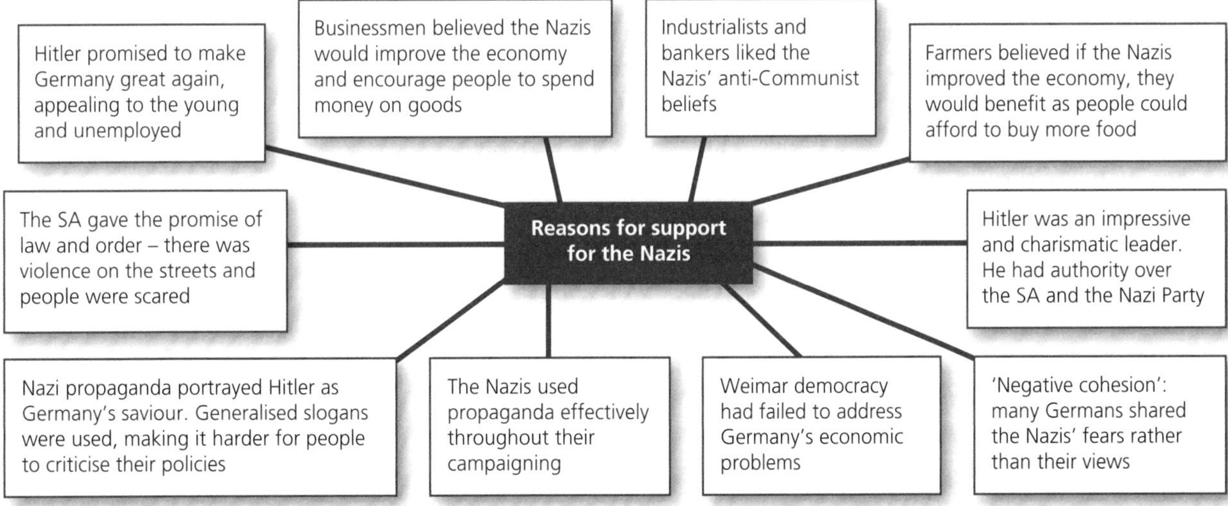

Reasons for support for the Nazis
Hitler promised to make Germany great again, appealing to the young and unemployed
Businessmen believed the Nazis would improve the economy and encourage people to spend money on goods
Industrialists and bankers liked the Nazis' anti-Communist beliefs
Farmers believed if the Nazis improved the economy, they would benefit as people could afford to buy more food
The SA gave the promise of law and order – there was violence on the streets and people were scared
Hitler was an impressive and charismatic leader. He had authority over the SA and the Nazi Party
Nazi propaganda portrayed Hitler as Germany's saviour. Generalised slogans were used, making it harder for people to criticise their policies
The Nazis used propaganda effectively throughout their campaigning
Weimar democracy had failed to address Germany's economic problems
'Negative cohesion': many Germans shared the Nazis' fears rather than their views

Checklist

Below is a list of reasons which may explain why attitudes towards the Nazi Party changed between 1920 and 1930. Tick or highlight those reasons which you know are *true*.

- Hitler continued to use force to seize power.
- The Depression made people turn against the Weimar Republic.
- Propaganda portrayed Hitler as Germany's saviour.
- The Nazis used slogans which were confusing.
- Before 1928, the Nazis won over the workers.
- People were more willing to vote for Hitler after the Depression because the SA gave the impression of providing stable law and order.

2.2 Nazi consolidation of power, 1933–34

Hitler became **chancellor** through electoral support and **political dealings**

- The Nazi Party increased its share of the votes in the July 1932 elections, winning 230 seats. This was more than any other party, but Hindenburg still refused to make Hitler chancellor as he was suspicious of him

↓

- Things seemed to be going worse for the Nazis – in the November 1932 elections they lost 38 seats

↓

- In December 1932, Hindenburg chose von Schleicher as chancellor, but he was forced to resign within a month. Hindenburg effectively ruled with the support of army leaders and industrialists

↓

- Hitler then struck a deal with Franz von Papen, another politician. Hitler would make von Papen vice-chancellor if von Papen could persuade Hindenburg to make Hitler chancellor

↓

- Hindenburg agreed to this, as he knew Hitler was popular. Both Hindenburg and von Papen believed that they could control Hitler. Hitler became **chancellor of Germany** on 30 January 1933

Key point

Hitler became chancellor in 1933, and by the end of August 1934 he was the *Führer*. Germany had moved from democracy to dictatorship.

The Nazis used the **Reichstag Fire** to remove the Communists

- In the 1933 elections, the Nazis controlled the media and banned any opposition meetings. The SA were also used to terrorise opponents.
- On 27 February 1933, the Reichstag caught fire. Marinus van der Lubbe, a Dutch Communist, was blamed for this. Hitler exploited the fire for his own purposes, and used it to stir up anti-Communist feeling in Germany.
- As a result of this, Hitler persuaded Hindenburg to pass the **Emergency Decree** on 28 February 1933, removing people's civil rights. Using the law, thousands of Communist supporters were thrown into prison.
- Elections took place on 5 March 1933, and the Nazis hoped that they would win enough seats to have an overall majority. They won 288 seats, but still didn't have a majority.
- Consequently, Hitler used the support of the Nationalist Party to gain a majority in the Reichstag and then banned the Communist Party.

The **Enabling Act** allowed Hitler to make laws without consulting the Reichstag

- The **Enabling Act** was passed on 24 March 1933 – it gave Hitler the right to pass laws for the next four years without having to get the support of the Reichstag. Hitler was a legal dictator.
- Trade unions were banned in May 1933, and all workers became part of the **German Labour Front (DAF)**.
- In July 1933, Hitler outlawed all other political parties – Germany became a **one-party state**.

Test yourself

1 Explain how Hitler rose to the position of chancellor.
2 Why did the Reichstag Fire help the Nazis?
3 What happened on the Night of the Long Knives?

Hitler successfully removed a threat to his power during the **Night of the Long Knives**

- Although the SA had helped Hitler to come to power, Hitler now saw it as a potential threat. Hitler believed Röhm, the leader of the SA, was becoming too powerful.
- The army were also suspicious of the SA and Röhm, and Hitler knew he would need the support of the army to remain in power. He therefore acted ruthlessly to deal with this threat.
- On the weekend of 29–30 June 1934, **SS** assassination squads murdered Hitler's potential SA rivals, including Röhm. Up to 400 people were killed.
- The SA became subordinate to the SS and many of its members were absorbed into the SS and army.
- Hitler declared his actions to be legal, as he argued that those killed were plotting to overthrow the government.
- The Night of the Long Knives was a triumph for Hitler, as it got rid of opposition and showed how ruthless the Nazis could be.

The death of Hindenburg led to the rise of Hitler as *Führer*

- President Hindenburg died in August 1934.
- Hitler used Hindenburg's death to combine the posts of chancellor and president.
- Hitler called himself ***der Führer*** ('the leader') of Germany.
- He also made himself the commander-in-chief of the army. From this point onwards, members of the armed forces swore an **oath of allegiance** (a promise of loyalty) to Hitler. Soldiers vowed to obey him and give their lives for him.
- The Weimar Republic was dead. Germany was a **dictatorship**.

Flow chart

Below is a blank flow diagram into which you must put the five key events that led to Hitler becoming *Führer* in 1934. The first one has been completed for you. A list of events that you could have chosen can be found on page 34.

The Great Depression

Practice question

Study Source A. Explain why this source was published in Germany at this time.

(5 marks)

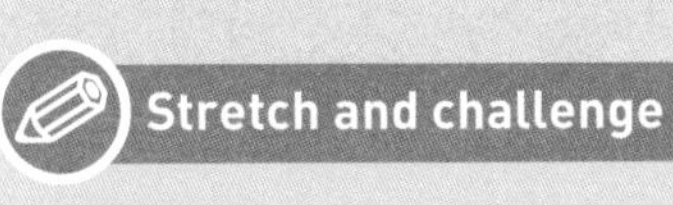

Stretch and challenge

Remember that in the exam you could also face a question about a source's usefulness. Can you identify how the election poster in Source A is useful when studying the rise of Nazi Germany?

SOURCE A *Nazi election poster, 1932. The text reads 'Work, Freedom and Bread! Vote for the National Socialists!'*

2.3 Nazi control through terror and propaganda

REVISED

Once in power, the Nazis set about turning Germany into a **police state**

- The Enabling Act meant that the government could read people's post, listen in on their conversations and search homes without notice.
- Germany was turning into a **police state**, whereby the police would supervise and restrict the activities of the Germans.
- Top jobs within the police were given to high-ranking Nazis.
- Civil servants who did not support the Nazis were sacked, and in 1934 the Law for the Reconstruction of the Reich was passed, giving the Nazis total power over local government.
- The legal system was controlled by the Nazis. Consequently, all judges were Nazis and there was no trial by jury.
- In March 1934, the **SD** (Nazi intelligence service) was set up under the initial command of Reinhard Heydrich, with the aim of spying on all Germans.

Key point

The Nazis maintained Germany as a totalitarian (one-party) state through the use of terror and propaganda. They aimed to create a *Volksgemeinschaft* (national community).

The Nazi Party also used **terror** to get the German people to **conform**

- The SS expanded under Himmler in the 1930s. It was completely loyal to Hitler and was feared by the German people.
- The first **concentration camps** were set up after 1933, initially to hold political prisoners.
- The **Gestapo** (secret police) was also feared. People were encouraged to report anyone to the Gestapo who they believed were anti-Nazi.
- The Gestapo was aided by local wardens, who would ensure that Germans were loyal to the Nazi regime.
- Most Germans were prepared to accept the new regime – either out of fear or because they agreed with the aims of the Nazis.

Test yourself

1 Give three examples of how Germany turned into a police state.
2 Why was Nazi propaganda effective?
3 How did the Nazis wish to create a *Volksgemeinschaft*?

As **minister of propaganda**, Goebbels aimed to **control** what the German people thought

- Goebbels was in charge of the Nazi 'propaganda machine', to promote the main Nazi ideas. He cultivated the '**Hitler myth**', which portrayed Hitler as saviour of Germany.
- Huge propaganda events such as the **Nuremberg rallies** gave the impression that the Nazis were bringing strength and order after a period of chaos.
- The Nazis promised to rebuild Germany through abolishing the Treaty of Versailles and restoring political stability. They promoted anti-Semitic and anti-Communist messages.
- Young people were more susceptible to Nazi propaganda, and the middle classes also responded positively.
- The Nazis' control of the media made it nearly impossible to access different views.

TIP

One of the key aims of the Nazis was to create a 'national community', or *Volksgemeinschaft*. Hitler believed in all Germans being one and working together. He wanted, in particular, to restore family values and Christianity to Germany in order to revive Germany after the Weimar Republic. The use of propaganda reinforced this, and aimed to convince members of the *Volksgemeinschaft* that they would work together to achieve Nazi goals.

In order to control people, the Nazis used a variety of **methods of propaganda**

Methods of propaganda used by the Nazis

- **Radio:** cheap radios ('People's Receivers') were manufactured so that most Germans could afford one. Broadcasting was controlled by the Nazis, and listening to the BBC was punishable by death
- **Films:** Goebbels ordered that all films, whether factual or fictional, had to have a pro-Nazi message. All foreign films were censored. Before each feature, there would be a newsreel made by Goebbels' film-makers
- **Books:** all books had to have Goebbels' permission to be published. In 1933, books which held ideas the Nazis didn't approve of were burned
- **Newspapers:** could not print anti-Nazi ideas. Editors were told what they could print. Circulation of newspapers fell by about ten per cent as they became dull to read
- **Art and music:** only Nazi-approved painters could show their work. Jazz was banned as 'black' music
- **Rallies:** the yearly rallies at Nuremberg were used to display unity, order and discipline
- **1936 Berlin Olympics:** used by the Nazis to suggest the superiority of the Aryan race

The Nazis hoped to create a *Volksgemeinschaft*

- The Nazis wished to create a *Volksgemeinschaft*, of Aryan Germans who were loyal to Hitler and the state.
- Their hope was that there would be no distinction between farmers, workers, and so on as they would just see themselves primarily as Germans. They would put the interests of their country before their own.
- In creating the *Volksgemeinschaft*, the Nazis hoped to restore pride and the belief that Germany was a racially and culturally superior nation.

Practice question

Study Source B. Explain how this source is useful to a historian studying Nazi Germany. (5 marks)

Considering usefulness

Below is a source on Hitler written in 1936 by David Lloyd George. Read the source, and consider how it is useful based on these criteria: content, provenance and context. Rate each one out of 10 and then explain why you think this source is useful to a historian or not.

SOURCE B *David Lloyd George paid Hitler a three-hour visit at the Berghof in September 1936. Later he wrote about him in the* Daily Express, *17 November 1936. Taken from D.G. Williamson,* The Third Reich, *2011.*

The old trust him, the young idolise him. It is not the admiration accorded to a popular leader. It is the worship of a national hero who has saved the country from utter despondency and degradation ... he is immune from criticism as a king in a monarchical country. He is something more. He is the George Washington of Germany – the man who won for his country independence from all oppressors. To those who have not actually seen and sensed the way Hitler reigns over the heart and mind of Germany, this description may appear extravagant. All the same it is the bare truth.

Content	Provenance	Context
What does this source reveal about attitudes towards Hitler?	Why is it significant that these comments were made by someone from Britain?	What knowledge can you include to explain why the source is useful?

Stretch and challenge

Do you think the Nazis would have stayed in power for so long without the creation of the police state? Explain your view.

2.4 Nazi economic and social policies

REVISED

Once in power, the Nazis sought to combat the **unemployment** problem and strengthen Germany

- The **National Labour Service** was set up. Men aged 16–25 were given jobs, and from 1935 it was compulsory to serve in this for six months.
- Hitler also established public work programmes. Unemployed men aided in the construction of **autobahns** (motorways), schools and hospitals.
- Due to the banning of trade unions, all workers had to join the German Labour Front.
- From 1935, **military conscription** was introduced for men aged 18–25. They had to serve for two years.
- In 1936, the **Four-Year Plan** was announced, which aimed to get the German economy ready for war.

Key point

The Nazis aimed to create a national community and went about making economic and social changes to every section of society.

Economic policies were set up to support the creation of a ***Volksgemeinschaft***

- The **Strength through Joy (KDF)** scheme provided workers with cheap holidays and leisure activities.
- The **Beauty of Labour** scheme improved working conditions in factories.
- The **Volkswagen** ('People's Car') Beetle Scheme meant Germans could save five marks per week to purchase their own car.
- Big businesses benefited as wages became stable and the role of trade unions diminished.
- All workers had to join the General Labour Front (DAF), run by Dr Robert Ley. This controlled the workers and striking was forbidden.
- Farmers played a key role in Hitler's rise to power, so he set up the **Reich Food Estate** in 1933. This meant that farmers had a market for their goods at guaranteed prices.
- The **Reich Entailed Farm Law** meant banks couldn't seize farms. It also had a racial aim, '*Blut und Boden*' ('Blood and Soil') – the belief that farmers were the backbone of the master race.

Not everyone benefited from the economic changes

- Workers couldn't strike, leading to grumbling and dissatisfaction with working conditions.
- By the late 1930s, workers were complaining that their standard of living was still lower than it had been before the Depression.
- Big businesses benefited, but it was harder for smaller businesses to survive.
- People moved from rural to urban areas because of the difference in wages, leading to a shortage of agricultural workers.
- Unemployment statistics didn't show 'invisible unemployment' – women and Jewish people were not counted.
- The Reich Entailed Farm Law only applied to twenty per cent of farms, and the law restricted farms expanding and modernising.

Test yourself

1. Give two examples of how the Nazis aimed to reduce unemployment.
2. How were farmers affected by Nazi economic policy?
3. Give two ways in which the education system was 'Nazified'.

The Nazis had **traditional ideas** about women which they supported with **policies, until war** broke out

- Women were expected to stay at home, raise children, cook for their families and go to church: ***Kinder, Küche, Kirche*** ('Children, Kitchen, Church').
- Women received medals for having children. They received a gold medal for eight children; a silver medal for six children and a bronze medal for four children.
- All these actions led to:
  - an increase in the birth rate from 15 per 1000 in 1933 to 20 per 1000 in 1939
  - an increase in pregnancies outside marriage.
- But once the war began, the male workforce was deployed and women were needed again in the workforce.

The aim of the **youth movements** and **education** was to create **committed** Nazis

- The Nazis wanted to ensure that young people remained loyal to the regime, and wanted to control them both at school and in their free time.
- In 1936, membership of the **Hitler Youth** was made virtually compulsory.
- Other youth organisations were banned.
- By 1939, there were 7 million members of the Hitler Youth, compared to 100,000 in 1933.
- The Hitler Youth was for boys and the focus was on military training. The League of German Maidens was for girls and the focus was on domestic service.
- Teachers joined the Nazi Teachers' League and swore an oath of loyalty to Hitler.
- The curriculum was rewritten to promote Nazi ideas, for example, in Biology they would learn how Germans were a superior race to the Jews.
- There was a greater emphasis on physical education, and fifteen per cent of the timetable was devoted to this.

Developing the detail

Below are a sample exam-style question and a paragraph written in answer to this question. The paragraph contains a limited amount of detail. Annotate the paragraph to add additional detail to the answer.

Explain how the Nazis used education to indoctrinate the German youth. (10 marks)

The Nazis used the education system in many different ways. For example, the curriculum was rewritten. In addition, teachers had to join the Nazi Teachers' League. Physical fitness was emphasised. Boys and girls were given different opportunities. Thus, the Nazis controlled all aspects of the education system and were able to influence what the German youth believed.

Practice question

Explain how workers were affected by Nazi economic policies.

(10 marks)

Stretch and challenge

Compare the experience of workers, farmers and businesses under Nazi rule and the Weimar Republic. How far did the Nazis improve things?

Do/don't list

Below is a list of factors you have to consider when answering 10-mark questions. Tick or highlight those factors which you know are *correct* when answering these types of questions.

- Come to a judgement which repeats everything you have said.
- Explain fully two clear reasons.
- Use precise evidence to support points made.
- Use lots of description.
- Include everything you know about a topic.
- Spend no more than ten minutes answering the question.

2.5 Opposition towards the Nazis, and Nazi treatment of minorities

REVISED

Even though the Nazis had a **tight grip** over Germany, there was still some **opposition**

- Underground networks were formed to try to organise industrial unrest.
- In 1937, Catholic priests read out a **papal encyclical** (letter) from the Pope, which condemned some Nazi ideas.
- Some youth opposition groups formed, for instance the **Edelweiss Pirates**. They rejected Nazi values and attacked the Hitler Youth.
- The **Swing Youth** rebelled against the Nazi control of culture, by listening to American jazz and dressing unconventionally.
- Some Germans expressed their dissatisfaction by refusing to give the Nazi salute, making anti-Hitler jokes and not hanging swastika flags.

Key point

Opposition towards the Nazis was limited. As soon as the Nazis took power they began their persecution of many minority groups, which grew increasingly violent.

There were reasons why **opposition** to Nazi rule was not greater

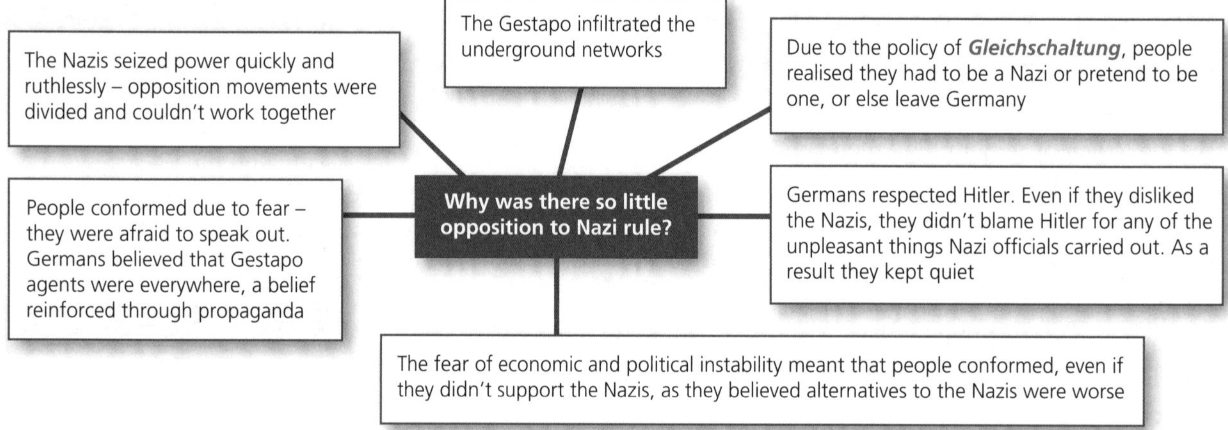

Why was there so little opposition to Nazi rule?
The Nazis seized power quickly and ruthlessly – opposition movements were divided and couldn't work together
The Gestapo infiltrated the underground networks
Due to the policy of *Gleichschaltung*, people realised they had to be a Nazi or pretend to be one, or else leave Germany
People conformed due to fear – they were afraid to speak out. Germans believed that Gestapo agents were everywhere, a belief reinforced through propaganda
Germans respected Hitler. Even if they disliked the Nazis, they didn't blame Hitler for any of the unpleasant things Nazi officials carried out. As a result they kept quiet
The fear of economic and political instability meant that people conformed, even if they didn't support the Nazis, as they believed alternatives to the Nazis were worse

The Nazis violently **persecuted** many **minority** groups within Germany

- Because of their belief in the superiority of the Aryan race, the Nazis sought to cleanse Germany of 'inferior' groups who challenged Nazi ideas.
- Many Gypsies were targeted. Five out of six Gypsies living in Germany in 1939 were killed by the Nazis.
- Jehovah's Witnesses were sent to concentration camps for religious reasons as they would not make Hitler their first loyalty and were opposed to war.
- Homosexuals were seen as a threat to family life and were sent to concentration camps. In 1936, Himmler set up the Central Office for the Combating of Homosexuality and Abortion.
- If there was the possibility of hereditary illnesses, **sterilisation** was enforced. Over 300,000 men and women were sterilised between 1934 and 1945 as the Nazis sought to remove 'genetic defects' from the gene pool.
- Mentally and physically disabled Germans were also targeted. A '**euthanasia**' programme was begun in 1939 and at least 5000 disabled babies and children were killed between 1939 and 1945.
- Around 72,000 mentally ill patients were gassed between 1939 and 1941, before public opposition to this grew and it was stopped.
- These racially based social policies were carried out because Hitler wanted to 'improve' the Aryan race through the Nazis' **eugenics** policies.

Hitler **hated** the **Jews** and immediately took steps against them when the Nazis took power

- Anti-Semitism had occurred in Europe for centuries – the Jews were blamed for the death of Christ and many people were jealous of well-educated Jews who ran successful shops and businesses.
- Hitler viewed the success of the Jews as a threat to the Aryan race.
- From 1933, the Nazis organised a **boycott** of Jewish businesses. Jews were prevented from entering certain professions, for example teaching.
- Jewish shops were marked with the Star of David and the word *Jüde* (Jew).
- Things escalated in 1935 with the passing of the **Nuremberg Laws**. Jews were no longer considered to be German citizens; Jews couldn't marry Aryans, and they had to wear a yellow star on their clothing.
- By 1938, Jews were no longer allowed in public places, and all Jewish children were banned from attending German schools.

Kristallnacht was a turning point in the Nazi treatment of the Jews

- In November 1938, a German diplomat was shot dead by a Jew in Paris.
- The Nazis retaliated, by ordering an attack on Jewish homes, businesses and synagogues.
- Between 9 and 10 November 1938, around 200 synagogues were burned down, thousands of businesses were attacked and 91 Jews were killed.
- In the following months, around 20,000 Jews were arrested and taken to concentration camps.
- Following *Kristallnacht* (the 'Night of the Broken Glass'), conditions for German Jews increasingly worsened.

Delete as applicable

Below are a sample exam-style question and a paragraph written in answer to the question. Read the paragraph and decide which of the possible options (underlined) is most appropriate. Delete the least appropriate options and complete the paragraph by justifying your selection.

'The passing of the Nuremberg Laws was the harshest measure the Nazi regime took against the Jews before 1939.' How far do you agree with this statement? (18 marks)

I agree to a great/fair/limited extent that the Nuremberg Laws were the harshest measure the Nazi regime took against the Jews. The passing of the Laws meant that German Jews were no longer seen as German citizens, marriage between Jews and non-Jews was banned, and Jews had to wear a yellow star on their clothing. This was a harsh measure because it restricted the rights of Jews and it started to turn anti-Semitism into a law. Additionally, the Nuremberg Laws were a harsh measure because

____

____

Test yourself

1 Give two examples of opposition to the Nazi Party.
2 Prioritise the reasons why opposition to the Nazi was largely ineffective.
3 How did the Nazis aim to 'cleanse' Germany?
4 Why are the Nuremberg Laws significant?
5 Outline the events of *Kristallnacht*.

TIP

Gleichschaltung refers to the Nazi takeover of parts of German society, such as the civil service, once they were in power. In practice, it meant the Nazification of society, for instance through the army oath and the replacement of the trade unions with the DAF. It allowed the Nazis to extend their control over Germany.

Stretch and challenge

Create a timeline which summarises the changing treatment of minorities, and identify times when persecution escalated. See if you can use contextual knowledge to explain these different periods.

Practice question

Explain why there was little opposition to the Nazi regime in the 1930s. (10 marks)

2.6 The impact of the war on Germany, 1939–45

REVISED

Hitler had **prepared** the Germans for war and initially Germany had many **successes**

- Morale was high when war was announced. The Germans had been prepared for war by the Nazi regime.
- Germany had great success at the start, invading Poland and France, as well as the majority of Europe.
- In June 1941, Hitler invaded the USSR and occupied the Baltic States. He wanted them as *lebensraum*.
- Bombing raids did not have too much of an impact initially.

Key point

The Second World War was a total war, which impacted on every part of German society. As the tide turned against the Germans, opposition grew, but so did persecution and the Final Solution was set in motion.

As the war continued, Germany suffered huge **losses** on the front and **hardships** at home

- Of the 18 million Germans who served in the armed forces, 5 million were wounded and 5 million were killed – 90 per cent of them on the Eastern Front.
- Rationing was introduced for clothing and food in 1939, and by 1942 the government rationed food more strictly.
- Working hours increased to over 50 hours per week.
- Foreign labour had to be used as workers were conscripted into the army.
- Due to the defeats in 1942, Albert Speer directed the economy to prepare for **total war**. All Germany's resources were directed to the war effort.
- All men not in the army had to join the ***Volkssturm*** (Home Guard).
- In 1942, the British and American air forces began to bomb German cities more heavily, disrupting lives even further.
- The bombing of Dresden in February 1945 killed between 35,000 and 150,000 people in just two days.

Women and young people became increasingly **involved** in the war effort as the war progressed

- The Nazis were torn between needing women workers and their traditional view of women.
- After 1941, the number of women in work did increase, especially in armaments factories, but not much.
- Youth movements focused on military drill and aiding the war effort.
- The age of conscription to the army decreased to sixteen.

Opposition increased as the war continued

- The activities of the anti-Hitler Youth movement, the Edelweiss Pirates, escalated. In 1944, in Cologne, twelve of the ringleaders were hanged.
- A student resistance group, the White Rose, distributed anti-Nazi leaflets. Its founders, Hans and Sophie Scholl, were executed in 1943.
- Catholic and Protestant Church leaders became more vocal with their opposition. For instance, Bishop Galen criticised the euthanasia policy. The Nazis were forced to stop this policy temporarily.
- Members of the army made several attempts to assassinate Hitler.
- One assassination attempt was the July Plot of 1944. Von Stauffenberg left a bomb in Hitler's conference room. The bomb did go off, but Hitler survived and the Nazis sought revenge, killing 5000 people.

Test yourself

1. Describe how morale changed between 1939 and 1942.
2. Why did opposition increase during the war?

Racial persecution towards the Jews escalated and ultimately led to the Final Solution

- In occupied countries, the Nazis set up ghettos, which were small areas of towns where Jews were gathered together. Conditions were terrible.
- After the invasion of the USSR in 1941, the Nazis found themselves with 3 million Soviet Jews to control. The ***Einsatzgruppen*** (SS death squads) organised mass executions of many of these Jews.
- The Wannsee Conference took place in January 1942, where the 'Final Solution' to the 'Jewish question' was discussed. The systematic killing of the Jews took place after this.
- **Death camps** were built, such as Auschwitz, to carry out the killing and cremation of mainly Jews, but also other groups such as Gypsies and homosexuals.
- There was some Jewish resistance, such as Gad Beck who led Jewish resistance in Berlin. Others led uprisings in the concentration and death camps.
- Some non-Jews and many Germans also helped Jews by hiding them and helping them to escape German territory.

Complete the paragraph

Below are a sample exam-style question and a paragraph written in answer to this question. The paragraph contains a point and specific examples, but lacks a concluding explanatory link back to the question. Complete the paragraph adding this link in the space provided.

Explain why opposition to the Nazi regime grew during the Second World War. **(10 marks)**

One reason why opposition to the Nazi regime grew during the Second World War was because the German army became disillusioned and dissatisfied with Hitler and the Nazis. As a result there were different attempts to assassinate ______________________________

____

____

Practice question

Study Sources C and D. Why do these two sources disagree? (10 marks)

SOURCE C *Perfect Aryan Family, Wolf Willrich, 1930s.*

SOURCE D *Women working in an armaments factory, Berlin, 1942.*

2.7 The impact of defeat and occupation of Germany, 1945–55

REVISED

Germany **surrendered** in May 1945 and was soon occupied by the Allies

- In 1945, Soviet forces entered Berlin and on 30 April Hitler killed himself. The war was over.
- Germany signed a full surrender on 7 May 1945, and the Soviets were the first to occupy Berlin.
- The Potsdam Conference took place in July 1945, where it was decided that Berlin would be split among the four occupying powers (USA, Britain, France and the USSR). Germany was to be denazified, demilitarised and democratised.
- Denazification included banning the Nazi Party; arresting any Germans seen as a threat to Allied control; introducing a new education system; and punishing Nazi criminals at the Nuremberg Trials.

Key point

After the German surrender and the process of denazification, Germany was divided into two states, with people living very different lives.

The Soviets and the Allies had **different** approaches to **denazification**

- People in Germany wanted to forget. *Trümmerfrauen* ('rubble women') cleared bombed buildings in preparation for Germany to be rebuilt.
- It was estimated that 12–14 million German speakers in Eastern Europe became refugees. They returned to Germany, where they were not welcome.
- The Soviets wanted to stamp out Nazism and all evidence of it was destroyed:
  - Nazi officials were sent to camps
  - one-third of German teachers were removed
  - around 30,000 Germans were convicted by commissions of being involved with the Nazis.
- In the Western zones:
  - leading Nazis were arrested
  - Germans over the age of eighteen had to reveal their political beliefs and past jobs
  - the Western Allies investigated senior officials, as well as members of the public sector
  - the German Review Board investigated around 3.5 million cases; about 4000 people were found guilty and just under 500 were executed
  - the Allies also wanted to re-educate the Germans, by making them understand the horror of the Nazi atrocities.

Test yourself

1. What is meant by 'denazification'?
2. Why was the division of Germany cemented in 1949?
3. Describe how life was different in East and West Germany after 1949.

The Allies had different ideas about **Germany's future**

- The Western Allies wanted to rebuild Germany, to prevent extremism rising again and to develop trade links.
- The Soviets, however, wanted reparations as compensation, and believed Germany should be divided.
- The Americans introduced Marshall Aid in 1947, which was money to help countries involved in the war recover. The Soviets refused Marshall Aid in their zone.
- This led to the Western zones becoming more prosperous, which made the Soviets fearful.
- Consequently, in 1948 the Soviets launched the **Berlin Blockade**, to cut off supply routes into West Berlin. This failed, and led to deeper resentment.

TIP

Remember, when revising how the Allies were discussing Germany's future, the Marshall Plan and Berlin Blockade, think back to what you know about these factors from your International Relations content.

Practice question

'Denazification had the biggest impact on Germany in the years 1939–46.' How far do you agree with this statement? (18 marks)

Between 1949 and 1955, East and West Germans led very different lives

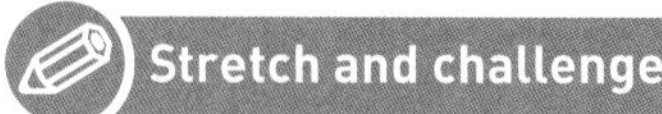

Stretch and challenge

Can you identify any ways in which there were similar experiences of democratisation in East and West Germany?

- The formation of two separate states cemented the division of Germany. The West formed the **Federal Republic of Germany** (West Germany); the Soviets the **German Democratic Republic** (East Germany).
- Between 1949 and 1955, life in West and East Germany was very different:

	Federal Republic of Germany	German Democratic Republic
Political	• Democracy • Basic Law – president had the power, but parties had to gain five per cent of the vote in order to send representatives to Parliament • Konrad Adenauer was chancellor from 1949 to 1963 • West Germany, alongside France, formed the European Coal and Steel Community in 1950 • In 1954 West Germany joined NATO	• Communist dictatorship • **Stasi** (secret police) was set up in 1950, keeping watch on potential enemies • Walter Ulbricht was installed as leader in 1949, a German and committed Communist • In theory, other political parties could exist, but the USSR ensured that the SED (German Communist Party) was the dominant force • By 1950, Ulbricht had reorganised the SED along the same lines as the USSR
Social	• Wages increased by more than 80 per cent between 1949 and 1955 • Industrial development led to more jobs • Government set up affordable housing schemes • Fewer strikes, as unions became less suspicious of managers • There was a growth in consumer goods, and the standard of living increased	• Lower living standards • Rationing had to be introduced • Germans forced into military service • Lack of consumer goods • Industrial unrest led to emigration of skilled people to West Germany • Any attempts to protest or to challenge Ulbricht were dealt with by the Stasi • Free education, as Ulbricht abolished private schools
Economic	• 'Economic miracle' – the economy grew by eight per cent each year between 1949 and 1954 • By 1955 unemployment had fallen to four per cent	• Few economic improvements • Stalin wanted East Germany to produce goods to help rebuild the USSR • Unlike in West Germany, there was no economic miracle

Which is best?

Below are two examples of answers to a 10-mark question for this paper. Read both, compare to the mark scheme on pages 180–2 and give both a mark out of 10. Underneath, explain why the one you have chosen is best.

Explain how the experiences of democratisation were different in East and West Germany. (10 marks)

a)	b)
In East Germany, a dictatorship was formed and there was a poor standard of living. In West Germany, Germans could vote for different political parties and there was a good standard of living.	*The experiences of democratisation in East and West Germany were different in many ways. For instance, in terms of politics, West Germany was a democratic state so Germans living there could vote for who they wanted, and had freedom to express their views. In comparison, East Germany was a dictatorship, with only the SED in power, and East Germans lived in fear of the Stasi, who kept watch over what was going on.*

3 The USA 1919–1948: The People and the State

3.1 The US economy in the 'Roaring Twenties'

REVISED

The **1920s** was a decade of great economic **affluence** in America

- In 1920, more people lived in towns than in the country.
- Average wages rose while working hours fell. This newfound leisure time was spent listening to music on the radio, dancing to jazz or at the cinema.
- Women gained a new freedom – the '**flapper**' (a woman who drank, smoked and partied) became one of the symbols of the 1920s.
- The boom in car ownership gave youth more freedom, helped the cities to expand and made more leisure activities possible.

Key point

After the First World War, the USA experienced an economic boom due to new technology and government policy, although not everyone benefited.

The **Republican Party** policies gave the **economy** room to **grow**

- President Hoover appointed experts from industry and business to help advise the government.
- He adopted a ***laissez-faire*** approach which meant less government interference. This, linked to '**rugged individualism**', meant that people were left to solve issues by themselves.
- The government put **tariffs** (taxes) on overseas goods. This protected the economy and encouraged people to 'buy American'.
- Low taxation meant that people kept more of their own money, which they could then spend on goods.

New industries boosted **production** and **decreased** the price of **luxury goods**

- The First World War showed the strength of the US economy to the world and helped to boost production levels. The USA overtook the industrial production of many of the fighting nations, and American banks benefited from loaning money to these devastated countries.
- Henry Ford's new car, the **Model T**, was made along a **production line**. This meant that each worker had one or two small jobs to do while the car moved past him along a conveyor belt. This sped up the process and made cars cheaper. By 1927, one car was produced every ten seconds.
- **Mass production** also applied to making luxury goods like radios and vacuum cleaners. This made them far more affordable.

Many of America's richest **businessmen** exploited US **natural resources**

- The USA was rich in oil, coal and iron, and these were used by many businessmen including:
  - Rockefeller – the boss of Standard Oil. The oil industry replaced coal as the most popular fuel, and car ownership was booming.
  - Carnegie – made his money from steel which was used to create cars, goods and skyscrapers.
  - Mellon – was a banker who gave investment to new industries such as electricity and aluminium, to help build cars, electrical appliances and aircraft.
- A new road network also employed many people and boosted the car industry.

Test yourself

1. What type of car did Henry Ford produce?
2. Why were goods cheaper in the 1920s?
3. Give an example of one failing industry.

People had newfound confidence in the economy

- People believed in the principle of **consumerism**. They felt they had a right to be successful and own the newest consumer goods.
- **Advertising** and the cinema encouraged people to buy more as they were shown **aspirational** images of what their lives could be like.
- People were allowed to buy on **credit**. This meant that they could pay in instalments over time and did not need the full amount at the time of purchase.
- With this confidence, many Americans bought shares in the **stock market**. They would use their own savings to buy small parts in companies with the view to selling them for a profit.

Practice question

Describe **one** example of Republican economic policies in the 1920s. (2 marks)

Not everyone benefited from the boom

Groups who did not benefit from the boom

Farmers
- Less food went overseas, which cut profits
- **Overproduction** meant that food went to waste
- Prices fell dramatically
- Competition from successful Canadian wheat farmers

The unemployed
- New machinery replaced workers
- Increased production did not mean increased jobs
- The government did very little to help

Traditional industries
- Coal was increasingly replaced, leading to a loss in jobs
- People in older industries had much lower pay
- New materials meant a loss of workers in the cotton industry

Support or challenge?

Below is a sample exam-style question which asks how far you agree with a specific statement. Below this are a series of general statements which are relevant to the question. Using your own knowledge and the information on the opposite page, place each factor in the box for 'agrees' or 'disagrees' with the stated view. As an additional challenge, you might want to think if any factors belong to both.

'Without the Republican policies, the prosperity of the 1920s would have been impossible.' How far do you agree with this view? (18 marks)

Factors leading to the economic boom:

- Low taxes set by the government meant that people had spare income.
- Tariffs on overseas goods meant that American goods were more appealing.
- The car industry employed a lot of people.
- People had confidence in the economy.
- The First World War had improved production levels.
- Advertising encouraged people to buy goods.
- The government left businesses to run themselves.
- People could buy goods on credit.
- Businesses were asked about policies.
- Mass production made a lot of goods much cheaper.

Agrees	Disagrees

Checklist

Decide whether or not each statement about the economic boom below is correct and put a tick in the appropriate box. Consider what evidence you can use to support your decision.

- The First World War helped cause the boom.
- People bought shares in the stock market.
- The Republicans interfered in the economy to make sure it worked.
- The production line made cars cheaper.
- The coal industry suffered in the 1920s.
- Farmers' exports decreased.
- Advertising encouraged consumerism.
- People lost confidence in the economy.

3.2 US society in the 1920s

REVISED

Women experienced some positive change in the 1920s

- Women gained the right to vote in 1920 after successful **Suffragist** campaigning. The First World War had also demonstrated that women had an important role to play in society.
- The political campaigning continued after the war through the League of Women Voters, which put forward over 600 pieces of legislation.
- During the war, women had provided a large proportion of the workforce in key industries. Many of these opportunities continued after the war, especially for urban middle-class women.
- New luxury goods gave women more free time and many decided to get a job. By 1929, there were 10 million women in work: this was a 24 per cent increase from 1920.

Key point

There was significant change in society during the 1920s, some of which was positive and some that led to violence and division.

- These new social and economic freedoms meant that women had increased wealth. Therefore, women were targeted by advertisers and new **Hollywood** role models were used to show them what to aspire to.
- For some women there was a new freedom from traditional roles. They could drink, drive, smoke and wear more revealing clothing. These young, urban women were called flappers – they summed up the positive changes for women.

However, there were still limitations for women

- Women lacked the opportunities that men had, and often their jobs were only in certain professions. In addition, women were paid less than men for doing the same job.
- Women had no political power beyond getting the vote. By the end of the 1920s, very few women had been voted to **Congress** (government).
- There was still a very strong religious and **conservative** (traditional) element to society, especially in the countryside. This meant that traditional views on women remained and they were expected to stay at home to raise a family.

Prohibition was introduced due to concerns about the effects of alcohol

- **Prohibition** was the ban on the sale and production of alcohol. It started in 1920 when the government passed the **Volstead Act** and did not end until 1933.
- The **Anti-Saloon League** and the Women's **Christian Temperance Movement** campaigned for prohibition as they were worried about the effect of alcohol on people's health and family life.
- Some business owners supported the idea of prohibition as they thought that workers would be more productive if they were always sober.
- It was also seen as **unpatriotic** (against your country's values) to drink:
  - Most breweries were run by German immigrants who were seen as the enemy after the events of the First World War.
  - Drink was also linked to the encouragement of **communism**.

There was a mixed reaction to prohibition

Positive impacts and reactions	Negative impacts and reactions
• Some officers were very effective in enforcing the law • Rural areas supported Prohibition • Consumption of alcohol fell in the USA • Some people were able to make a lot of money by smuggling alcohol into the USA (**bootlegging**)	• Ordinary people became criminals when they visited **speakeasies** (illegal bars) • Prohibition was difficult to enforce in the cities • Bootlegging increased as alcohol was smuggled across the border • People made their own alcohol ('**moonshine**') which was often poisonous • Officials seemed **corrupt** as they were paid to keep quiet about illegal activities • **Gangsters** became more common as gangs formed to smuggle alcohol • Rich people felt that prohibition did not apply to them and ignored the law

Gangsters led to the end of the 'noble experiment'

- Al Capone made around $60 million a year from his speakeasies.
- He bribed corrupt officials so he did not have to worry about being arrested.
- It is thought that Al Capone was responsible for around 300 murders.
- The **St Valentine's Day Massacre** in 1929 was the final straw. This mass killing of members of a rival gang was too much violence for people in the USA. Many people thought prohibition needed to end to stop the violence.
- In addition to this, when America suffered an economic depression people argued that the reintroduction of alcohol would create new jobs.

Evaluate the source

Below is a sample exam-style question. Use your own knowledge and the information on the opposite page to evaluate the source using the table below.

Study Source A. How useful is this source to a historian studying the lives of women in the 1920s? (5 marks)

SOURCE A *An advertisement for stockings in the 1920s. Although the caption says silk they were actually rayon.*

Issue to think about	How this makes the source useful
Message	
Context (knowledge that supports or goes against the source)	
Provenance (who, why and when)	

Test yourself

1. When did women get the vote and why?
2. Which famous gangster led to the end of prohibition?
3. In what ways did ordinary people become criminals?

Practice question

Explain why life changed for some women in the 'Roaring Twenties'. (10 marks)

Stretch and challenge

Go back through this spread and find evidence that supports and challenges the following statement: 'America was a divided society'. You should then consider the extent to which you agree with this statement – you may want to write a paragraph explaining your thinking.

3.3 Prejudice and discrimination in 1920s' society

REVISED

Immigrants experienced prejudice due to the fear of new political beliefs

- When people arrived from other countries, they tended not to **integrate**. They lived in the same areas of cities as other immigrants from their countries. They were also more likely to live in poor housing and be unemployed.
- In the 1920s, a new type of politics started in Russia in the **Communist Revolution**. Americans were afraid that people from Russia and Eastern Europe would bring radical Communist ideas to the USA. This reaction was the '**Red Scare**'.
- When the economy got worse, workers went on **strike**, refusing to work until wages improved. People saw this as a sign of communism starting in America.
- People who did not believe in any type of government (**anarchists**) conducted bombing raids in many cities. One bomb nearly killed Attorney-General Palmer.
- During the 1920s, 60,000 suspected Communists were rounded up, investigated and accused; 10,000 were deported. This was often done on very little evidence.

Key point

Even though the economy was strong, the USA was still very divided both racially and politically. Those who did not fit the American ideals suffered discrimination and violence.

Sacco and Vanzetti were executed because of their origins and political beliefs

- In 1920 two men, Sacco and Vanzetti, were arrested, put on trial, and executed for armed robbery and murder.
- At the end of the trial, the judge admitted that there was very little evidence that the men were guilty, but that they should be executed anyway.
- The judge sentenced them on the grounds that they were Italian and anarchists. He felt they went against the American way of life.
- They were executed in 1927 and the US government faced huge public outrage.
- However, the government was passing laws to introduce **quotas** (limits) on the number of immigrants allowed, due to public fears of new political ideas. The total number of people allowed into the USA every year was limited. The largest quota was people from north-western Europe. No Asians were allowed.

Practice question

Explain why the execution of Sacco and Vanzetti in 1927 was controversial.
(10 marks)

African Americans faced discrimination and violence

- The **Jim Crow Laws** made **segregation** legal. This meant anyone could separate black and white citizens. Furthermore, African Americans were prohibited from voting and had worse access to education and jobs.
- The **Ku Klux Klan (KKK)** believed in '**white supremacy**' and therefore discriminated against African Americans with extreme violence. The organisation was revived in the 1910s and had increasing political power.
- Cases of **lynching** increased. African Americans were hanged publicly without trial and many members of the white community would gather to watch. There were thousands of lynchings in the 1920s, many of which were in the southern states.
- The extreme levels of violence and discrimination forced many African Americans to move from the racist South to the more accepting North.

Test yourself

1. Why were Sacco and Vanzetti executed?
2. What was the Red Scare?
3. What does NAACP stand for and what did it do?

There were some improvements for African Americans in the 1920s

- Things were better for those African Americans who moved North. There were more jobs and greater access to education.
- Famous black Americans such as Paul Robeson and the jazz musicians of Harlem served as positive role models.
- The **NAACP (National Association for the Advancement of Colored People)** was founded by W.E.B. DuBois. The organisation campaigned for equality and desegregation and at its peak had 90,000 members.
- Marcus Garvey established the **UNIA (Universal Negro Improvement Association)**. It encouraged African Americans to take pride in their heritage and gave money to help them start their own businesses. By 1921 it had over 1 million members.

Stretch and challenge

Make a short profile on all of the key people or groups mentioned in this topic (Sacco, Vanzetti, immigrants, KKK, Garvey, DuBois, anarchists, Communists). In each profile, include a detail about what they did and a sentence about how much discrimination they faced.

Despite political progress there were still huge differences between races

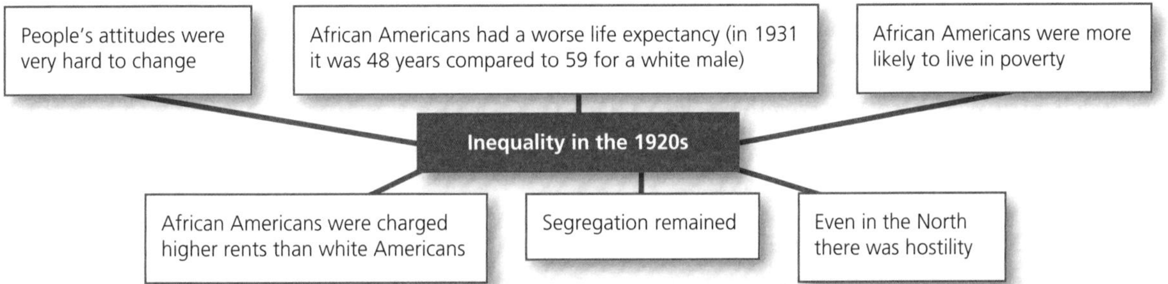
People's attitudes were very hard to change
African Americans had a worse life expectancy (in 1931 it was 48 years compared to 59 for a white male)
African Americans were more likely to live in poverty
Inequality in the 1920s
African Americans were charged higher rents than white Americans
Segregation remained
Even in the North there was hostility

Complete the paragraph

Below are a sample exam-style question and a paragraph written in answer to this question. The paragraph contains a point and specific examples, but lacks a concluding explanatory link back to the question. Complete the paragraph adding this link in the space provided.

Explain why many African Americans migrated to towns in the northern USA in the 1920s. (10 marks)

One important reason why so many African Americans moved North during the 1920s was because of the violence of the KKK. The membership of the Klan was at its highest in the 1920s and thousands of African Americans were lynched. This resulted in people moving North because ... ______________________________

____

____

Turning assertion into argument

Below is a sample exam-style question and a series of assertions. Read the question and then add a justification to each of the assertions to turn it into an argument.

Explain why the execution of Sacco and Vanzetti in 1927 was controversial. (10 marks)

The fact that there was no evidence of their guilt made it controversial because ...

The two men were Italian immigrants and this made it controversial because ...

The two men were anarchists and this made the case controversial because ....

The fact that the judge was clearly prejudiced made the case controversial because ...

3.4 The Depression

REVISED

The Wall Street Crash led to a considerable loss in confidence in the American economy

- In the autumn of 1929, investors began to lose confidence in the US economy. As a result they began to sell stocks.
- This led to other investors panic selling their stocks, dramatically reducing their value. This was known as the **Wall Street Crash**.
- As a result of **shares** losing value too quickly, people lost a lot of money in a short space of time. If they had loans or debts to pay, then it was likely they would also lose houses and businesses.
- Government **tax cuts** helped to restore some productivity and stability, but people did not trust the economy any more – 659 banks closed in 1929, with a further 1352 shutting in 1930. People felt their money was safer at home.
- People did not spend their money on goods so businesses suffered. People keeping their money at home meant banks did not have money to loan. Businesses went **bankrupt** and failed.
- Wages also fell – between 1928 and 1933 they fell by 60 per cent. Farm production fell by 40 per cent. There were 14 million unemployed by 1933. This period was termed the '**Great Depression**'.

Key point

The Wall Street Crash led to significant hardships for the majority of Americans and there was anger at the way the Republicans handled the problems in the economy.

The Depression caused hardship in both the countryside and towns

Effects of the Depression in the countryside	Effects of the Depression in the cities
• Farmers had already suffered in the 1920s • They had lower incomes • They had to pay back loans to the banks • Lots of farms went bankrupt • They had to leave their farms and therefore their homes • They had tough journeys looking for work • Over-farming and drought led to **dustbowls** – large areas of infertile land • **Malnutrition** became more common as people struggled to find food	• There was a rapid rise in unemployment • In 1932, 80 per cent of the people of Toledo were unemployed • Many were forced out of their homes • Some people left their homes to look for work • There was an increase in homelessness • **Hoovervilles** (shanty towns) emerged in most towns • People scavenged for food in the rubbish • Soup kitchens were set up

Anger at Hoover led to an opportunity for Roosevelt to become president in 1932

- Hoover had tried to restart the economy with tax cuts and by asking businesses to keep wages high.
- However, he was a **Republican** and believed that government intervention was not the answer. He even blocked an act to spend $2.1 billion to help create jobs.
- In June 1932, he refused to meet with protesting First World War soldiers who were asking for their war pensions early. He ordered troops to deal with them and the protest ended in violence.
- Roosevelt was a **Democrat** and promised to: spend money to help the poor, use government schemes to create jobs and consult businesses to get the best advice.
- He also promised a '**New Deal**' to improve the economy. He had a warm personality and led a very active campaign.
- Roosevelt's campaign worked and he gained a 7 million majority. It was the worst defeat ever for the Republicans.

Test yourself

1. Which political party was Roosevelt a member of and which was Hoover a member of?
2. What were Hoovervilles?
3. What new approaches to the economy did Roosevelt suggest?

Delete as applicable

Below are a sample exam-style question and a paragraph written in answer to this question. Read the paragraph and decide which of the possible options (underlined) is most appropriate. Delete the least appropriate options and complete the paragraph by justifying your selection.

'Hoover lost the election because of his position as a Republican president.' How far do you agree? (18 marks)

I agree to a great/fair/limited extent that Hoover lost the election because of his Republican policies. Aside from tax cuts and encouraging businesses to maintain higher wages, he did very little to help the ordinary American. Republicans believed that the government should not interfere in the economy and that issues would resolve themselves. Therefore, he lost the election because ... ______

______

______

______

Opposing views

Below you will find two examples of opinions on the 1932 presidential election. Both are very strong views one way or another. You need to read those views and highlight or underline those parts of the statements which you agree with. Once you have done this, write a third view underneath which is a balanced view of the election which incorporates aspects of both views.

View 1: Hoover lost the election due to his own poor management of the Depression and his inability to listen to the needs of the people. He ignored pleas for help from First World War veterans and blocked plans to spend money to create jobs. He showed no interest in helping the poor and was so ineffective that anyone would have been able to win against him.

View 2: Roosevelt won the election because of his own strengths as a candidate. He showed the people of America that he had a plan to improve the economy and that he would also improve their living conditions. He travelled across the country to give speeches and tell people about his New Deal. Roosevelt was always going to win, regardless of who he was running against.

Stretch and challenge

Read this topic again and find evidence to decide who suffered most as a result of the Depression. Challenge yourself by writing a convincing argument for either side. This will help develop your conclusions in essays.

Practice question

Study Source B. What is the message of the source? (5 marks)

SOURCE B *A cartoon by the US artist John McCutcheon, 1932. McCutcheon won a Pulitzer Prize for this cartoon.*

3.5 The New Deal

REVISED

Roosevelt immediately set to work in his first 'Hundred Days'

- In Roosevelt's election campaigning he had promised a New Deal to:
  - get people back to work
  - protect savings and property
  - provide relief for the sick, old and unemployed
  - restart agriculture and industry.
- In his first '**Hundred Days**' he worked with his advisers (the 'Brains Trust') to do the following:
  - close all the banks
  - reopen trustworthy banks and passed the Emergency Banking Act and the Securities Exchange Commission to prevent speculation
  - create **FERA (Federal Emergency Relief Agency)** and the **CCC (Civilian Conservation Corps)** to immediately assist the poor and unemployed young men.

Key point

Roosevelt had promised America a New Deal which would get people back to work and help the poor. There was a mixed reaction and the New Deal had a varied level of success.

The **First New Deal** set up a range of measures called the **Alphabet Agencies**

- Roosevelt wanted to make the banks more secure and so in his first 'Hundred Days' he closed all banks. He then reopened trustworthy banks and introduced the **Emergency Banking Act**. This made sure banks had enough funds to cover a crisis.
- FERA was established to give $500 million for soup kitchens and blankets for the poor.
- The CCC was designed to get young men into jobs. It worked for 2.5 million Americans.
- Roosevelt also wanted to help farmers. The **AAA (Agricultural Adjustment Administration)** set quotas to reduce production and therefore helped to stabilise food prices.
- In industry, the **PWA (Public Works Administration)** used government money to build new infrastructure like schools. This provided a lot of jobs in the short term. In addition, the **NRA (National Recovery Act)** improved conditions for those already in work.
- The **TVA (Tennessee Valley Authority)** was created to build a dam in the Tennessee Valley. This would provide more jobs and improve farming land in the area.

Some **criticisms** of the **New Deal** forced new **measures** in the **Second New Deal** in 1936

- The first new measure related to tax. The **Revenue Act** introduced a 79 per cent tax on incomes over $5 million a year and increased taxes on businesses.
- The **Wagner Act** allowed trade unions to form and therefore allowed workers to strike for better pay and conditions.
- The **Social Security Act** gave pensions to the elderly and widows, provided government aid for the sick and disabled, and insurance for the unemployed.
- The **WPA (Works Progress Administration)** organised the different agencies from the **First New Deal** that helped people to get jobs. It made the process easier.
- Both the **RA (Resettlement Administration)** and the **FSA (Farm Security Administration)** helped farmers, the first by providing better land and the second by helping farmers to buy their own land.

Test yourself

1. What was Huey Long's criticism of the New Deal?
2. What was the TVA?
3. What was the aim of the New Deal?

The **New Deal** was **criticised** by people for a **range** of reasons

- Some people thought that the New Deal did not do enough to help people. Huey Long felt that the very poorest and African Americans were still living in extreme poverty. He set up '**Share our Wealth**', which called for limits to top wages.
- Some felt that the New Deal was doing too much. Republicans and businessmen thought that Roosevelt was interfering too much. They argued that the reforms were more like Communist reforms, that Roosevelt behaved like a dictator and that too much state help would make people lazy.
- Roosevelt was upset at the criticism and angry at personal attacks. However, voters were on his side and he easily won the 1936 presidential election.
- The **Supreme Court** had the final say on legal matters. They decided that the New Deal broke the rules of the **American Constitution** and, before changes in 1936, made life very hard for Roosevelt.

The **New Deal** had both **successes** and **failures**

Successes of the New Deal	Failures of the New Deal
• Improved people's faith in the economy and government • There was no corruption reported • Workers' rights were protected • Helped to create millions of jobs • Stabilised the banks • Improved the standard of living in some places • Some African Americans gained work • Slum clearances improved the standard of living • Some women were placed in prominent roles • Eleanor Roosevelt (wife of the president) publicly helped the poor • The **Indian Reorganization Act** (1934) helped Native Americans buy land	• It undermined local government • Trade unions were still met with violence • 6 million were still unemployed in 1941 • Only involvement in the Second World War ended unemployment • Big business remained very powerful • It never dealt with underlying economic issues • There was still discrimination against African Americans (higher unemployment rates) • There was nothing specifically aimed at helping women • Native Americans were mostly ignored • Led to accusations of communism and being anti-American

Doing reliability well

Below are a series of attributions from various sources. Consider the attribution and make a comment about its reliability after having rated it. Consider the following concepts and try to use them in your evaluation of the attribution.

- **Vested interest**: the source is written so that the writer can protect their power or their financial interests.
- **Second-hand report**: the writer of the source is not an eyewitness, but is relying on someone else's account.
- **Expertise**: the source is written on a subject which the author (for example, a historian) is an expert.
- **Political bias**: the source is written by a politician and it reflects their political views.
- **Reputation**: the source is written to protect the writer's reputation.

Source	Rating	Reason for rating
A cartoon published by the American Liberty League (ALL) in 1935. The ALL was a group of Democrats who were unhappy with Roosevelt's policies	/10	
An extract from a book by the prominent businessman Howard E. Kerschner, called *The Menace Roosevelt and His Policies*, published in 1936	/10	
A cartoon from the British magazine *Punch*, published in 1935. The caption read: The Illegal Act. President Roosevelt: 'I'm sorry but the Supreme Court says I must chuck you back again'	/10	

3.6 The Second World War and the economy

REVISED

Wartime **production** levels **improved jobs** and **wages**

- By the end of the war, the USA was producing twice as much as its enemies combined.
- From 1941 to 1945, the USA made 250,000 aircraft, 90,000 tanks, 350 destroyers and 200 submarines.
- The USA made 50 per cent of all of the world's weapons, plus clothing, food, cars and engines.
- Not only did this directly benefit these industries themselves, but it also helped associated industries that supplied them. For example, glass, leather and steel all increased production too.
- The war also encouraged new businesses and therefore improved employment levels.
- Farmers benefited from increased demand for food in Europe.

Key point

The USA entering the Second World War after the attack on Pearl Harbor in 1941 did more to help restore the economy than the New Deal ever did.

The **government encouraged** workers to help in the war, but most were **happy** to do so

- People were so eager to help in the war that they took to hardships, like the **rationing** of food, with enthusiasm. The biggest problem was finding things for people to do.
- People purchased **war bonds** – this meant that they gave money to the government to spend on the war, and they got their money back whenever it ended, along with interest.
- Anti-Nazi and pro-American **propaganda** helped the government gain support and encouraged people to sign up.
- The propaganda effort was aided by the Japanese attack on Pearl Harbor on 7 December 1941. This helped convince people to help the war effort.
- The entertainment industry in Hollywood also proved a useful propaganda tool.
- The wartime economy was government controlled and government spending was doubled. To help, the **Victory Tax** was passed in 1942: this was a tax on savings, wages and luxury goods.
- In January 1942 the **War Production Board** was set up. Experts in businesses consulted on what the government needed to do to meet the demands of the war.

Test yourself

1 What were war bonds?
2 Why did the war benefit farmers?
3 How many more women were in work by the end of the war?

There were many more **jobs** available, especially for **women**

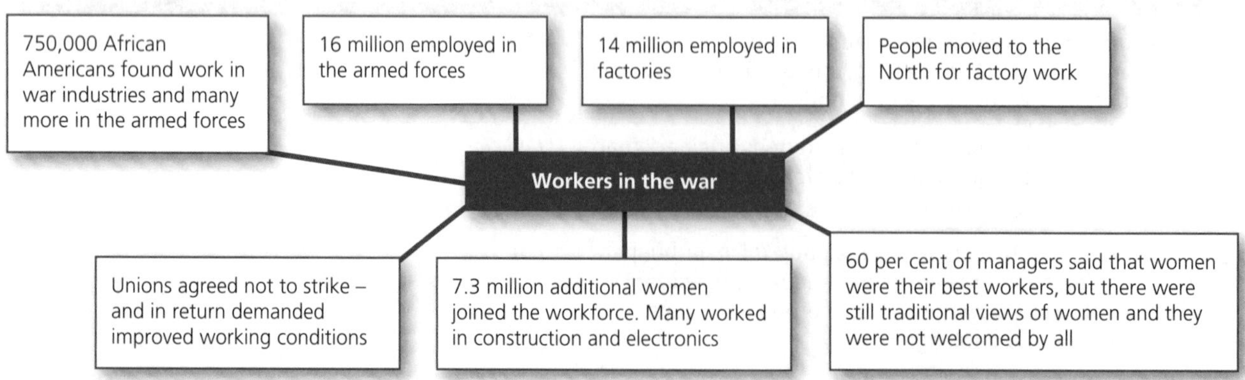

Workers in the war
750,000 African Americans found work in war industries and many more in the armed forces
16 million employed in the armed forces
14 million employed in factories
People moved to the North for factory work
Unions agreed not to strike – and in return demanded improved working conditions
7.3 million additional women joined the workforce. Many worked in construction and electronics
60 per cent of managers said that women were their best workers, but there were still traditional views of women and they were not welcomed by all

Checklist

Below is a list of events, facts and issues relating to the economy during the Second World War. Tick or highlight those events which you know are right.

- Unemployment levels fell during the war because of work in industry.
- Women were often respected by their bosses.
- African American workers did not get more jobs during the war.
- There were over 7 million more women in work during the war.
- Women were accepted by men.
- People supported the war effort.
- People were happy to buy war bonds from the government.
- Women were no longer bound by traditional views of their roles.

Stretch and challenge

Read this chapter again. Make a spider diagram with any examples of how the war was helping workers more than the New Deal. For each example, explain how far it was improving the lives of American people.

Complete the paragraph

Below are a sample exam-style question and a paragraph written in answer to this question. The paragraph contains a point and a link back to the question, but no specific examples to support the point. Complete the paragraph adding relevant examples in the space provided.

Explain why the economy was helped by the Second World War. **(10 marks)**

The economy was helped by the Second World War because it provided jobs.

____

____

____

This helped the economy because it provided people with spare income. This meant that they could spend it on goods, making America richer, or war bonds, which gave the government more to spend on the war.

Practice question

Study Sources C and D. How similar are these sources? (10 marks)

SOURCE C *A wartime poster featuring Rosie the Riveter.*

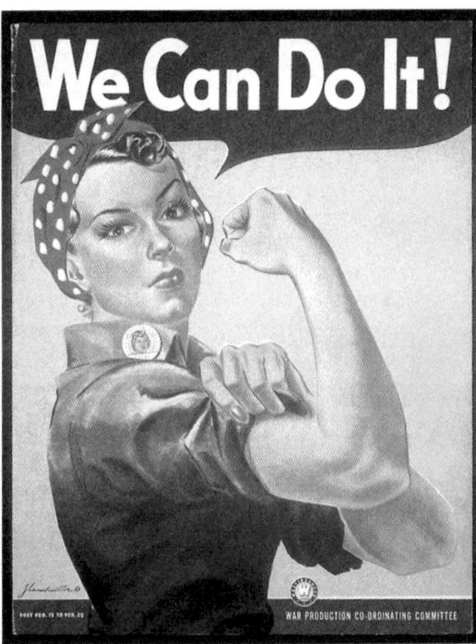

SOURCE D *An official US government photograph of women riveting in an aircraft factory.*

3.7 Division in the war

REVISED

Some people did not give full support to the war

- Howard Zinn took a different view of the way Americans responded to the war effort. In his book *A People's History of the United States* he said that:
  - Strikes took place, even though they were not meant to. Workers were frustrated that wages had been frozen.
  - Some people refused to fight at all. Many were **conscientious objectors** who said they disagreed with the very idea of war. Many of these were sent to prison – a greater number than during the First World War.
  - The government passed strict laws (such as the **Smith Act** in 1940) which made it illegal to encourage people to refuse to fight or to encourage them to overthrow the government.

Key point

While many Americans supported the war effort, not all benefited from new jobs, and racial discrimination remained a serious issue.

Japanese Americans were treated very poorly

- Due to the Japanese attack on Pearl Harbor there was strong anti-Japanese feeling, particularly on the West coast.
- Around 120,000 Japanese Americans in the West were **interned**: this meant they were placed in camps in remote parts of the country. They weren't allowed any form of property.
- This discrimination made no distinction between those who were born in Japan and had moved to America (***Issei***) and those who were American-born Japanese (***Nisei***).
- It became clear that this policy was racist, rather than being about the security of the USA.
- However, Japanese Americans remained very patriotic, and over 33,000 volunteered to fight in the US army as soon as they were allowed to do so in 1943.

African Americans faced discrimination in the workplace

- There were opportunities available in the North for those who needed employment, and on average wages doubled to $1000 a year.
- Some groups campaigned for the end of discrimination in the workplace by threatening walkouts by African American workers.
- As a result, Roosevelt Passed **Executive Order 8802**. This said that any businesses involved in the war effort had to end discrimination in their workplace. But there were instances of white workers walking out in protest when this order was implemented.
- There were **race riots** in 47 cities during the war when both white and African American workers violently clashed due to racial tension in the workplace.
- While the experience of many workers in the war was poor, this period also saw the start of the **civil rights movement**. African Americans wanted the same protection from racism that they were fighting for in Nazi Germany.

Practice question

'Overall, the people of the USA supported the government in the war effort.' How far do you agree with this statement? (18 marks)

Test yourself

1. What was internment?
2. What were the two executive orders passed by the government during the war?
3. What caused the race riots?

Stretch and challenge

Re-read this chapter. Write a short introduction that helps you answer the following question: 'How far do you agree with the view that the war solved the economic problems, but created tension in society?'

African Americans faced discrimination in the armed forces

- African Americans were eager to help fight against the racism of Nazi Germany and about 1 million joined the armed forces.
- However, African Americans faced many issues throughout the conflict:

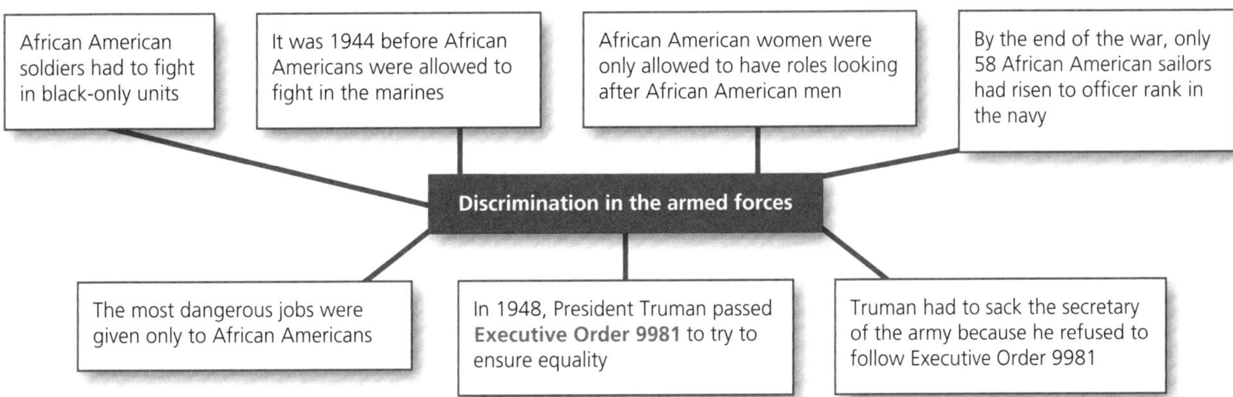

Discrimination in the armed forces
African American soldiers had to fight in black-only units
It was 1944 before African Americans were allowed to fight in the marines
African American women were only allowed to have roles looking after African American men
By the end of the war, only 58 African American sailors had risen to officer rank in the navy
The most dangerous jobs were given only to African Americans
In 1948, President Truman passed Executive Order 9981 to try to ensure equality
Truman had to sack the secretary of the army because he refused to follow Executive Order 9981

- Some units in the army were mixed race and the African American units distinguished themselves at the **Battle of the Bulge** and **Iwo Jima** but these were small victories and did not lead to lasting equality or change.

Support or challenge?

Below is a sample exam-style question which asks how far you agree with a specific statement. Below this are a series of general statements which are relevant to the question. Using your own knowledge and the information on these pages, place the letter of each factor in the box for 'agrees' or 'disagrees' with the stated view. As an additional challenge, you might want to think if any factors belong to both.

'Overall, the people of the USA supported the government in the war effort.' How far do you agree with this statement? (18 marks)

Write the letter of each factor.

A There was a big reaction to calls to increase production during the war.
B 7.3 million women went to work.
C Morale was high.
D Japanese Americans were interned.
E People wanted to fight to combat racism.
F 33,000 Japanese joined up to fight.
G There was segregation in the armed forces.
H People spent a lot of money on war bonds.
I People ignored the executive orders to improve equality.

Agree	Disagree

Do/don't list

This is an example of question 4 from the non-British depth study paper:

'Overall, the people of the USA supported the government in the war effort.' How far do you agree with this statement? (18 marks)

Below is a list of ideas that you might consider when writing the answer to this question. In the boxes marked 'Do' and 'Don't', write the letter of each instruction, then use these to write your own instructions for how you should approach this question.

Write the letter of each factor.

A Include at least two paragraphs.
B Include a brief conclusion which indicates clearly your opinion.
C Look at both sides of the argument.
D If you can't remember the facts, guess.
E When using evidence, follow it with an explanation of how that issue answers the question.
F Tell the story of what happened.
G Write one big paragraph with everything you can remember.
H Be careful not to be too forceful with your own ideas.

Do	Don't

4 The USA 1945–1974: The People and the State

4.1 The Red Scare

REVISED

The **international** context after the Second World War led to a **fear** of new **political ideologies**

- Despite being allies and working with the **Soviets** to defeat Germany in the Second World War, after 1945 **America** and the **USSR** became rivals. As a result, many Americans saw **communism** as a threat.
- In 1949, the USSR developed a powerful **atomic bomb** which came as a surprise to the Americans. They felt threatened that there was now a rival to their own **nuclear** weapons programme.
- In the same year, China also became Communist. There was now a nation of 500 million people who were also Communist. America was shocked once again by this development.

Key point

A post-war fear of new political ideologies led to division and discrimination in US society.

- It also became clear that communism was spreading. Other countries in South-East Asia were also turning Communist, such as Indonesia and Burma.
- Between 1950 and 1953, the USA was involved in the **Korean War**. Communist North Korea had invaded the South and America organised a counter-attack.

Global issues combined with **internal politics** and led to the **Red Scare**

- The 1930s had seen American society unite and there was cooperation between the main political parties. However, by the end of the war racial tensions were on the rise, there were tensions between unions and employers and between and within political parties.
- As the fighting between politicians increased, so did suspicion. People started to think that their opponents might be Communist. They also found that calling someone else a Communist was a good way to damage their reputation.
- The phrase '**Red under the bed**' conveyed the belief that Communists could be anywhere.
- In 1949, eleven leading members of the **Communist Party of the USA** were arrested and accused of violating the **Smith Act** of 1940 (this had made it illegal to ask for, plan or attempt to overthrow the US government).
- The case was widely reported. They were all imprisoned and fined $10,000. It showed that there was no tolerance for communism in America.

Government **agencies** hunted for **suspected Communists**

- The **Federal Bureau of Investigation (FBI)**, led by J. Edgar Hoover, was strongly anti-Communist and had been investigating the threat of communism since the Russian Revolution.
- In 1947, Hoover set up the **Federal Employee Loyalty Program** which allowed the FBI to investigate government employees to see if they were Communists.
- From 1947 to 1950, around 3 million people were investigated. Of these, 212 were deemed security risks and lost their jobs.
- The **House of Representatives** established the **HUAC** (House Un-American Activities Committee) which investigated suspected Communists for the FBI.
- At one point, the FBI was convinced that Hollywood actors, directors and producers were members of the Communist Party.
- This '**Hollywood Ten**' became famous as they refused to answer the questions of the HUAC. They knew that it was not illegal in America to be a Communist and challenged their 'trial', arguing that it broke their right to freedom of speech. Ultimately, they were all jailed and never worked in Hollywood again, showing the power of the HUAC.

Test yourself

1. What did the HUAC do?
2. What was the importance of the Hollywood Ten?

High-profile cases only increased the fear surrounding communism in the late 1940s and 1950s

- In 1948, Whittaker Chambers faced the HUAC and admitted he had been a member of the Communist Party in the 1930s. He accused Alger Hiss of being a member too – Hiss was an important member of the US government.
- Hiss accused Chambers of lying but a young politician called Richard Nixon investigated further and found evidence that the two men had known each other. Hiss was found guilty of perjury (lying in court) and was sentenced to five years in jail.
- When the USSR developed an atomic bomb in 1949, there was a fear that it had been given information by US spies. In 1950, a man was convicted of doing just this and accused a couple (the Rosenbergs) of passing information too.
- The Rosenbergs were found guilty and were executed in June 1953, even though there was very little evidence against them.
- These two cases encouraged the government to pass the **Internal Security Act of 1950**. It was controversial but was eventually made law. It decreed that Communist organisations had to register with the government and that no Communist could work in the security forces or hold a US passport.

Stretch and challenge

Read through this topic and look for the specific cases mentioned (for example, the Hollywood Ten). For each of them, summarise the case in fifteen words and then write a sentence explaining how it added to the Red Scare.

Practice question

Describe **one** example of the actions of the HUAC. (2 marks)

There was a mixed reaction among the public to the Red Scare

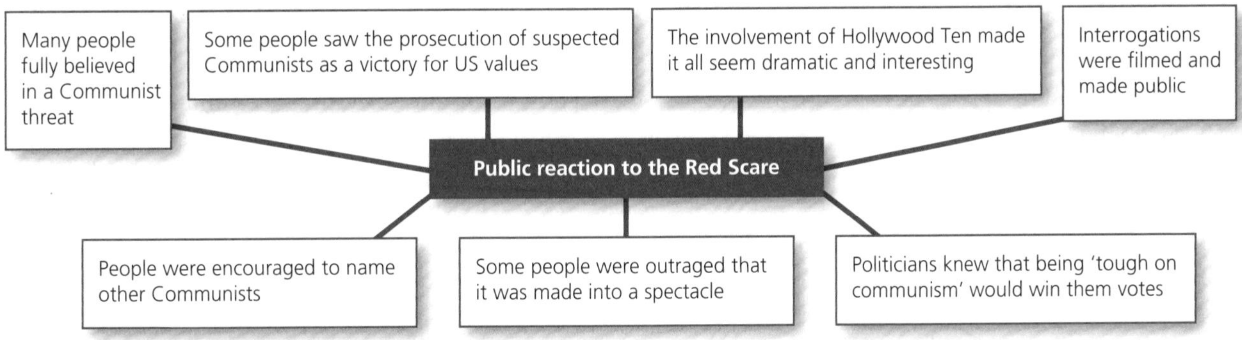

Public reaction to the Red Scare
Many people fully believed in a Communist threat
Some people saw the prosecution of suspected Communists as a victory for US values
The involvement of Hollywood Ten made it all seem dramatic and interesting
Interrogations were filmed and made public
People were encouraged to name other Communists
Some people were outraged that it was made into a spectacle
Politicians knew that being 'tough on communism' would win them votes

Checklist

Below is a list of events that may relate to the Red Scare. Tick or highlight those events which you know *did* take place. You may also want to consider what you might write in an essay to explain why these events contributed to the Red Scare.

- People feared capitalism.
- Lots of other nations became Communist after the Second World War.
- The HUAC interviewed people suspected of communism.
- There was a fear of the USSR after they developed the H-bomb.
- The Hollywood Ten were shunned from Hollywood after the accusations made against them.
- The Rosenbergs were executed for being spies for the Soviets.
- The FBI defended people who were accused of communism.

Complete the paragraph

Below are a sample exam-style question and a paragraph written in answer to this question. The paragraph contains a point and specific examples, but lacks a concluding explanatory link back to the question. Complete the paragraph adding this link in the space provided.

Explain why there was a fear of communism in America after the Second World War. (10 marks)

There was a fear of communism at the end of the Second World War because the USSR developed their atomic bomb in 1949. This was sooner than American advisers had suggested. Therefore …

____

____

4.2 McCarthyism

REVISED

Senator **McCarthy** rose to fame when he **claimed** there were **Communists** within the **government**

- In 1950, Senator Joseph McCarthy claimed that he had a list of over 200 Communists working within the US government. He said that this list had been compiled by the FBI's **loyalty board investigations**.
- By the time the list was made public there were only 57 names and 35 of these had already been cleared.
- McCarthy saw an opportunity and wanted to push on with these accusations in the forthcoming elections. Anti-Communist speeches helped to gain votes.
- A Democrat, Millard Tydings, was critical of McCarthy and said there wasn't enough evidence that any of the government workers accused were Communist. McCarthy said that Tydings was '**un-American**'. This tactic worked and the Republicans were very successful in the 1952 Senate elections.

Key point

McCarthyism illustrated the extent of the US fear of communism, but the extreme nature of his claims led to the decline of the Red Scare.

Test yourself

1 Why did *Captain America* come back?
2 How did McCarthy make his name?
3 Why did McCarthyism end?

- McCarthy was made the head of a new organisation (a White House committee) which investigated suspected Communists. It did a similar job to the HUAC.

Anti-Communist messages and the **media** increased the **suspicion** and **fear** directed at others

- McCarthy used this platform to accuse many influential people. He claimed that General Marshall was involved in a Communist plot to overthrow President Eisenhower.
- Thousands of others were also accused, and the investigations into their lives became known as '**witch-hunts**'. False accusations led to them being **blacklisted**. Over 100 university lecturers were fired due to pressure to reduce Communist activity.
- In Hollywood, 324 personalities were blacklisted by the HUAC and many producers, including Walt Disney, refused to employ anyone listed.
- Hollywood also made anti-Communist films, which sent a message that people were about to be invaded. This added to the hysteria surrounding **McCarthyism**.
- One good example of the media spreading fear of communism was the comic book ***Captain America***. This character had been killed off at the end of the Second World War, but in 1953 the superhero returned, this time battling the Communists.

McCarthy also faced some **strong opposition** to his Communist **witch-hunts**

Opposition to McCarthy

Government and the media
- Many other senators spoke out against McCarthy
- Some newspapers wrote articles that damaged McCarthy's credibility

Hollywood
- Many big names in Hollywood protested about the treatment of people in the industry
- Films were made that commented on the paranoia around communism
- Arthur Miller wrote a play (*The Crucible*) about the real witch-hunts. People knew he was criticising McCarthy

Owen Lattimore
- Lattimore was a professor who was an expert on Communist China. He had been an adviser to President Truman
- He was questioned by the HUAC for twelve days, protesting his innocence all the time
- He was found guilty of **perjury** (lying under oath)
- He was finally found innocent in 1955

Ed Murrow
- Murrow was a journalist who was critical of McCarthy
- In 1954 he broadcast a show that attacked McCarthy
- He was critical of his methods and showed damning footage
- The show was important in changing people's minds about the senator

McCarthy took his **accusations** too far and ultimately this led to the end of the **Red Scare**

- Many people started doubting McCarthy when he turned his accusations on the army. He said there were Communist sympathisers at the highest level.
- In televised hearings, McCarthy was made to look foolish by lawyers. They showed that he had no evidence and said he had 'no decency'.
- McCarthy had lost all credibility. People were still scared of communism but saw that McCarthy's methods were causing more harm than good.
- By the end of the 1950s, the HUAC had lost its power and profile. People were publicly critical of it and President Truman called it 'un-American'.
- McCarthyism had a huge impact during the 1940s and 1950s. Historians have criticised McCarthy heavily and some have argued that he actually made it harder to catch spies.

Practice question

Explain why Senator McCarthy rose to prominence in the 1950s. (10 marks)

Eliminate irrelevance

Below are a sample exam-style question and a paragraph written in answer to this question. Read the paragraph and identify parts of the paragraph that are not directly relevant to the question. Draw a line through the information that is irrelevant and justify your deletions in the margin.

Explain why Senator McCarthy rose to prominence in the 1950s. (10 marks)

McCarthy rose to prominence in the 1950s because of his accusations of communism against people working in important government positions. He had a list of over 200 names, which then reduced to around 90 names before eventually becoming only 57 names. Even then, 35 of these had been cleared and only 22 of the people were still being investigated by the FBI. He was asked to lead his own enquiries into prominent people and these were widely reported. He was helped by the context of the time. Other nations had become Communist. China had turned Communist in 1949, and then places such as Indonesia and Burma followed. People were worried that the Communists around the world were planning to attack. Films and comics added to this hysteria and made people believe that not only was McCarthy right, but he was the only one who could 'save them'.

Opposing views

Below you will find two examples of opinions on McCarthy. Both are very strong views one way or another. You need to read those views and highlight or underline those parts of the statements which you agree with. Once you have done this, write a third view underneath which is a balanced view of McCarthy which incorporates aspects of both views.

View 1: McCarthy was a man who was trying to save America from the threat of Communist attacks or spies. There is evidence to suggest that some people did sympathise with the Communist Party, and therefore the USA's enemy, the USSR. McCarthy was hugely patriotic and wanted to defend his nation from those who might want to attack an American way of life. He genuinely believed that there were people who wanted to harm the nation and the president.

View 2: McCarthy was an opportunist. He wanted to be remembered and wanted to win his seat in the 1952 election and he knew that the Red Scare, which followed the Second World War, gave him an opportunity to increase his popularity. He used accusations of communism to discredit people who opposed him, and he rarely had evidence against those he publicly blacklisted. You might even suggest that he didn't even believe his own accusations, but just wanted fame and power. He made it more difficult to identify real threats as there were so many ridiculous accusations.

4.3 The position of African Americans in US society

REVISED

African Americans had made **little progress** due to the **continuation** of **the Jim Crow Laws**

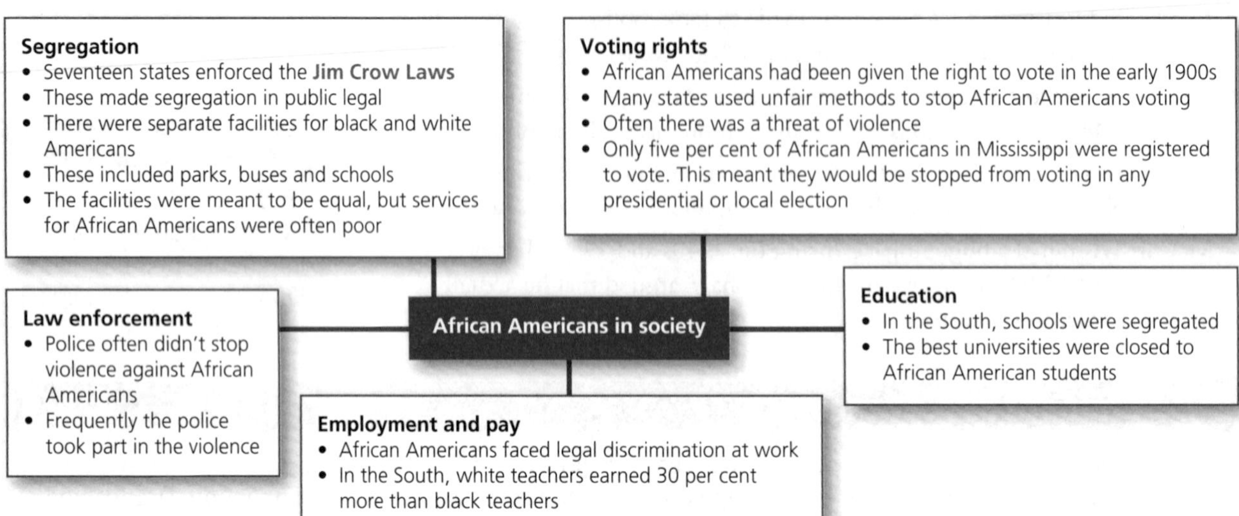

Segregation
• Seventeen states enforced the Jim Crow Laws
• These made segregation in public legal
• There were separate facilities for black and white Americans
• These included parks, buses and schools
• The facilities were meant to be equal, but services for African Americans were often poor
Voting rights
• African Americans had been given the right to vote in the early 1900s
• Many states used unfair methods to stop African Americans voting
• Often there was a threat of violence
• Only five per cent of African Americans in Mississippi were registered to vote. This meant they would be stopped from voting in any presidential or local election
Law enforcement
• Police often didn't stop violence against African Americans
• Frequently the police took part in the violence
African Americans in society
Education
• In the South, schools were segregated
• The best universities were closed to African American students
Employment and pay
• African Americans faced legal discrimination at work
• In the South, white teachers earned 30 per cent more than black teachers

The **threat** of **violence** encouraged some people to demand **improvements**

- The threat of violence from **white supremacists** meant that some key individuals felt it was time to say something. In 1949, the HUAC decided to investigate the dangers of Communist influence on minority groups like African Americans:
  - Paul Robeson was a leading African American actor. He said that African Americans would not fight the USSR for the USA because of the discrimination they faced.
  - The baseball star Jackie Robinson was called as an extra witness. He partially disagreed with Robeson and said he would fight. However, he agreed with Robeson and criticised the treatment of African Americans.
- Schools were segregated and those schools for African Americans were far worse. In 1952 the **NAACP** challenged the **Board of Education** in Kansas. A student named Linda Brown had to travel many miles to go to school because she was not allowed to attend an all-white school nearby.
- In 1954 the judge, Earl Warren, said segregated education was not equal education and therefore that all schools had to be desegregated and fully integrated as soon as possible.

Key point

The position of African Americans in society had shown no real progress by the start of the 1950s, but some improvements emerged by 1957.

The **Montgomery Bus Boycott** was maintained throughout the **early 1950s**

- The murder of the fifteen-year-old Emmet Till showed that there was still a lot of racist violence. He was brutally killed in 1955 by local men for flirting with a white woman. Those accused were found not guilty.
- The same year saw the **Montgomery Bus Boycott**. The town in Alabama had a law that African Americans could only sit nearer the back of the bus, and had to give up their seats to white passengers. In 1955, Rosa Parks refused to give up her seat.
- In response, the **Montgomery Improvement Association (MIA)** was set up to continue the protest by **boycotting** the buses.

- On the first day the buses were empty and 10,000–15,000 people listened to the new president of the MIA speak – Martin Luther King.
- The boycott was a success: the bus company lost 65 per cent of its income, and **non-violent direct action** had been shown to be effective. However, the people involved faced legal action and violence.
- But, in December 1956, the court ruled that segregated bus travel was illegal and that therefore all public segregation was illegal.

The **government began** to take **interest** in the **civil rights movement**

- The Montgomery Bus Boycott raised the profile of the civil rights movement. After the boycott, there was a push for a **Civil Rights Act** that would force states to end segregation.
- Eisenhower showed his support for civil rights in 1957 at Little Rock, Arkansas. The court demanded that the state should work harder to end segregation. It said that Governor Faubus had to let nine African American students attend a white school.
- Faubus resisted and used the **National Guard** (soldiers) to stop the students entering. He only backed down when Eisenhower sent **federal** troops to protect the students.
- Despite resistance, Eisenhower introduced the Civil Rights Act in 1957. It aimed to end segregation, and made it easier to report if people were stopped from voting.
- It was badly enforced. The number of African Americans voting only increased by three per cent. However, it showed that the president was willing to listen and cooperate with civil rights leaders.

Stretch and challenge

There were five key areas of discrimination towards African Americans before 1950. These were: segregation, voting, employment, education and law enforcement. Re-read this topic and try to find evidence that shows any form of progress for African Americans in the 1950s. You could then give each of the five areas a mark out of five for how much progress they demonstrate.

Turning assertion into argument

Below are a sample exam-style question and a series of assertions. Read the question and then add a justification to each of the assertions to turn it into an argument and link it clearly back to the question.

Explain why progress was made in civil rights between 1949 and 1967. (10 marks)

Progress was made as a result of legal challenges because ...

Progress was made because of Martin Luther King because ...

Progress was made because of the interests of Eisenhower because ...

Progress was made as a result of violence against African Americans because ...

Test yourself

1 What was the outcome of the Montgomery Bus Boycott?
2 Why was the case of Emmet Till important?
3 What were the two aims of the 1957 Civil Rights Act?

Practice question

Describe **one** example of the early success of the civil rights movement by 1957. (2 marks)

4.4 The civil rights movement, 1960–68

REVISED

Continued **frustration** after the **1957** Civil Rights Act led to more **direct action**

- In 1960, Eisenhower introduced the new Civil Rights Act. This allowed federal agents to inspect voter registration and made it a federal crime to stop someone from voting.
- A lot of campaigners continued to put pressure on the government:
  - Martin Luther King established the **SCLC (Southern Christian Leadership Conference)** in 1957.
  - Soon afterwards the **SNCC (Student Non-violent Co-ordinating Committee)** and **CORE (Congress of Racial Equality)** were also started. These three groups worked together to organise protests.
- In 1960, SNCC members decided to protest about **segregated** seating in restaurants in Greensboro. Four African American students sat in seats meant only for white customers.

Key point

After the success of non-violent direct action in the 1950s, a range of civil rights campaigning groups pushed further for equality and legal protection in the 1960s, with some success.

- The non-violent tactic of '**sit-ins**' spread to other towns. By the end of 1960, segregation in restaurants had ended in 126 cities.
- In May 1961, CORE activists led **Freedom Rides**. Segregation on buses had not ended, so protesters rode on buses in Birmingham, Alabama to make a point. They faced violence, and 200 were arrested.
- In 1962, James Meredith, an African American student, was rejected from attending Mississippi State University. He won an appeal to attend. Federal troops were sent to make sure he could go to class. He faced increasing violence, but eventually attended.

By 1962 there had been **some progress**, but the following **three** years saw **dramatic changes**

- By 1962, there were a lot of positives about the civil rights movement. However, racism and violence were also still everyday issues for African Americans.
- In Birmingham, Alabama, the situation was particularly bad, so in April 1963, Martin Luther King organised a protest march in the town. Police Chief 'Bull' Connor ordered violent action be taken against the protesters. In the end, President Kennedy had to step in and order the police to make changes.
- King called for stronger civil rights laws. Kennedy saw this differently and wanted to make sure African Americans could vote.
- The **March on Washington** maintained pressure on government. In August 1963, 200,000 African Americans and 50,000 white Americans marched to Washington, DC to call for a civil rights bill.
- This worked. Kennedy was assassinated in 1963, but his successor Johnson continued the commitment to civil rights and passed the 1964 Civil Rights Act. This made it illegal for local government to discriminate in areas such as housing and employment.

The **Civil Rights Act** of 1964 was not the **end** of the **struggle** or the **campaign**

- The focus of the civil rights movement remained on voting rights. In the so-called '**freedom summer**' of 1964 the SCLC and white Americans helped people to register and within the first twenty months after the new law was passed, 430,000 African Americans did so.
- A voting rights march was organised in Selma, Alabama as discrimination was rife there. The sheriff, Jim Clark, was openly racist and only 2.4 per cent of African Americans were registered to vote.
- The march was banned. When 600 people marched anyway, they were brutally attacked. Most of the USA was shocked by the scenes.
- Martin Luther King was criticised for not marching in Selma. However, the government passed the **Voting Rights Bill** in 1965. It made it easier to control voting registration and ended literacy tests.
- The increase in African American voting led to five major cities having black mayors and Jim Clark lost his job as sheriff in Selma.

Martin Luther King has been remembered for his impact

- In 1968, Martin Luther King was assassinated. His death marked an end of an era in civil rights.

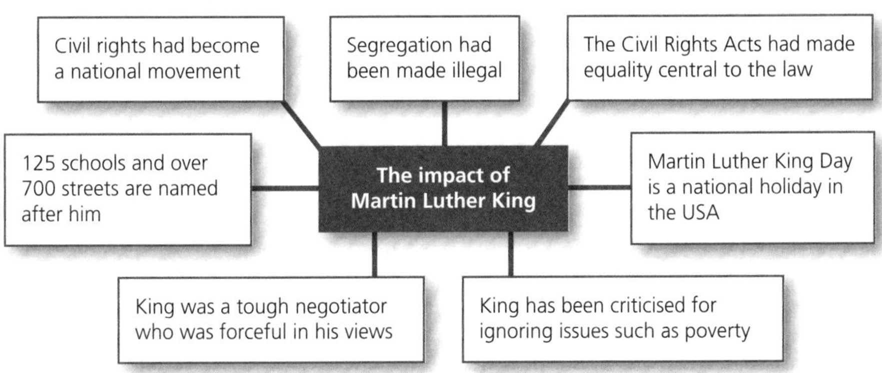

The impact of Martin Luther King
Civil rights had become a national movement
Segregation had been made illegal
The Civil Rights Acts had made equality central to the law
125 schools and over 700 streets are named after him
Martin Luther King Day is a national holiday in the USA
King was a tough negotiator who was forceful in his views
King has been criticised for ignoring issues such as poverty

Test yourself

1 Where were the sit-ins?
2 Why did the SNCC start the 'Freedom Rides'?
3 What were the aims of the Selma march and what was its consequence?

Considering usefulness

Below is a source relating to the civil rights march in Birmingham in 1963. Look at the source and consider how useful it is to a historian investigating the purpose of the march based on the criteria of: content, provenance and context. Rate each one for usefulness out of 10 and then explain why you think this source is useful to a historian or not.

SOURCE A *Martin Luther King, commenting on his tactics in Birmingham, Alabama, in 1963. Critics had accused him of deliberately stirring up violence.*

Instead of submitting to surreptitious cruelty in thousands of dark jail cells and on countless shadowed streets, we are forcing our oppressor to commit his brutality openly – in the light of day – with the rest of the world looking on. To condemn peaceful protesters on the grounds that they provoke violence is like condemning a robbed man because his possession of money caused the robbery.

Content	Provenance	Context

Stretch and challenge

Re-read this chapter, and think what you found out on these two pages. Think about issues of segregation, voting rights, government, violence and protest and how much progress there has been in each section. Complete this statement and explain your judgement:

'I think there was more/less progress in civil rights in the 1960s than the 1950s because ...'

Practice question

How useful is Source A in telling us about the events of the Birmingham civil rights march in 1963? (5 marks)

4.5 Other key issues in civil rights

REVISED

The **Black Power movement** had **positive** and **negative** impacts on the progress of civil rights

- The **Black Power movement** was also active during the 1960s. It believed in 'black **nationalism**' and that African Americans should be justified in using violence in the fight for equality with, and the separation from, white Americans.
- Malcolm X was a supporter of the **Nation of Islam** who fought for a separate black state.
- The most extreme campaigners were the **Black Panthers**, who had a private army of around 2000. They believed weapons should be used to force white Americans to give up power.
- In the North, some disillusioned African Americans responded to the message of the Black Power groups and a series of violent riots took place from 1965 to 1967.
- The riots mostly focused on tension between African Americans and the police. A report into the riots concluded that there were two Americas: a black one and a white one.
- Many believed that Black Power was damaging to civil rights as it frightened and alienated white Americans from the civil rights cause.

Malcolm X also had a **significant** but **different** role to play in the **civil rights movement**

- Malcolm X never led a mass movement in the way that Martin Luther King did. He was, however, able to inspire and energise the disillusioned young African Americans who were frustrated with King's campaign.
- He was important in bringing the issue of civil rights to Northern cities. This made it even more of a national movement, rather than one confined to the South.
- Malcolm X gave many African Americans a self-belief and made them proud of their heritage again. He also raised the profile of the Islamic faith among African Americans.
- Before he was assassinated in 1965, Malcolm X was able to unite and co-ordinate a range of campaigning groups. His leadership was strong enough that he was able to bring them together to work more effectively.

Other groups also deserve **credit** for their **role** in the **civil rights movement**

- As well as the bigger organisations that took part in protests, there were also a large number of individuals, both black and white, who participated. They faced violence and intimidation but did what they thought was right.
- Diplomats from African nations were also important. They travelled from New York to Washington along **Route 40** and faced discrimination. They were frequently stopped by police due to the colour of their skin and they were refused service in restaurants and hotels.
- Many other countries criticised America for this treatment of foreign officials. The USSR could use the racism shown by American in their anti-American propaganda. This was embarrassing for the presidents.
- The anger about the treatment of the diplomats on Route 40 added to the pressure to pass the 1964 Civil Rights Act.

Key point

There were other significant groups in the campaign for civil rights, including three presidents who passed various pieces of legislation to establish equality.

Test yourself

1 Why were some people frustrated by the campaign of Martin Luther King?
2 What was affirmative action?
3 What was the importance of Route 40?

Practice question

'Presidents did more than campaigners in achieving civil rights for African Americans between 1960 and 1968.' How far do you agree with this statement? (18 marks)

The presidents of the 1960s and early 1970s had varying degrees of success

President	Positive contributions	Limitations
John F. Kennedy, 1961–63	• He supported the aims of the civil rights movement • He made high-level black appointments to government • He stood up to governors of Southern states during the Freedom Rides • He ensured James Meredith went to university • He made public commitments on TV to civil rights • He challenged segregation in airports • He laid the way for Johnson to pass the Civil Rights Act	• Civil rights was not a priority for him • He moved too slowly on issues • His first proposed Civil Rights Bill was moderate and disappointed activists • He knew he couldn't be too radical and was careful not to alarm the public
Lyndon Johnson, 1963–69	• He gave large amounts of government money to reduce poverty which helped African Americans • He managed Congress so difficult laws were passed • He made the 1964 Civil Rights Act more radical than Kennedy had planned • He passed the Voting Rights Act in 1965 which banned literacy tests and allowed more people access to voting • There was a record number of African American officials in important positions in his presidency	• He was an aggressive and difficult man
Richard Nixon, 1969–74	• Desegregation in schools went from being a requirement to a reality • He extended the **Voting Rights Act** in 1970 and banned literacy tests nationally • He bought in quotas for the number of African American students and numbers employed in local office. This was called **'affirmative action'** • He set up the **Office of Minority Business Enterprise** which gave government contracts to African American and Hispanic businesses	• There was still segregation in housing • The Watergate scandal overshadowed his achievements • He had a poor relationship with civil rights leaders • He cooperated with Southern governors who weren't following the law • He tried to appoint judges who were pro-segregation

Spot the mistakes

Below is a paragraph that is part of an answer to the question:

Explain why some people joined the Black Power movement. **(10 marks)**

There are some factual errors in the answer. Find them and replace them with more accurate examples.

Some people would have joined the Black Power movement because they were resident in the South of the USA and Martin Luther King was mostly focused on the North. Therefore, they would have seen the appeal of people that were more focused on their needs in their particular parts of the USA. In addition, people were keen to join an organisation that had a great focus on their heritage. The Country of Islam believed that African Americans should leave and return to Africa and that this would provide them with greater equality. The Black Tigers went even further and thought that African Americans should use force to get what they wanted. Therefore, the Black Power movement gave an alternative to those people who wanted more than the civil rights movement was offering.

Stretch and challenge

There were three main presidents who had a role to play in civil rights: Kennedy, Johnson and Nixon. Give each one a mark out of 10 for how much they achieved (1 = worst; 10 = best). Explain your decisions using specific examples to support your judgements.

4.6 The fight for equality for other minority groups

REVISED

The late 1960s saw the first **attempts** to **co-ordinate** protests among **Hispanic Americans**

- There had been a long history of immigration from Mexico into the USA. By 1978, 33 per cent of Los Angeles' population were migrants from Mexico who had moved to the USA for better jobs and pay.
- Mexican immigrants faced the same intolerance as African Americans. They suffered from high unemployment, ill treatment, low wages, poor housing, segregated education and police discrimination.
- Mexican Americans were also discouraged from voting and were under-represented at all levels of politics. The community felt disengaged from American politics and started to call themselves '**Chicanos**' rather than Mexican Americans.
- There was a campaign to restore the national pride and identity of the Chicanos. Reies Tijerina launched a legal campaign to have large parts of New Mexico returned to the Chicano people.

Key point

The Civil Rights Act of 1964 started to shift attitudes and other groups, such as Hispanic and Native Americans, also campaigned for equality with mixed success.

- It was defeated in the courts but it did highlight the issues facing Chicanos and inspired the young to become more nationalist.
- Rodolfo 'Corky' Gonzales also established the **Crusade for Justice** in 1966 which campaigned for better treatment of the Chicanos. In 1968, he led Chicano representatives on the **Poor People's March on Washington**.

There was **some progress** for **Chicanos** but by the end of the 1960s **many issues remained**

- In 1966, the head of the **United Farm Workers (UFW)**, Cesar Chavez, led a strike of Californian grape pickers to fight for better pay and conditions. The public supported the strike and boycotted grapes while the strike went on for five years.
- Chavez gained support from Senator Robert Kennedy. This led to a settlement in the early 1970s which gave workers better wages, but the Chicanos remained one of the poorest sections of society.
- Most Chicanos realised that education would help to lift them from poverty. However, few went to college, many dropped out of school and segregated education meant poor teaching.
- In March 1968, students organised a mass walkout of Chicanos from high schools in Los Angeles – 20,000 students took to the streets to protest. However, the protests ended in violence.
- The protests didn't fulfil their aims. The police forced the students back into school. There were no changes to the education standards for Chicanos. Further walkouts in 1971, 1972 and 1974 also failed and there are still issues remaining in the community today.

There had been a **long** history of **discrimination** against **Native Americans**

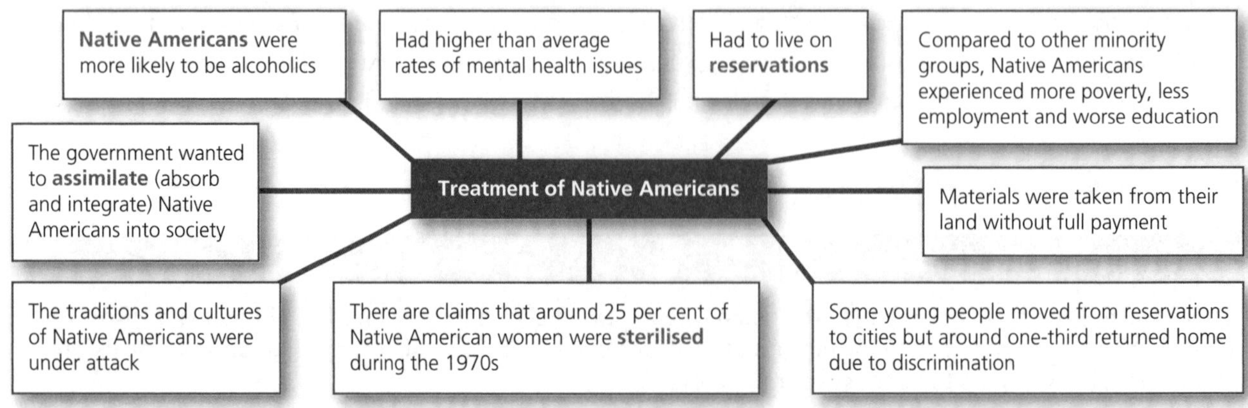

Treatment of Native Americans
Native Americans were more likely to be alcoholics
Had higher than average rates of mental health issues
Had to live on reservations
Compared to other minority groups, Native Americans experienced more poverty, less employment and worse education
The government wanted to assimilate (absorb and integrate) Native Americans into society
Materials were taken from their land without full payment
The traditions and cultures of Native Americans were under attack
There are claims that around 25 per cent of Native American women were sterilised during the 1970s
Some young people moved from reservations to cities but around one-third returned home due to discrimination

Continued discrimination led some Native Americans to organise protest marches

- There were calls for **Red Power**, along the lines of Black Power. The protests mostly revolved around trying to reclaim land that white European settlers had taken or bought for next to nothing from the Native Americans.
- In 1972, the **American Indian Movement (AIM)** marched on Washington and took over the offices of the **Bureau of Indian Affairs (BIA)**.
- In 1973, the AIM occupied **Wounded Knee**, where Native Americans had been slaughtered in 1890. It protested against discrimination.
- Specifically, it said that the head of the BIA was corrupt, that reservation police acted like an army and that there were too many environmental impacts of mining in Dakota.
- The siege failed after 73 days and two deaths. However, there was huge publicity and lawyers then pushed issues of land ownership through the courts.
- President Nixon had to act:
  - he appointed a Native American as a **Commissioner for Indian Affairs**
  - 48,000 acres of land were returned to tribes
  - the **Child Welfare Act** of 1974 prevented children being taken from their families by the government
  - the **Indian Self-Determination Act** of 1975 meant that Native Americans were free to govern themselves.

Test yourself

1. What did Chicano students do in 1968, 1971, 1972 and 1974, and why?
2. Which organisation did Cesar Chavez lead?
3. Give two examples of measures introduced by Nixon to help Native Americans.

Practice question

Explain how far Native Americans and Chicanos made progress in the years 1954–74. (10 marks)

Essay style

Below is a sample exam-style question. Use your own knowledge and the information on these two pages to produce a plan for this question using the template below. Your extended essay should contain two main paragraphs. Once you have planned your essay, write the introduction and conclusion for the essay. The introduction should introduce your opinion and the main points you will make. The conclusion should come to an overall judgement and link the factors you have explored.

Explain how far Chicanos and Native Americans made progress in the years 1954–74. (10 marks)

Introduction	**Set out your opinion**	*I think there was no/some/significant progress for Chicanos and Native Americans between 1954 and 1974 because …*
Paragraph 1: Chicanos	**Point**	
	Evidence	
	Link to question	
Paragraph 2: Native Americans	**Point**	
	Evidence	
	Link to question	
Conclusion	**Come to a judgement and link the issues**	

Stretch and challenge

There a series of important protests in this period:

- the Poor People's March on Washington
- the United Farm Workers' strike
- the school walkouts
- the siege of Wounded Knee.

For each them, decide if the motivation was **social** or **economic** and then reach a judgement on how successful each protest was in meeting its aims.

4.7 Women's rights, gay rights and poverty in the USA

REVISED

Changes in the **role** of women **post-1945** led to a demand for an end to **discrimination**

- Between the Second World War and 1960 there was around a 30 per cent increase in the number of women in the workplace.
- However, 95 per cent of managers were men and women only earned 50–60 per cent of the wages of men. Women's work was low paid, part time and low level.
- But there began to be a shift in attitudes. Before the Second World War most women wanted to marry, have children and stay at home. After the war, women either didn't want that family life, or wanted to carry on working once married.
- In 1963 a **Status Commission Report** on employment and wages led directly to the **Equal Pay Act**. The Civil Rights Act of 1964 also prohibited discrimination against women.

Key point

The political activism of the civil rights movement, the Chicano national movement and Native Americans led to a push for other social groups to gain more rights and equality.

- The **women's movement** emerged. This was a collection of many different women's groups with a variety of goals and tactics who wanted to see these goals fully implemented.
- In 1966, the feminist Betty Freidan established **NOW (National Organisation for Women)**. It adopted peaceful protest and co-ordinated with other groups challenging discrimination in the courts.

The **women's movement** made some **progress** but there was also **opposition** to equality

- NOW was relatively popular but was traditional in its outlook and methods. Younger women started the **Women's Liberation movement**, which was far more radical.
- One key campaign for all radical feminists centred on legalising **abortion**. Many felt that it was discriminatory and unsafe to make it illegal.
- The legal case was started by Estelle Griswold in Connecticut. The lawyers argued that stopping abortion was an invasion of a woman's privacy. The case of ***Roe* v. *Wade*** went all the way to the Supreme Court and in 1965 abortion was legalised.
- In the 1960s there was a push to add an extra clause to the **constitution** that would make sure men and women were equal and 63 per cent of the population supported this.
- However, an organisation founded by Phyllis Schlafly led a campaign to stop this. She said a women's role was devalued by making her equal to a man. She slowed down any changes to the constitution and the move was defeated in 1982.

A **shift in attitudes** about **homosexuality** was helped by the **emergence** of **Gay Activists** and **Gay Pride**

- The 1969 raid on a gay bar, called the Stonewall Inn, New York, showed the extent of anti-gay feeling in America. Homosexuality was still a crime, it was seen as a psychological condition and was treated with shock therapy.
- Gay people were angry and fearful about the way they were treated. The **Stonewall raid** led to violent demonstrations, which lasted a week.
- The police continued to raid gay establishments. In 1970 the **Snake Pit raid** led to 170 arrests and a death. This shocked many people.
- Following this and **Gay Liberation Front (GLF)** campaigning, the **American Psychiatric Association** stopped classifying homosexuality as a disorder and the first **Gay Pride marches** took place in New York and Los Angeles.
- These raids pushed many gay men into action. Three gay newspapers were established. The GLF was formed and the **GAA (Gay Activists Alliance)** campaigned for gay rights in a co-ordinated manner.

The **young** were a powerful voice **against discrimination**, inequality and the **Vietnam War**

- Students formed **Students for a Democratic Society** in 1959, with members campaigning in colleges for better education. Many student groups also protested for civil rights and women's liberation, and against the society their parents had created.
- There were a number of anti-war protests relating to the war in Vietnam. Over 40,000 students were involved in these protests in 1968 across university campuses. The protests would frequently involve burning the US flag – an illegal rejection of American values.
- In 1970, at Kent State University, a protest against invading Cambodia became so heated that the National Guard opened fire on the demonstration and killed four students. The USA was horrified.
- The **hippy movement** became a form of protest. Hippies' clothing, hair, lifestyle and music were seen as a rejection of the rest of society. People were concerned by this attitude.
- Many people thought these crises were the end of the American society that the country had fought to protect in the Second World War.

Politicians also worked to make changes in society, particularly to solve **poverty**

President	Aim/focus	Successes	Limitations
John F. Kennedy, 1961–63	• To unite Americans • To make America a fairer place • To create a **'New Frontier'**	• Increased the minimum wage • The **Housing Act** gave money to clear slums • **Social Security Act** helped the elderly and unemployed • The **Manpower Deployment and Training Act** retrained the unemployed	• Minimum wage only helped those with a job • The housing loans didn't help the poorest • There were housing shortages due to slum clearances • Many poor black Americans moved north for work, but faced discrimination there
Lyndon B. Johnson, 1963–69	• To take Kennedy's work further and create a **'Great Society'** • A 'war on poverty' • An 'end to racial injustice'	• The **Medical Care Act** funded health care for the elderly • Gave money to help the poorest with their children • Multiple agencies founded to create jobs in cities • The Elementary and Secondary Act increased funding to education in poorer areas	• Still very high unemployment levels • Social tensions • Anti-war protests • High government spending
Richard Nixon, 1969–74	• Critical of Johnson's 'Great Society' • Welfare measures	• **Supplemental Security Income (SSI)** guaranteed an income for the elderly and disabled • Twenty per cent increase in government spending on social security • Tax reform to help the poorest • Return of the **Food Stamp programme**, making food aid more available to the poorest	• Some policies never became law or were not implemented as Nixon had to resign because of political scandal

Stretch and challenge

Some people argue that in the 1960s parts of American society was in crisis because of civil unrest. Re-read this chapter. What evidence can you find of:

- People disobeying law?
- Progress in society?
- People challenging what had previously been accepted?

Come to your own judgement: how far was America in crisis in this period?

Test yourself

1. What did people find worrying about the hippy movement?
2. What was NOW?
3. What did *Roe* v. *Wade* legalise?

Section 2 Thematic studies

What the British thematic study is about and how it will be examined

Overview of the British thematic study

The focus here is on change and continuity across a long period of history. In this book we cover all the British thematic studies.

Thematic studies require you to make appropriate judgements about change and continuity:

- You will need to have a clear understanding of significant characteristics of individual periods within the timeframe – this will allow you to make links and draw comparisons.
- You will need to be able to explain key themes or developments.
- Key turning points should be identified (that is, points at which the 'narrative' changes).
- You will want to consider factors that caused change (or even why change did not happen at specific points) and the type of change.

Key skills needed for the British thematic study

'Second-order concepts' are thought processes that allow us to study the past. They do so by providing us with a way to organise 'big ideas' in history.

Below you will find guidance on the second-order concepts **most** relevant to the thematic studies. It important to acknowledge that some of the points below are **generalisations**; there are exceptions to all.

Significance – 'Significance' is not the same as 'importance'. When **evaluating** historical significance you may consider **consequences**; **parallels** with another period; **remembrance**. You must use **criteria** (such as those previously mentioned) to support judgements you make about the significance of an event, person or development. Useful words: 'magnitude', 'durability', 'relevance'

Continuity – This is the idea that some things **stay** as they were, even across long periods of time. This concept tends to be more important when you are looking at a **longer period** of time. For example, the British. Useful words: 'maintained', 'remained', 'unaltered'

THE THEMATIC STUDY

Change – What you will be examined on is the **nature**, **extent** and **significance** of change. Can you say **how** relations between the monarch and the people changed in the UK? To address this question you might consider how relations **improved** or **deteriorated**; the type of change and how important this was. Useful words: 'developed', 'evolved', 'switched'

Cause – Causation addresses **why** things happened. There is always a **variety** of reasons for events taking place. Your job will be to **explain** reasons. The 24-mark question may involve you explaining which **factors** were most **important**; the best answers may explore how factors **link** together and the **relationship** between them. Useful words: 'created', 'produced', 'prompted'

Main question types in the British thematic study

This is Paper 2. It is worth 50 marks in total. You will be asked the following types of question.

1 **Describe two examples of ...** *(4 marks)*

This is a basic describe question. One mark will be awarded for an example and another for development/description (as 4 marks are available you will be expected to do this twice).

You do not need to go into a huge amount of depth for this type of question: the development/description just needs to add depth to the example you have identified.

2 **Explain why, by ... X had happened/ Explain why there were ...** *(8 marks)*

This question will come from a different period than that focused on in the previous question.

A full-mark answer would explain more than one feature in relation to the question with a good amount of supporting detail.

The focus is not on the number of examples explained. You should concentrate on producing an explanation which is focused on the second-order concept identified by the question (for example, cause, consequence, change): this type of response would reveal a detailed understanding of the issue.

3 **How significant a change was X? Explain how significant X was** *(14 marks)*

This question will always focus on the significance of an event.

When answering this question you can consider significance in a variety of ways, for instance, for the example question above you could consider who was affected by the Glorious Revolution, and how power structures were changed (see page 74 for information on significance as a second-order concept).

A full-mark answer would explain more than one feature in relation to the question with a good amount of supporting detail.

4 **Statement + how far do you agree?** *(24 marks)*

This question will always be focused on more than one period: it is a question about change over time. The periods covered by the question will be consecutive.

Arguments in response to this question should pick up the similarities and differences across the periods concerned.

For a full-mark answer you should consider both sides of the argument, but make sure that you support your response with examples that span the entire period in question.

How we help you develop your exam skills

The revision tasks help you to build understanding and skills step by step. For example:

- **Change over timeline** will allow you to assess trends and turning points across periods. You will also use this to plot how historians' views changed over the period.
- **Which is best?** will allow you to consider the demands of exam question types.
- **Support or challenge?** will help you to use content to inform your judgement in an essay question.
- The **practice questions** give you exam-style questions.

Plus:

- There are annotated model answers for every practice question online at **www.hoddereducation.co.uk/myrevisionnotes** or use this QR code to find them instantly.

5 War and British Society c.790 to c.2010

5.1 Viking raids and the Norman Conquest

REVISED

The Vikings were a **nomadic** people who attacked and conquered much of the British Isles

- The **Vikings** were a people from what is now modern Norway and Denmark who had developed a culture of raiding coastal settlements. Initially, they tended to return to Scandinavia after a successful raid, but the climate of the British Isles began to encourage them to stay.
- The **Anglo-Saxons** were unprepared for this, especially as during the ninth and tenth centuries there was not an 'England', but several smaller kingdoms which fought each other frequently.
- The people of England, most notably in the north-east, lived in fear of Viking raids. Archaeological evidence suggests that the region experienced a very large degree of looting, fighting and death.

Key point

From the eighth century, the Anglo-Saxon kingdoms withstood centuries of attacks and invasions by the Vikings until finally William of Normandy conquered England in 1066.

- The Anglo-Saxons called the Vikings 'Northmen' and seem to have feared them greatly. Much of the evidence we have is from monks who chronicled various invasions and wars, and their fear comes across very strongly.

The Anglo-Saxons **resisted** their invaders with some success

- Following centuries of raids, the Vikings launched a full-scale invasion around AD865, beginning in the north-east and conquering the kingdoms of Mercia (the Midlands) and East Anglia, to leave themselves in control of half of England.
- The kingdom of **Wessex** was nearly conquered too, but their king, Alfred the Great, survived several attacks and a peace was agreed.
- Knowing that the Vikings would eventually come again when they were prepared, Alfred reorganised his forces, and created several **Burhs** (fortified towns) across Wessex. These proved a much better resistance to the Viking attacks.
- Alfred's daughter Aethelflaed and son Athelstan built on these successes, pushing the Danes (as the Vikings were now known) out of **Mercia**, and establishing the **Witan** (a form of ruling council).
- Ultimately, peaceful coexistence seems (we are not certain) to have descended between 955 and 990 and eventually intermarriage and the blending of cultures began to take place.
- Thirty years later, the Vikings returned, and defeated the Anglo-Saxons under the leadership of Aethelred. Unable to protect his people, he was eventually forced into exile.
- In 1016, King Cnut seized the kingdom. He did not establish a purely Danish kingdom, but kept several Anglo-Saxon barons, including Godwin. When Cnut died, the Anglo-Saxon Edward took power.

Harold Godwinson defeated Hardrada, but was defeated himself by the **tactics** of William, Duke of Normandy

- When Edward the Confessor died in 1066, three rivals claimed the throne:
  - Harald Hardrada, the King of Norway
  - William, the Duke of Normandy
  - Harold Godwinson, the Earl of Wessex.
- Harold Godwinson was appointed by the Witan. He was then forced to fight Harald Hardrada at Stamford Bridge before bringing his exhausted army to fight William outside of Hastings.
- William and his Norman army were successful because: the Norman army was better equipped than the English army, the Normans could change tactics more easily than the English, who were using century-old tactics and William's supporters were a very loyal group.
- William's tactics tricked the Anglo-Saxons into a suicidal charge that was easily cut down, killing Harold. William became King of England, although he had to continue to fight some rebels.

The Normans took **control** of England through force, and protected their control with castles

- William dealt with rebellions effectively, but initially did not punish the rebels who rose up against him.
- However, the Anglo-Saxons kept resisting, especially in the north. In 1069, the King of Scotland and a Viking fleet came to the aid of the English earls there.
- William was not willing to allow this to continue, so in late 1069, the **Harrying of the North** took place. Entire towns were destroyed and hundreds of people and animals were killed. The resulting starvation killed tens of thousands.
- Following this brutal assault, the Normans built hundreds of **motte and bailey** castles in most of England's towns and larger villages. William then distributed the land of England and control of these castles to the men who had supported him in his invasion.
- Most people were peasants, and their lives undoubtedly became harder as rents rose, their power was taken away and the Norman invaders imposed their will on the kingdom.

Test yourself

1 Which was the only English kingdom to avoid conquest by the Vikings?

2 Who did William defeat at the Battle of Hastings?

3 What kind of castles did the Normans build to keep control of England?

Stretch and challenge

It is really important to understand who was ruling in England at this time, and more importantly when 'England' became an identifiable kingdom with a single ruler. Make yourself a timeline showing who was ruling, and when the smaller kingdoms such as 'Wessex' and 'Mercia' became 'England'.

Developing the detail

Below is a sample exam-style question and a paragraph written in answer to this question. The paragraph contains a limited amount of detail. Annotate the paragraph to add additional detail to the answer.

Describe two examples of the impact of Viking raids on the British Isles in the period 790–1000 on the population of Britain. (4 marks)

The most obvious short-term impact was the looting and violence which took place. The long-term impact was that some of the Anglo-Saxon kingdoms were weakened by the attacks.

Complete the paragraph

Below are a sample exam-style question and a paragraph written in answer to this question. The paragraph contains a point and specific examples, but lacks a concluding explanatory link back to the question. Complete the paragraph adding this link in the space provided.

Explain why King William used such excessive tactics to suppress the Anglo-Saxons. (8 marks)

After initially attempting to be conciliatory in his approach, William realised that the Anglo-Saxons would continue to resist unless he made an extreme show of force. Therefore he …

____

____

____

____

Practice question

How far was the Norman invasion of 1066 significant for Britain? (14 marks)

5.2 Feudal society

REVISED

Medieval society was organised into the **feudal system** to control the people and the kingdom

The **king** was the ruler of the English kingdom, but he required the support of each of the levels of the **feudal system** beneath him to be able to rule effectively and manage land efficiently

↓

Tenants-in-chief were the barons and bishops who took charge of areas of the kingdom on behalf of the king and ensured that order was maintained and rents from tenants on their lands were collected. This group evolved to become the **nobility**. There were about 100 of these in the medieval period

↓

Sub-tenants were knights or lords of the manor who were soldiers in the king's army, and later became responsible for leadership of small areas such as villages. There were between 1000 and 2000 of these in the medieval period. They followed the **chivalric code**

↓

Peasants were the people who were granted or had to rent land from knights to grow food to feed everyone. These were the majority of people of England, between 1 and 2 million in this period

Key point

Feudal society saw centuries of relative peace, interrupted only by conflict between wealthy and powerful nobles who wanted to take power back from the king.

Other aspects of life served to **support** the feudal system

- Castles were an essential part of the feudal system:
  - they acted as a base for the armed forces from which they could put down any potential revolt
  - they served as seat of power for the local baron
  - they projected authority and fear over the population.
- The Church was an incredibly important part of the medieval world. Every member of English society was deeply religious, and the Church helped to maintain order and loyalty through prayer and sermon.
- It was not always perfect, some nobles and knights mistreated their people and often got away with it, and there were numerous feuds and conflicts between them which the king often had to step in to deal with.

Test yourself

1 What is the name given to the social system in England?

2 Who fought for control of England after the death of King Henry I?

3 In what year was the Magna Carta signed?

The system broke down with a **civil war** between **Stephen** and **Matilda**

- King Henry I died in 1135 without a legitimate heir. His daughter Matilda and the richest baron in England, Stephen Blois, fought for control of England.
- After fifteen years of civil war, both sides were forced to compromise. Stephen was allowed to take the throne, but it was Matilda's son, Henry, who would become king on Stephen's death.
- Because Stephen lacked **royal authority** (the right of a monarch to use their power) this led to a period known as the '**Anarchy**' during which law and order broke down almost completely.
- Henry II was crowned in 1154 and immediately set about restoring royal authority by confiscating 40 castles and returning them only to those barons who had proved their loyalty.

Practice question

'Between 790 and 1215, war did not have a significantly negative effect on the English people.' How far do you agree with this statement? (24 marks)

The **Magna Carta** limited the power of English kings

- Fifty years later, Henry's son King John had taken over the throne after the death of his elder brother Richard the Lionheart. John was not a good king, being harsh, greedy and cruel.
- Richard had been killed in a war against the French King Philip II in 1199. In 1204, John lost control of Normandy, which caused great upset to the barons.
- By 1215, John and his barons went to war over his rule of the kingdom. There were no open battles, and many barons seem to have been in two minds about which side to choose. To end the conflict, John signed the **Magna Carta** in 1215. This put the king under, and not above, the law.
- John quickly chose to ignore the Magna Carta, and went about trying to destroy the barons once more, but the conflict came to an end when he died of dysentery. He was succeeded by his nine-year-old son, who became Henry III.

Stretch and challenge

You will be required to study a castle as part of this course. It is worth looking at what was happening to your castle during this period, as it will have seen a great deal of change. Have a look at the material your teacher has given you on this year's castle, and write five bullet points about the changes that took place in your castle in this period.

Complete the diagram

Use the information on these pages to complete the diagram below, explaining the feudal system and the role of each group.

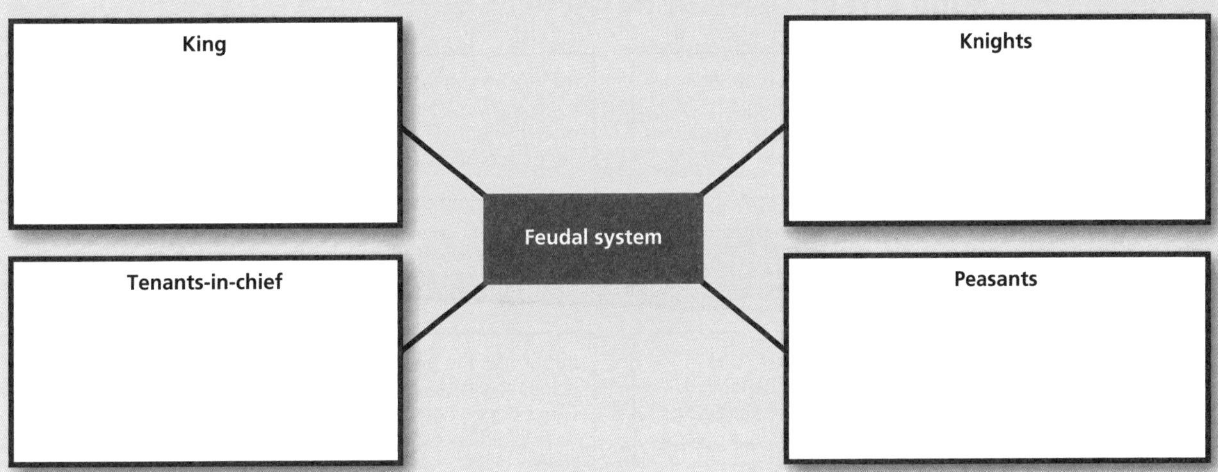

You're the examiner

Below are a sample exam-style question and a paragraph written in answer to this question. Read the paragraph and the mark scheme provided on pages 180–2. First decide which level you would award the paragraph. Then decide where in the level you would place it. Write the level below, along with a justification for your choice.

Explain why the feudal relationship between king and barons broke down in the reign of King Stephen. (8 marks)

The main problem was King John's personality. He was selfish and harsh to all those around him, and he failed to realise that all his predecessors had worked to ensure a good relationship with the barons. He was also untrustworthy; he signed the Magna Carta and then ignored it.

Level: ☐

Reason for choosing this level: ____________________

____

____

5.3 War and medieval society

REVISED

The **age of chivalry** saw Edward I invade both Wales and Scotland

- In the thirteenth century, the chivalric code became even more significant and knights took on a larger role, thanks to the enthusiasm of King Edward I. In 1276, he took a force of 1000 knights and 15,000 **infantry** to Wales. The Welsh surrendered without a fight.
- In 1282, Daffydd ap Gruffydd led a revolt against English rule, which had imposed deeply unpopular laws and taxes. This united the Welsh in a way that had never been seen before (there has never been a united, independent Wales).
- Edward defeated the Welsh in a long winter campaign that was funded by extra grants of tax from Parliament. He recaptured Wales and then captured Daffydd, who was executed for treason. Edward then imposed heavy taxes on Wales to pay for the war.
- Edward attempted to do the same to Scotland. At first he was successful, but a rebellion, initially led by William Wallace, succeeded in freeing Scotland. Edward eventually died of illness leading his fourth invasion of Scotland.

Key point

Edward I's desire for war led to a distinct change in English society, as the cost and impact of war began to erode the feudal system.

Warfare had a **huge effect** on many aspects of medieval society

Impact of Edward's wars on England

Impact on the bystanders: when armies marched through enemy countryside, looting, damage and violence were common. Even the army that was on 'your' side might do damage or at the very least steal everything it could

Impact on the whole country: the sheer cost of mobilising so many men, so many horses and so much equipment, repeatedly, placed a huge financial burden on the kingdom. Taxes were raised repeatedly and were deeply unpopular

Impact on the government: in 1295, to gain continued support and taxation for his wars, Edward summoned the 'Model **Parliament**' and created a chamber for the **Commons**. This allowed him to give a voice to the people and thus made them more willing to pay

Impact on the people: the invasions of Wales and Scotland helped to create a sense of national identity in those countries. England too began to develop some sense of English identity, though at the cost of those who were seen as 'other', notably **Jews**

The Hundred Years' War led to many changes to **feudal warfare**

- Beginning in 1337 and ending in 1453, the Hundred Years' War was in fact a series of wars between the French and English for control of France. There were moments during this period where either side could have won.
- Nearly 120 years of conflict saw great changes in warfare:
  - The nobility chose to offer money as opposed to service. Knights on horseback were now less important – Henry V won the **Battle of Agincourt** thanks to the skill of his archers.
  - Now knights and soldiers could make a living, so they fought more for their own profit than from loyalty.
- The constant warfare against the French killed off the use of the French language at court, and helped to build a sense of 'English' identity. At the same time, it reduced the appetite for war, while also reducing England's ties to Europe.
- Defeat in the Hundred Years' War was a key trigger to the period of civil war termed the **Wars of the Roses**, which only ended when a Welsh exile named Henry Tudor seized the throne at the Battle of Bosworth in 1485.

Test yourself

1. What was the code that obliged nobles and knights to raise armies to fight for the king?
2. Who was the Welshman who led a revolt against the English in 1282?
3. Between which years was the Hundred Years' War fought?

Turning assertion into argument

Below are a sample exam-style question and a series of assertions. Read the question and then add a justification to each of the assertions to turn it into an argument.

How far was new technology responsible for the end of the feudal system? (14 marks)

The extended nature of the wars meant that Edward I was forced to …

Henry V's archers' destruction of the French cavalry proved that …

The growing wealth of the nobility meant that instead of providing leadership and soldiers, they were now providing money. This meant …

Event overview grid

Complete a one-sentence summary of the events listed in the grid below.

Event	Summary
Viking attacks on England	
Cnut's capture of England	
The Norman Conquest	
The Harrying of the North	
The feudal system	
Civil War between Matilda and Stephen	
The Magna Carta	
Edward's invasion of Wales	
Edward's wars in Scotland	
The Hundred Years' War	

Practice question

Explain why feudal warfare had such a significant effect on English society in the period 1276–1337. (8 marks)

Stretch and challenge

The term 'English' comes up a great deal in this section. Write an explanation of why it was significant that people would now consider themselves 'English'.

5.4 The war with Spain

REVISED

Catholicism was a **powerful force** in Europe and Elizabeth I's religious **settlement** threatened it

- The **Catholic Church** was an exceptionally large and dominant institution in Europe (see Topic 9.1, pages 152–3 on the nature of the Church), and the advent of the **Renaissance** and the **Reformation** led to a century of religious conflict.
- In England, the **Tudors** had swung the country between **Protestantism** and **Catholicism** before Elizabeth I finally settled on a Protestant religion with concessions to Catholicism. This did not appease England's enemies however, notably Spain.
- Elizabeth faced a series of plots against her by Catholics who were secretly being funded by the Spanish. Elizabeth was **excommunicated** by the Pope, giving licence to Catholics to attempt to assassinate or overthrow her.
- At the same time, Elizabeth's cousin, Mary Queen of Scots, was under house arrest in England. She was a Catholic and had a claim to the throne as Henry VII's granddaughter.

Key point

Elizabeth fought costly but successful battles against Catholic dominance throughout her rule.

Test yourself

1 Why did Elizabeth's excommunication increase Catholic plots against her?
2 What was a privateer?
3 List three impacts of war on Elizabethan society.

Privateering and war in the Netherlands led to the failed invasion of the Spanish Armada

- In 1567, England seized 400,000 crowns (almost ten times Elizabeth's annual tax revenue) from a Spanish ship that had landed at Torquay in a storm. This was meant to be the pay for the Spanish soldiers who were occupying the Netherlands at the time.
- Elizabeth then granted licences to several English ships to become **privateers** (government-approved pirates). This became a source of income for the English Crown, and essentially an undeclared war between England and Spain.
- Eventually, Philip II of Spain had had enough, and sent a huge **Armada** (fleet of ships) to invade England. The plan was to seize power, remove Elizabeth I, and make England part of the Spanish Empire.
- The attack failed, however, thanks to attacks by the small but well-trained English fleet, and the effects of bad weather. The Armada had to return to Spain, with the loss of over 10,000 soldiers and sailors.

Practice question

To what extent were wars popular with the English population in the period 1000–1600? (24 marks)

The **threat** of Catholicism continued through Spain and **Ireland**

- Although England had not been invaded, it remained vulnerable to the considerably more powerful Spain. Elizabeth sent an expedition to attack the remains of the Armada, but it was unsuccessful and much of the fleet was destroyed.
- Throughout the 1590s, there was a fear that Spain might try to invade again. Privateers continued their attacks. In 1596, an English fleet captured the Spanish port of Cadiz and destroyed a fleet that had been intended for an invasion of England.
- There was a fear that Spain would use religion to gain a foothold in Ireland, which was still deeply Catholic. The Spanish lent their support to Hugh O'Neill, who led a major rebellion in the north of Ireland in 1595.
- Elizabeth spent nearly £1.9 million quelling the rising, and died before it finally ended.

Stretch and challenge

If you are studying 'War and Society', you will not be studying 'The Reformation', but it is worth looking at the first section (see pages 152–3) to help you understand the significance of religion and the Church at this time.

Continued warfare had many **effects** on the English **nation**

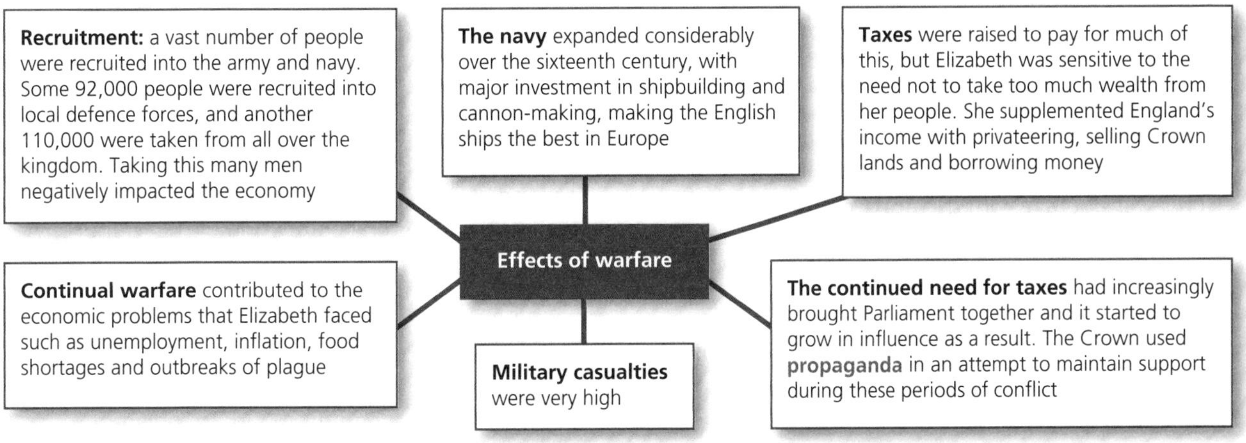

Effects of warfare

Recruitment: a vast number of people were recruited into the army and navy. Some 92,000 people were recruited into local defence forces, and another 110,000 were taken from all over the kingdom. Taking this many men negatively impacted the economy

The navy expanded considerably over the sixteenth century, with major investment in shipbuilding and cannon-making, making the English ships the best in Europe

Taxes were raised to pay for much of this, but Elizabeth was sensitive to the need not to take too much wealth from her people. She supplemented England's income with privateering, selling Crown lands and borrowing money

Continual warfare contributed to the economic problems that Elizabeth faced such as unemployment, inflation, food shortages and outbreaks of plague

Military casualties were very high

The continued need for taxes had increasingly brought Parliament together and it started to grow in influence as a result. The Crown used **propaganda** in an attempt to maintain support during these periods of conflict

Complete the paragraph

Below are a sample exam-style question and a paragraph written in answer to this question. The paragraph contains a point and specific examples, but lacks a concluding explanatory link back to the question. Complete the paragraph adding this link in the space provided.

Describe two examples of the impact of the war with Spain, 1585–1603. **(4 marks)**

Recruiting 385,000 men put a huge burden on the English government and economy. Not only did the Crown have to pay the salary of a very large number of people, but also …

Developing the detail

Below is a sample exam-style question and a paragraph written in answer to this question. The paragraph contains a limited amount of detail. Annotate the paragraph to add additional detail to the answer.

Explain why England was able to survive the war with Spain between 1585 and 1603. **(8 marks)**

England was extremely lucky during the war with Spain. When the Armada attacked, some ships got sunk by the English navy, and some of the rest were destroyed by a storm. After this, the English destroyed another fleet that the Spanish were building. Throughout the war, the queen had been recruiting many people for the army and navy.

5.5 The British civil wars

REVISED

England descended into **civil war** in 1642 as Parliament clashed with the king

- Charles wanted to change the English Church to make it look more beautiful, like a Catholic Church. This was popular with the peasantry, but many of the nobility and gentry were appalled, and feared a return to Catholicism.
- During the reign of Elizabeth, and to an extent James I, Parliament had become more important. King Charles I alienated Parliament by hardly calling on it at all.
- At the same time, the king refused to tolerate criticism and arrested, imprisoned and tortured those who spoke out against him.
- War broke out over Charles' demands for yet more taxes to pay for armies to put down rebellions in Scotland and Ireland (Charles was king there as well as England). The wars would consume all three kingdoms for the next decade.

Key point

The English civil wars were devastating to England, Scotland and especially Ireland, and ultimately led to the restoration of the monarchy.

Practice question

Explain why the English civil wars were so devastating to the population in the period 1642–51. (8 marks)

People chose sides between the **Parliamentarians** and the **Royalists**

- Both sides very quickly resorted to terror tactics against their enemies, but the problem was that all of their people were English.
- Unlike many civil wars, this conflict did not divide England neatly in half. It was much worse as it divided regions, towns, and sometimes even families. If you were in the minority where you lived, life could be very hard. Or very short.
- Raising armies used the same methods as Elizabeth had used: recruiting and conscripting people. The problem was that both sides would try to recruit from the same area, and the people and their gentry could find themselves victims of retribution from both sides.
- The same issue was found in terms of tax. In areas held by just one side during the war, demands were high. In border areas though, both sides would make excessive demands and when people could not pay, they would extract goods and materials.

The nature of the conflict was **violent** and **ruthless**

- There were over twenty major battles, and a handful of very major battles in the three civil wars, across England, Ireland and Scotland. There were dozens of battles and sieges and hundreds of skirmishes.
- The technology of war was moving on rapidly. Gunpowder was now relatively commonplace, and so muskets and cannon were becoming very important, though swords, shields and cavalry were still more important.
- The military leader of the **Parliamentarian** forces was Oliver Cromwell, who developed the **New Model Army**. It had professional leadership, good training and would serve anywhere in the kingdom. Its quality was the undoubted reason for Parliamentarian success.
- The fighting was especially savage, with thousands of civilians caught up in the conflict, and prisoners and traitors were treated extremely poorly.

The short- and long-term **effects** of the conflict were **huge**

- The war claimed 180,000 lives. Rampant pillaging led to a group of armed civilians called **Clubmen** forming in the south-west and south Wales. They were formed to keep out both sides.
- Because the war took place entirely on British soil, the conflict caused severe damage. It also damaged the economy as troops expected '**Free Quarter**' – they expected to be fed and housed by local inhabitants for free.
- Scotland managed to avoid the fighting in the First Civil War, but experienced terror in the Second. In Ireland, famine, disease and destruction claimed the lives of almost 40 per cent of the population.
- Psychologically, the execution of the monarch was deeply traumatic for many people, and the years of the **Interregnum** (a period without a monarch) also saw many injustices. For this reason, Charles II was asked to take the throne in 1660.

Spot the mistake

Below are a sample exam-style question and a paragraph written in answer to this question. Why does this paragraph not get into Level 3? Once you have identified the mistake, rewrite the paragraph so that it displays the qualities of Level 3. The mark scheme on pages 180–2 will help you.

Describe two examples of where the English people were treated poorly by the combatants in the Civil War. (4 marks)

Many English villages were visited by both sides of the Civil War and made to pay taxes and give goods to the armies. Very often when the other side came they punished them for having helped the first side.

Test yourself

1 What was the name for the period when Charles ruled without Parliament?
2 What did Oliver Cromwell develop that led to Parliamentary victory?
3 Roughly how many people died during the civil wars?

Support or challenge?

Below is a sample exam-style question which asks how far you agree with a specific statement. Below this are a series of general statements which are relevant to the question. Using your own knowledge and the information on these pages, place each factor in the box for 'agrees' or 'disagrees' with the stated view. As an additional challenge, you might want to think if any factors belong to both.

'Between 1300 and 1700, wars were supported by the population.' How far do you agree with this statement? (24 marks)

Factors which affected the support of the English population for war:

- The wars against Spain were defensive and therefore 'right'.
- The wars with Spain and intervention in Ireland by Queen Elizabeth were extremely expensive.
- Queen Elizabeth treated the people well and was a well-loved monarch.
- Wars against France were popular as France was an enemy and victory brought the possibility of wealth.
- The wars against Spain had a religious character and defeat would mean the reimposition of Catholicism.
- The civil wars were devastating to England, Scotland and especially Ireland.
- Both sides in the civil war treated non-combatants appallingly.

Agrees	Disagrees

TIP

The civil wars:

- First Civil War 1642–46: the main conflict, which led to a Parliamentarian victory. Charles I was restored to power by Parliament, but he quickly attacked again.
- Second Civil War 1648–49: a considerably shorter conflict, and another Parliamentarian victory. Charles I was executed as a result.
- Third Civil War 1649–51: a different conflict, largely fought against Scottish and Irish forces led by Charles II.

Stretch and challenge

With the exception of the wars of the late twentieth and early twenty-first centuries, the Civil War is the best example of a **deeply** unpopular war, in contrast to almost every other war. Create a detailed mind map which shows the reasons why this conflict was so unpopular with the people.

5.6 The changing relationship with Scotland

REVISED

Key point

In 1707, the Act of Union created Great Britain out of England and Scotland.

For most of the last 1000 years, Scotland was an **independent kingdom**, and often England's enemy

- You have studied wars fought against the Scottish by Edward I, and Scotland's involvement in the English civil wars. There were also invasions and raids across the border throughout the fifteenth and sixteenth centuries.
- You will have noted that sometimes Scotland came under the control of England.
- The town of Berwick-upon-Tweed is a few miles from the border, and swapped between English and Scottish control frequently, mostly because of the importance of its shipping and fishing port.
- **Reivers** from the southern counties of Scotland and northern counties of England attacked each other throughout the fifteenth and sixteenth centuries, leading to many feuds.

Border warfare was dominated by the actions of the reivers

- The reiving became a way of life for clans on both sides of the border. It was similar to the Viking raids of the Anglo-Saxon kingdoms eight centuries earlier. Livestock, goods and sometimes people were stolen, and villages were severely damaged.
- Henry VIII encouraged the English reivers in an attempt to make a Scottish invasion more difficult. In 1543 alone, towards the end of his reign, reivers destroyed 192 buildings and stole over 10,000 cows.
- Border counties were known as 'Marches'. **Wardens of the Marches** were employed by both governments to limit the impact of the reivers. This failed as the Scottish wardens tended to join the raids, and the English wardens were ignored.
- The reiving ended with the accession to the throne of James, who became King James VI of Scotland and James I of England. This fighting became pointless as the two countries were united and any remaining reivers were executed.

By 1707 most people were ready to accept the **union of England and Scotland**

- Scotland faced religious divisions: southern counties favoured Protestantism, while the Highlands in the north preferred Catholicism. James I tolerated this, but his son Charles I did not.
- The Scottish people were spared the horrors of the First English Civil War, but they joined Charles I in the Second. In the Third Civil War, they launched an invasion of England, and reached Worcester in the Midlands, where they were heavily defeated by Cromwell.
- Charles II was restored in 1660. When he died, his brother James II took the throne and attempted to impose Catholicism on both sides of the border. This led to his overthrow. Many Scottish people were unhappy and supported James; they became known as the **Jacobites**.
- In 1707, the **Act of Union** united Scotland and England to create **Great Britain**. (Note that Wales was thought of as part of England, which is why it is not represented on the flag.) It notably improved the economy of Scotland, and so the majority accepted this.

Test yourself

1 What is the name of the town that switched between England and Scotland frequently?

2 What is the term for raiders from either side of the Anglo-Scottish border?

3 In what years were the two Jacobite Rebellions?

Two eighteenth-century rebellions for Scottish independence ultimately failed

- In 1714, Queen Anne died without child. This caused a crisis as the next in line to the throne would have been James Stuart, but he was a Catholic. For this reason, Prince George of Hanover was placed on the throne as King George I.
- In response, a group of Jacobites launched a rebellion that briefly succeeded in taking control of Scotland. They were not popular with the southern Scottish who were Protestant, and eventually retreated into the Highlands.
- In 1745, a second rebellion was launched by Charles Stuart ('Bonnie Prince Charlie'). Most of the British army was fighting in European wars, so England was relatively undefended. The rebels were unable to take advantage of this and fled back to the Highlands.
- The Jacobite force was defeated at the **Battle of Culloden** in April 1746. Charles escaped to France. The defeat shifted the power of Scotland to the southern Protestants who had remained loyal. The Highlanders' military skill became of key use to the British army around the world.

Practice question

Explain why the Jacobite rebellions of 1715 and 1745 were unsuccessful. (8 marks)

Event overview grid

Complete a one-sentence summary of the events listed in the grid below.

Event	Summary
Reiving in Scottish Borders	
King James became King of England	
The Act of Union	
The Rebellion of 1715	
The Rebellion of 1745	

Change over timeline

Using the information in this section, create a timeline which shows the views of the question over a given period of time.

'Between the thirteenth and eighteenth centuries, the relationship between Scotland generally improved.' How far do you agree with this statement? (24 marks)

Annotate on your timeline why trends change at given points.

1.2
1.0
0.8
0.6
0.4
0.2
0
13th century 14th century 15th century 16th century 17th century 18th century

TIP

Great Britain: it is important that you are careful to refer to **England** before 1707, and **Britain** after this date.

Stretch and challenge

It is worth considering how much impact the wars and rebellions in Scotland had on England. Make yourself a table showing the major wars that involved England between 1300 and 1750, and indicate which of those were helped by Scotland, and those that were made worse.

5.7 Imperial warfare

REVISED

The **Seven Years' War** between Britain and France established Britain as a dominant European power

- The rivalry between Britain and France developed as the latter saw Britain as an increasing threat to its power in Europe.
- Britain's **Thirteen Colonies** were extremely valuable, although rivalry with France's colony of Louisiana was growing. The French had a larger population and were allied with Spain, but Britain had Prussia as an ally.
- Britain's strong navy had made it easier to develop overseas colonies in the Caribbean, Africa and India, and to seize French and Spanish possessions in the Caribbean.

Key point

Victories over France in the Seven Years' and Napoleonic Wars established Britain as the dominant world power: a reputation it maintained through the Crimean and Boer Wars.

- In the end, the French were forced to surrender in the Treaty of Paris. Britain took much of French Canada, took control of India and built up heavy debts. Some of these debts they tried to pay off with taxes on goods, which helped spark the **American Revolution**.

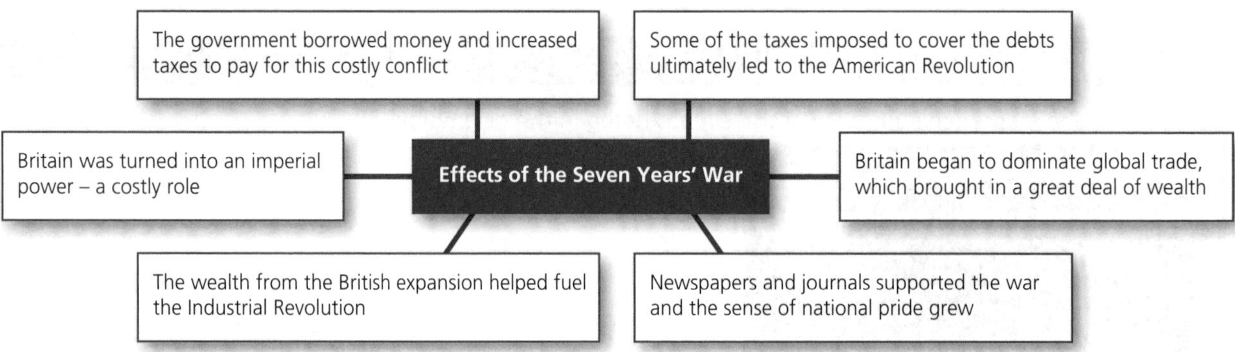

Effects of the Seven Years' War
The government borrowed money and increased taxes to pay for this costly conflict
Some of the taxes imposed to cover the debts ultimately led to the American Revolution
Britain was turned into an imperial power – a costly role
Britain began to dominate global trade, which brought in a great deal of wealth
The wealth from the British expansion helped fuel the Industrial Revolution
Newspapers and journals supported the war and the sense of national pride grew

The **Napoleonic Wars** cemented Britain's dominance of the world

- France had helped the revolutionaries in the American Revolution, but at huge cost to itself. The resulting taxes led to the **French Revolution**. France's neighbours, Britain, Prussia and Austria, attempted to invade to restore the monarchy, but were defeated.
- The **Revolutionary** and **Napoleonic Wars** saw France come close to the total conquest of Europe. A crucial moment, however, came in 1805, with British naval victory at the **Battle of Trafalgar**. Without a strong navy, France could not seriously threaten an invasion of England.
- Britain did not get involved in land battles, except for a campaign in Spain in 1808.
- Finally, Britain (with Prussian assistance) won a victory at the **Battle of Waterloo**.
- The war had been a major boost to British technology and trade.
- Britain had had to put a great deal of pressure on its population. This led to some resistance and periods of social unrest. However, the war was generally popular, and supported through the media.

The **Crimean War** was more **publicised** and **criticised** than previous conflicts

- In the 1850s, Britain faced a new rival – Russia. The Russians were becoming a threat against British possessions in India. In response to this, and Russian attempts to seize power and territory from the **Ottoman Empire**, the British and French declared war on Russia, and invaded the Crimea.
- As a result of the conflict, the British and French discovered that the Russian forces were poorly trained and equipped.
- In 1856, Tsar Alexander II asked for peace and the Treaty of Paris was signed.

- Britain's navy was excellent, but although modern, its army proved poor and was criticised for a number of reasons:

Britain was a more literate and democratic society so people were more willing to question the government's actions

↓

The number and success of newspapers had grown – this was the first war to have media coverage

↓

People were therefore able to learn of the incompetencies of some military leaders, which led to criticism of their decisions

- However, there were also positive outcomes to the Crimean War:

Through the media, the actions of the troops became known to the general public for the first time and their bravery was applauded and commemorated

↓

Some army reforms were passed in response to public criticisms

↓

The government realised the importance of public opinion

↓

The work of Florence Nightingale and Mary Seacole led to significant developments in the hygienic treatment of wounded soldiers

The **Boer Wars** were very controversial, but generally well **supported** by the **public**

- The '**Scramble for Africa**' had caused much colonial conflict. The First Boer War (1880–81) was a rebellion by the Dutch-descended **Boers** who rebelled against British rule. It happened at a time when the British were engaged elsewhere, so Britain allowed the Boers to rule themselves in Transvaal and the Orange Free State.
- The **Second Boer War** (1899–1902) was much more serious. Britain suffered some humiliating early defeats, but after reinforcements, the tide seemed to turn. The press supported the conflict.
- The war ground on as the Boers resorted to **guerrilla** warfare. The British responded harshly, establishing **concentration camps** to hold the families of the Boer soldiers hostage – 20,000 women and children died in these camps.
- The war had a considerable impact on the army – 22,000 British soldiers died, largely through incompetence. Afterwards, the British army was reformed, leaving it better prepared for the First World War than it would have otherwise been.
- There was also a significant impact on British society: it cost the country a huge amount of money and put the government into debt; it exposed a lot of underlying health problems in British soldiers which led to reform of healthcare in Britain; it led to the defeat of the Conservative government in the 1905 election.

Test yourself

1. Where did the Seven Years' War take place?
2. Which were the two decisive battles of the Napoleonic Wars?
3. What did the British use to hold families of Boer soldiers?

Practice question

How far did new technology change the impact of war on the British people 1750–1900? (14 marks)

Stretch and challenge

Most of the wars here were popular, with the exception of the Crimean War. Explain why Crimea was the exception.

Event overview grid

Complete a one-sentence summary of the events listed in the grid below.

Seven Years' War	
American Revolution	
French Revolution	
Napoleonic Wars	
Crimean War	
Boer Wars	

5.8 The First and Second World Wars

REVISED

The First World War was fought for **dominance**; the Second World War was fought for **defence**

- The creation of the German Empire by Prussia in 1871 dramatically changed the balance of power in Europe. Britain and Germany became rivals, and that rivalry drove a division between them and their allies.
- Britain, France and Russia went to war with Germany and Austria-Hungary largely out of the belief that the war would be brief and that there was something to be gained. The outbreak of war was celebrated in every combatant country.

Key point

The First and Second World Wars were devastating conflicts which brought about huge changes to Britain.

However

- In contrast, the Second World War was a war to prevent Hitler conquering Europe, and the British and French had attempted to prevent it. (For more details see Topic 1.4, page 12.)
- Britain and France did not launch an invasion of Germany. Their military forces were simply not ready, a fact that nearly cost them and the world very dearly.

The **attitudes** of the government and people to each war were significantly **different**

- To help win the First World War, Britain used the might of its global empire against Germany.
- During the Second World War, conflicts took place in Europe, Asia, Africa and Australasia.
- The United States supported Britain in both wars. In both cases its aid was with material, goods and food for the first two years of the war, changing to full military alliance. Both Woodrow Wilson (the First World War) and Franklin Roosevelt (the Second World War) had wanted to enter the war earlier.
- Both wars had support from the media and the public:
  - The First World War was seen as a conflict in which Britain stood up for smaller nations, and against a military-dominated Germany.
  - Initially, there was enthusiasm to fight the war, but when casualty levels rose this turned to determination. Only after the Battle of the Somme was there criticism levelled at the government, but the public never turned against the war effort.
  - The Second World War was a conflict against an enemy that people believed should be resisted and people remained patriotic, but fearful. The public also believed they would be rewarded with social improvements after the war.

The **lessons** of the First World War were quickly **applied** in the Second

- **Total war** was an idea that slowly took hold in Britain during the First World War. It involved:
  - conscription replacing recruitment when targets failed
  - compulsory **rationing** when voluntary rationing failed

- the deployment of women in the workforce when a manpower shortage occurred
- the introduction of **DORA** to restrict people's everyday lives
- the strict **censorship** of the news, although the press largely censored itself
- clashes within industries when the government tried to move workers into jobs needed for the war effort.

- As a result of the First World War, when the Second World War began Britain was better prepared:
  - a **coalition** government (formed of several parties) took over to avoid partisan politics
  - conscription began *before* the war started
  - rationing was introduced from the start and was more comprehensive
  - eight times more women were involved in the war effort than in the First World War
  - children were **evacuated** from cities to the countryside
  - the news was censored, but the radio was introduced to inform the public
  - trade unions worked with the government from the start of the conflict.

Both wars led to significant **social and political change** in Britain

- After the First World War, the government recognised that the people should be rewarded for their war effort and should have a say in government.
- In 1918, the **Representation of the People Act** gave all men, and married women, over the age of 21 the vote.
- As the war continued, the public also realised that more government intervention was needed in society to improve people's lives.
- The rise of the **Labour Party**, which represented the **working class**, replaced the Liberal Party. The massive cost of the war saw several strikes and other issues arising from the working class demanding fair treatment.

However

- Following the Second World War, the class differences in Britain became much clearer and people demanded that the government truly respond to demands for a better country following the conflict.
- The **Beveridge Report** recommended the creation of a **welfare state**.
- With the Labour Party victory in the 1945 election, the welfare state and a series of welfare reforms came into being.

Test yourself

1 The creation of which country led to increased tension in Europe?
2 Which nation gave support to Britain in both world wars?
3 What did the majority of adults receive at the end of the First World War?

Practice question

How far was the British response to the Second World War the same as its reaction to the First?
(14 marks)

Stretch and challenge

Make a table which shows the similarities and differences between the two wars, especially the attitudes of the British public.

Event overview grid

Below is a list of ideas that may be true about Britain in the First and Second World Wars. Tick or highlight those which you know *are* correct.

- Britain expected to win the First World War quickly.
- Britain went to war in 1939 to defend Czechoslovakia.
- DORA allowed the British government to turn the country into a total war economy.
- The creation of the Italian Empire in 1871 led to tension between the powers.
- Both wars were popular with the people, but for different reasons.
- Britain was entirely self-sufficient in both wars.
- Women's position in society was improved after both world wars.
- The working class only saw improvements after the Second World War.

5.9 War since 1945

REVISED

The **Cold War** saw the **end** of Britain's role as a **world power**

- Immediately following the Second World War, Britain was bankrupt, and could no longer afford an empire. India was granted **independence** (freedom to rule itself) in 1947, and this began a process of retreat from empire that ended with the independence of Zimbabwe in 1980.
- Britain became a key ally of the United States in the **Cold War** (see Topic 1.6, pages 17–18). Britain allowed US military and nuclear forces to be stationed in the UK.
- Britain also developed its own nuclear weapon in 1954 at great expense. The **Campaign for Nuclear Disarmament** protested this for several decades.
- The British attempted to seize control of the **Suez Canal** in Egypt in 1956, expecting to be able to continue to act in an imperial manner. They were condemned by the Americans, and forced to withdraw their forces.
- The United States put pressure on Britain to get involved in fighting the **Vietnam War**. Britain stood firm and refused to deploy British forces there.

Key point

Since Britain's decline as a world power it has been plagued with issues of terrorism at home and abroad.

Northern Ireland became the scene of 30 years of violent **ethnic** conflict

- In the 1920s Ireland was partitioned: the largest area was independent of British rule and became the Republic of Ireland in 1949.
- In the late 1960s, violence erupted in Northern Ireland, and two fighting groups emerged: the **IRA** (Irish Republican Army) on one side and the **Ulster Unionists** on the other.
- Both sides used guerrilla tactics:
  - The IRA targeted British forces, and from 1973 until 1994 they carried out attacks on the British mainland, including a mortar attack on Downing Street in 1991.
  - British troops in Northern Ireland committed several attacks on innocent people, notably the **Bloody Sunday** attacks of 1972.
- Life was, at times, extremely difficult for the people of Northern Ireland, with military presence and the threat of bombings and shootings. Even mainland Britain saw frequent bomb threats. In all cases, however, there was simply an attempt to get on with life.
- Eventually, negotiations led to the 1994 **Good Friday** agreement, which brought much of the conflict to an end with a semi-independent Northern Ireland assembly. It has been largely successful, though at the time of writing it is still slightly unstable.

The reasons for British involvement in the **Iraq War** were eventually proved to be **unfounded**

- Following the invasion of Afghanistan in 2001 (see Topic 1.11, page 28), the **Bush Administration** in the USA built a case for **regime change** in Iraq, against Saddam Hussein. Tony Blair's UK government backed this plan.
- Blair compared Hussein to Hitler and claimed that there was evidence that Iraq possessed **WMDs** (weapons of mass destruction). This was the case for war that was presented to Parliament. Both Parliament and a small majority of the British population agreed to war.

- The invasion of Iraq was a resounding success in March 2003. It took only weeks for the capital Baghdad to fall.
- But the Western powers did not have the support of the local population. From that point on, attempts were made to establish a Western-style democratic government while fighting guerrilla resistance. As of 2017, this is still an on-going issue.
- As it slowly emerged that there had never been any WMDs in Iraq, public opinion turned against the entire Iraq War.
- The 2016 **Chilcott Report** concluded that Tony Blair had known this in 2003 and had lied to Parliament and the electorate. As a result, this conflict weakened the relationship between the government and the British people.

The **War on Terror** at home and overseas has led to many changes in Britain's laws

- Al-Qaeda (see Topic 1.11, page 28) considered Britain to be one of main Western powers who were attempting to destroy Islam, and made it a target for terrorism. Britain's involvement in the invasions of Afghanistan and Iraq exacerbated this.
- Between 2003 and 2011, there were at least eight major attempted acts of terrorism – seven of which were stopped or failed.
- On 7 July 2005, four men detonated **suicide bombs** on the London Underground and a bus in central London. Over 700 people were injured and 52 killed. These men had been **radicalised** by people with links to al-Qaeda.
- In response, the UK government:
  - dramatically increased security in major airports, railway stations and ports
  - used electronic intelligence from **GCHQ** to foil potential attacks
  - increased the number of days a suspect can be held by the police without being charged from two days to fourteen in 2003 and finally to 28 days
  - increased police powers to search and use surveillance.
- Many of these increased police powers have repeatedly been shown to be unpopular with the British public.
- But tensions remain high as press coverage has heightened fears and fuelled **Islamophobia**.

Test yourself

1. Where did Britain refuse to send troops, despite American pressure?
2. What agreement reduced terrorism in Northern Ireland?
3. On what date did four terrorists detonate homemade bombs on London Transport?

Practice question

How much impact did warfare have on British governments in the twentieth century? (14 marks)

Stretch and challenge

The War on Terror is an on-going situation, and new information is being revealed all the time. During your revision, have a look at a news website to see if any further revelations can be added to your knowledge.

Spot the mistake

Below are a sample exam-style question and a paragraph written in answer to this question. Why does this paragraph not get into Level 5? Once you have identified the mistake, rewrite the paragraph so that it displays the qualities of Level 5. The mark scheme on pages 180–2 will help you.

Explain why Britain faced terrorist attacks from the late 1960s onwards. (8 marks)

Britain experienced terrorism as a result of the on-going 'Troubles' in Northern Ireland. The Catholic majority made up 70 per cent of the population, while the Protestant minority represented 30 per cent. The British government then escalated the situation by deploying the British army as an army of occupation for nearly 30 years.

5.10 Think thematic!

REVISED

War has always had a considerable impact on Britain, and has generally been popular with the people

Here are some examples of divisions from across the time period:

Review questions

1 Look back at the divisions listed and consider the reasons for them.
2 Can you track any examples of change or continuity from c.790 to 2014?
3 Can you use this information to suggest:
   a) when conflict was within Britain or outside it?
   b) when the patterns of support for war were?
   c) when war led to a notable change for the British people?

AD790–1500

- In the ninth and tenth centuries, there was no 'England', and the small kingdoms, such as Wessex, were constantly in fear of invasion and attack from Vikings.
- William's conquest of England came through the power exerted by building hundreds of motte and bailey castles, and from the projection of fear.
- The control established by William broke down in the 1130s–50s as a civil war erupted between Stephen and Matilda. Matilda's son, Henry II, took back a great deal of control, by seizing many castles.
- The struggle between King John and the barons led to civil war, which led to increased power for the nobility, but greater cooperation with the king.
- The Hundred Years' War was a huge drain on England's resources, and defeat in 1453 led directly to the Wars of the Roses, which eventually put Henry VII on the throne.

c.1500–c.1750

- Religious instability led to war with Spain, which was extremely costly, but also generally popular with the people of England. It also helped to trigger rebellion in Ireland.
- Anger about King Charles' personal rule and religious changes led to civil war in England, Scotland and Ireland. It was utterly devastating to all three kingdoms.
- Unlike all previous conflicts, this war was extremely hard on the people of England, with whole communities destroyed and over 180,000 people dead.
- The aftermath of the war ultimately saw greater power in the hands of Parliament, which ended civil war in England.
- Conflict between England and Scotland had been waged intermittently for centuries, and more frequently on a local level with reiving across the border.
- The accession to the throne of King James I brought England and Scotland together, although they retained separate laws and parliaments.
- The Act of Unity in 1707 abolished the Scottish Parliament and brought Scotland into the English Parliament. Reaction to this in Scotland led to the Jacobite Rebellions of 1715 and 1745.

c.1750–c.2010

- Rivalry with the French in North America led to the Seven Years' War, which in turn led to the American Revolution.
- The conflicts of the nineteenth century were, in general, popular with the British people. Victory in the Napoleonic Wars and Crimean War was supported by the size and power of the British Empire.
- Propaganda disasters and military setbacks in the Boer Wars led to reforms which meant that Britain was more prepared for the First World War.
- Support for the First World War was maintained through attempting to avoid defeat by Germany, and by a mixture of propaganda and heavy authoritarian control under the Defence of the Realm Act.
- Many lessons on how to fight total war were put in place as soon as the Second World War began. Support for the war was, in general, stronger as a result of the direct attacks on the UK and the sense of justification from the threat of the Nazis.
- Since the war, there have been conflicts that have centred around terrorism, both in Northern Ireland because of religious conflict, and in England as a result of terror linked to al-Qaeda. Both of these have led to increased security and governmental powers.

The nature of conflict has changed across time

From the seventh to the eleventh century there was conflict over who would control England, from Vikings and Anglo-Saxons and then the Norman invasion of 1066	→	War in the period from the Norman Conquest to the end of the Wars of the Roses was split between civil conflict to decide control, wars to conquer Wales and Scotland, and finally the Hundred Years' War with France. These wars were fought with small armies	→	From the civil wars onwards, wars were fought on a much larger scale, with larger armies doing considerably more damage. This escalation continued to the mass destruction of the First and Second World Wars	→	In the twentieth century, the nature of warfare was such that it led to reforms for the people of Britain. With the beginning of the Cold War, this changed dramatically as nuclear weapons meant mass conflict was no longer an option

It is worth noting the following ideas however:

- The various wars for control of England in the Middle Ages were between different groups of powerful nobles and did little to help ordinary people. The war between Stephen and Matilda, the conflict between King John and the barons, and the Wars of the Roses were all such conflicts.
- The development of England's navy made a big difference to England's (and later Britain's) ability to fight from the sixteenth century onwards.
- The conflicts to secure control of Wales and Scotland took centuries of political upheaval and military conflict.

Review questions

Study the exceptions to the generalisations then try to reword each generalisation in one sentence to account for the exceptions.

The nature of warfare has evolved from internal to external

During the medieval period (c.790–c.1500), England's wars were internal: • The wars over control of England from the Viking invasions to the Norman Conquest were about the right to control all of England • The civil wars for control of England were frequent, and were largely about who would dominate, both in England but also for control of Wales and Scotland	→	**From c.1500 to c.1750, the nature of war changed from small localised wars to wars which were much more deadly to the English people:** • Elizabeth's wars with Spain and in the Netherlands coincided with a major rebellion in Ireland • The civil wars devastated England and did severe damage in Scotland and Ireland	→	**From c.1750 to 2010, wars were conducted on a larger scale:** • In the nineteenth century, various laws made Parliament more representative • In the 1990s, Wales, Northern Ireland and Scotland were given greater political freedom

Review questions

Look at the three boxes above. Each of the statements is a generalisation. See if you can find information to challenge the statements and add this to your diagram. Add Post-Its to each to make a new generalisation that incorporates all of the evidence provided.

Review questions

1 Sort the points below into one of the three periods you have studied (c.790–c.1500, c.1500–c.1750 and c.1750–2010):
- The Jacobite Rebellions.
- The terror bombings in London on 7 July.
- Anglo-Scottish border wars.
- Viking coastal raids.
- The Boer Wars.
- The Wars of the Roses.
- England's involvement in wars in the Netherlands.
- Conflict in Northern Ireland.
- Conflict between the barons and King John.
- The First and Second World Wars.
- The civil wars.

2 Rate each example of conflict in terms of the following:
- How much change came about for ordinary people as a result (1 = very little change; 10 = very extreme change).
- How popular this conflict was with ordinary people (1 = not very successful; 10 = very successful).

Use your ratings to write a response to the following statement: 'Over time, challenges to those in power became more extreme, but less successful.'

3 Colour code your responses to show whether they were internal or external conflicts. (Note that Scotland is **external** until 1707.)

6 Power: Monarchy and Democracy in Britain c.1000 to 2014

6.1 Anglo-Saxon England, c.1000–1066

REVISED

People at the top of society held the power in Anglo-Saxon England

- The king was chosen by the **Witan** and was usually one of the most important men in the country.
- The Earl of Wessex was the biggest landowner in England and was often made king.
- The English people saw the king as their defender – it was his job to raise armies and to produce laws to help him govern the country.
- The relationship between the king and important **nobles** and **churchmen** was important to the successful running of Anglo-Saxon England.

Key point

Anglo-Saxon England was well organised and effectively run, but there were many power struggles.

Anglo-Saxon England had a strong system of government

- The king would give land and influence to important nobles and churchmen, and they would give him loyalty and troops for an army, and govern the shires for the king.
- By 1000, Anglo-Saxon England had efficient administration and trade was prosperous.
- England was divided into shires, and the shires were subdivided into hundreds – each hundred had its own law courts and would provide the king with an army when needed.
- The **lesser nobles** (or **thegns**) carried out administration for the king (they might act as bailiffs, estate managers or tax collectors).
- By 1000, Anglo-Saxon England was famous for its coinage.

The Vikings had threatened peace in Anglo-Saxon England for a long time

- The **Vikings** attacked Anglo-Saxon England often.
- Anglo-Saxon kings tried to defend England against the Vikings by paying them **Danegeld** (a payment to prevent raids) – this was often advised by the Witan.
- Alfred the Great managed to bring relative stability to England and the Vikings settled in the north and east. This area became known as the **Danelaw**.
- By 980, Vikings raiders had started to attack the coasts of England again.

There were troubles at the end of Aethelred's reign

- Aethelred found it difficult to maintain good relationships with some of his subjects.
- Some of the local lords did not believe that Aethelred could protect England from Viking raids.
- The Witan advised Aethelred to pay Danegeld to the Vikings in 991, however they returned in 994 with the hope of being paid off again.
- In 1002, Aethelred gave an order that all Danes living in England should be killed – this was unpopular with nobles who ruled over Danish people, and many refused.
- In 1013, Sweyn Forkbeard, King of Denmark, led a full-scale invasion of England and Aethelred went into exile.

England changed under Cnut and Edward

- When Sweyn Forkbeard died in 1014, English nobles asked Aethelred to return to the throne.
- Aethelred died in April 1016 and by October 1016 Cnut (Sweyn's son) had conquered England.
- Cnut executed several Anglo-Saxon nobles and gave their lands to his loyal followers, but most Anglo-Saxons were allowed to keep their land.
- Cnut divided England into four earldoms: Northumbria, East Anglia, Mercia and Wessex.
- Throughout Edward's reign, Godwin, Earl of Wessex, caused problems.
- In 1051, Godwin went into exile with his sons after a failed attempt to overthrow Edward.
- Godwin returned to England in 1052 and was successful – Edward was forced to back down and Godwin effectively became the ruler of England.
- After Godwin died, his son Harold Godwinson took over Wessex.
- Edward the Confessor died without an heir – although the Witan chose Harold Godwinson, there were other claimants to the throne.

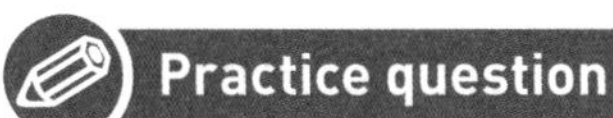

Practice question

Describe **two** examples of the Church's importance in Anglo-Saxon England. (4 marks)

Stretch and challenge

Go back through this spread and highlight any weaknesses or anything that was threatening Anglo-Saxon England. Then answer the following question: 'What presented the biggest threat to the stability of Anglo-Saxon England?'

Test yourself

1. Give one feature of government in Anglo-Saxon England.
2. Who was the Earl of Wessex?
3. Why were there problems at the end of Edward the Confessor's reign?

Checklist

Decide whether or not each statement below is correct – tick those which are. Consider what evidence you can use to support your decisions.

- Normal people had a lot of power and representation in Anglo-Saxon England.
- There was an efficient system of government in Anglo-Saxon England.
- There was a hierarchy of power in Anglo-Saxon England.
- Churchmen were in charge of tax collection.
- The Vikings successfully took over England in 980.
- England stabilised during Aethelred's reign.
- Cnut divided England into five earldoms.
- Cnut let many Anglo-Saxons keep their land.
- By 1052 Godwin effectively ran England.
- The Witan favoured Harold Godwinson as ruler of England.

Developing the detail

Below you can find a generalised summary of the role of the king in Anglo-Saxon England. Highlight the parts that may need more supporting evidence; if you get stuck try to evidence the underlined parts of the text:

> Anglo-Saxon kings had a lot of power and authority. But there other important people in Anglo Saxon England that the king needed on side for effective running of the country. The king would also take advice from a council.
>
> The king was seen as the country's defender. It was also important for the king to make sure that England had effective administration, and that it was prosperous.

6.2 The Norman Conquest and its impact

REVISED

Key point

The Norman Conquest brought change at the top of society, but many features of Anglo-Saxon England remained.

1066 was a year of turmoil

- Edward the Confessor died without an heir, but reportedly promised the throne to two people: Harold Godwinson and William of Normandy.
- Harold was crowned by the Witan, they wanted a strong leader to defend the country.
- William claimed that Edward had promised him the throne in 1051, and that Harold had sworn to uphold this promise in 1064. William began to plan his invasion of England.
- Another **claimant** (someone with a claim to the throne), Harald Hardrada, attacked the north of England – Harold Godwinson marched north to meet him and defeated him at the **Battle of Stamford Bridge**.
- William landed in the south unopposed. Harold rode back to the south and gathered a new army – they met William's army at the **Battle of Hastings**. Harold was defeated.
- William was crowned King of England on 25 December 1066 after defeating another claimant (Edgar Atheling).

Norman consolidation of power was swift

- There were many rebellions in England against Norman rule between 1067 and 1075.
- Most of the rebellions were easy to put down as they lacked co-ordination or strong leadership.
- William's treatment of rebels became harsher over time: at first he accepted some rebels' surrender without harsh repercussions, but later he devastated parts of the country and killed rebels (such as in the **Harrying of the North**, 1069).
- The Normans built **castles** to show the England that they were a permanent presence. Later, many castles were painted white so that they would be visible for miles around.
- Castles were **garrisoned** (stationed with troops) and used to control the surrounding area.
- William rewarded the loyalty of family and closest friends with land. This land had been taken from English thegns.

The Norman Conquest brought a lot of change

- Although there were some fortified houses and enclosures in Anglo-Saxon England, castles did not exist before the Conquest.
- In return for loyalty, William distributed land to his followers, who would then divide their land to reward their followers – this later became known as **feudalism**.
- The majority of Anglo-Saxon thegns (between 4000 and 5000) lost their land.
- A lot of English **sheriffs** and other officials were replaced by Normans, as were important English **bishops** and **abbots**.
- The Normans carried out a huge church rebuilding project and church architecture more closely resembled that of Normandy.
- William compiled the **Domesday Book** so that he could organise more efficient systems of taxation.

There were some examples of **continuity**

- The Church was still important to the king. William spent a lot of time after 1075 fighting in France and he left England in the hands of his barons and a group of churchmen (including Lanfranc, **Archbishop of Canterbury**).
- William made use of efficient systems of Anglo-Saxon administration (such as tax collection, writs, the gathering of armies, and dealing with law and order).
- The number of **serfs** (people owned by their lord) rose sharply after the Conquest, but there had been many slaves in Anglo-Saxon England.

Practice question

Explain the ways in which England changed as a result of the Norman Conquest. (8 marks)

Stretch and challenge

Historians argue about the extent to which England changed after the Norman Conquest. Look back through this spread and record examples of change and continuity, and then consider whether or not England benefited from each change you have identified.

Test yourself

1 What was the Witan?
2 What methods did William the Conqueror use to consolidate power?
3 Why was the Church important to the king?

Support or challenge?

Decide if each piece of information listed below supports or challenges the following statement – put a tick or a cross in the appropriate box to demonstrate your thinking:

England did not change after the Norman Conquest.

	Supports	Challenges
Anglo-Saxon systems of administration were used by the Normans		
Lots of castles were built		
Slaves had existed in Anglo-Saxon society		
Religion was still important to the king		
A lot of Anglo-Saxon land was confiscated		
Anglo-Saxon churchmen were replaced by Normans		

Complete the paragraph

Below is a paragraph written in answer to the exam-style question above. The paragraph below is missing specific detail to support the point. Complete the missing section.

When William took over as King of England he changed who was in control.

Therefore, William changed the ruling classes in England.

Section 2 Thematic studies

6.3 Struggles over power in the medieval period

REVISED

The **barons** gradually gained **greater rights** during the medieval period

- When Henry I took the throne the barons had favoured his brother, Robert. When Robert returned from crusade, Henry imprisoned him. The barons were unhappy about this.
- Henry I's **Coronation Charter** of 1100 made some concessions to the barons to win them over. For example, the king had less control over the marriage of their barons' and earls' daughters.
- Henry II did not impose harsh taxes on his barons, and would often forgive rebellious barons.
- King John did not have a positive relationship with his barons, partly because he taxed them heavily.
- The barons under John became resentful of his abuses of power. John began to sell 'justice' (this meant he allowed himself to be bribed during court cases), and often ruled in favour of the nobles.
- In 1215, a civil war broke out after disputes between John and his barons could not be solved.

Key point

There were many challenges to the power of monarchs during the medieval period.

- John was forced to admit defeat and he accepted the barons' demands in a document known as the **Magna Carta** ('Great Charter') which limited the power of the king, for example, the king could no longer accept justices.
- The signing of the Magna Carta embedded the principle that everyone (including the king) was subject to the law. This was the first time the relationship between monarchs and their subjects had been arranged as such.

Parliament emerged in the thirteenth century

- By the first half of the thirteenth century an extended council of barons were consulted by the king.
- During Henry III's reign, lesser nobles and representatives from towns were included in his councils.
- In 1251, Simon de Montfort and a group of barons forced Henry to accept the **Provisions of Oxford**. The Provisions stated that the king had to rule with the advice of a council of 24 advisers, and **Parliament** had to meet three times a year.
- After Henry gained support from some barons he challenged de Montfort. De Montfort was successful and Henry was detained.
- De Montfort ruled for a brief period in which he created the first Parliament which met in 1265.
- Some people thought de Montfort was too radical and he was killed at the **Battle of Evesham** in 1265. Henry was then reinstated as king.
- Henry continued to summon Parliaments until his death in 1272 and he openly accepted the terms of the Magna Carta at the start of each Parliament.
- Edward I was a strong and effective ruler. He summoned Parliament regularly, and in 1295 he called the **Model Parliament**. Knights and representatives (**burgesses**) from major towns were invited and this group made up the **Commons**.
- A pattern emerged whereby kings used Parliament to listen to the concerns of their subjects, and Parliament would give the king the money needed for wars and other things.

Test yourself

1. Who did Henry I offer concessions to in his coronation charter?
2. What did Simon de Montfort do in 1251?
3. What was the Model Parliament of 1295?

The **barons** had enough **power** to **depose** Richard II

- Richard II became king at the age of ten and so a **council of barons** ruled on his behalf.
- In 1381, Richard was challenged by the **Peasants' Revolt**: this was triggered by high taxation for the war with France.
- Richard broke his promise to give in to some of the peasants' demands and he ordered the deaths of more than 5000 people in retaliation.
- The situation became worse when Richard began to promote some low-ranking men to positions of power.
- Some nobles (including Henry Bolingbroke of the Lancaster family) staged a rebellion. By 1387, Richard had been defeated and was forced to execute some of his allies.
- Over the next decade, Richard restored his power and gained support from some noble families.
- In 1397, Richard arrested some of the nobles who had opposed him in 1387.
- Richard confiscated Bolingbroke's inheritance and Bolingbroke responded by raising a force and defeating Richard in 1399. Bolingbroke was crowned Henry IV in October 1399.

The **Wars of the Roses** reveal that **monarchs** were **losing power**

- Henry V acceded (took over from) Henry IV and had a successful and peaceful reign.
- Henry VI was recognised as a weak and ineffective king; during his reign he lost a lot of land in France.
- The Dukes of York and Somerset began to quarrel about who should be Henry VI's chief adviser; Somerset was killed in battle.
- The **Lancastrians** (Henry's family) and **Yorkists** began to form armies. The Duke of York was killed but his son deposed Henry VI and became Edward IV.
- Edward IV had a relatively stable reign but began to quarrel with one of his close allies – the Earl of Warwick. Warwick rebelled, and was killed in 1471.
- After Edward IV's death his son became King Edward V. Three months later his uncle seized the throne and was crowned Richard III (Edward and his brother disappeared).
- Richard III faced opposition from Henry Tudor (a relative of Henry VI). In August 1485, Henry killed Richard III at the **Battle of Bosworth**.

Identify an argument

The three extracts below are all responses to the question:

Why did people begin to challenge the monarchy in the medieval period?

Each one demonstrates one of the following:

- assertion – a general point that is unfocused
- description – some relevant factual detail that does not tackle the focus of the question
- argument – a response which is specific to the question and has a clear focus.

Decide which feature you would apply to each extract.

1. There were lots of examples of challenge to the monarch in the medieval period. The peasants revolted against Richard II in 1381, the barons and King John had a civil war, and Simon de Montfort challenged the power of the king through the Provisions of Oxford.
2. The monarchy ruled over the people in the medieval period but the barons did not always like the monarchy.
3. People began to challenge the monarchy in the medieval period because they were unhappy with the amount of power the king had. At some points the nobles disagreed with the king's right to raise taxes, and at other times the nobles did not like the fact that they were not fully represented.

Stretch and challenge

This spread contains a lot of information about how monarchs were challenged, and how Parliament developed. Make a list of the ways in which Parliament developed and annotate each one to explain whether or not this showed the monarchy was losing power.

Practice question

How significant a change was the Magna Carta for Britain? (14 marks)

6.4 Tudor government

REVISED

Henry VII limited the power of the nobles

- Henry VII's changes to government meant that the king had the upper hand.
- Under Henry VII, important decisions were made in the **Royal Court**. If nobles did not attend, they could not be part of these decisions.
- Henry disciplined nobles in the **Star Chamber** (a special court).
- Henry avoided expensive wars, and used taxes to build up the wealth of the Crown.

Key point

Power shifted back to the monarchy in the Tudor period.

- Henry got nobles on side through **royal patronage** by offering promotions or land.

Henry VIII extended the power of the monarchy, but he had to work with Parliament

- Henry VIII ruled with close assistance from key nobles, but he always made sure their power was kept in check.
- In 1487 and 1504, Henry restricted the number of **retainers** a nobleman could have.
- Henry used the nobles he was close to, to force decisions in Parliament to go the way he wanted.
- Henry worked closely with Parliament and made sure that he sanctioned his actions by making them law.
- Henry waged wars with France and Scotland, and used heavy taxation, approved by Parliament, to finance them.
- In 1534, Henry passed the **Act of Supremacy** (this removed England from the Catholic Church). The **Church of England** was created, and Henry was recognised as its head.

Henry VIII had a turbulent relationship with key nobles

- Henry made Thomas Wolsey Archbishop of York, and later **chancellor** (the chief minister). Wolsey used his influential position to acquire a lot of wealth.
- Wolsey could not convince the Pope to annul Henry's marriage to Catherine of Aragon.
- In 1529, Wolsey was arrested after having been charged with treason. Wolsey died before facing trial.
- Henry appointed Thomas Cromwell as his **chief minister** in 1534. In this role, Cromwell had a lot of power over other nobles.
- After Cromwell's leadership of the **break with Rome** and **Dissolution of the Monasteries**, Henry made him Earl of Essex.
- Cromwell was arrested and executed without trial in 1540 after the marriage he arranged between Henry and Anne of Cleves failed to bring political union with France.

Elizabeth I was a strong leader and overcame many challenges in her reign

- Elizabeth I took advice from nobles to ensure that people felt they were being listened to.
- Elizabeth's sister, Mary, was Catholic. Some people were worried about the frequent changes in religion but Elizabeth did not strictly persecute Catholics, and only enforced moderate Protestantism.
- Elizabeth's **Religious Settlement** helped to repair many religious divisions during her reign.
- In 1569, Elizabeth defeated the rebels who wanted to see Mary Queen of Scots on the throne – 750 people who had been involved in the **Northern Rebellion** were executed.
- Elizabeth spread anti-Catholic propaganda to deal with the threat of Catholic spies and traitors.
- Elizabeth never married but she used her status as the '**Virgin Queen**' to gain support – her subjects knew that she had dedicated her life to her country.

Elizabeth I had a **positive** relationship with Parliament

- Elizabeth worked closely with her **Privy Council** to pass laws and agree taxes.
- Elizabeth saw Parliament as her point of contact with the people – **MPs** (Members of Parliament) were allowed to raise questions about important issues (such as succession and taxation).
- Elizabeth's positive relationship with Parliament was aided by William Cecil, who brought order and stability to the Royal Court.
- Parliament supported Elizabeth's views on religion.

Practice question

Describe **two** examples of ways in which Henry VIII extended the power of the monarchy. (4 marks)

Stretch and challenge

Go back through this spread and find any evidence that can be used to support the following statement: 'The power of the monarchy grew under the Tudor monarchs'.

Test yourself

1 What was the Act of Supremacy?
2 What changes did Thomas Cromwell manage for Henry VIII?
3 What was the Northern Rebellion?

Turning assertion into argument

Below are a sample exam-style question and a series of assertions (general points that are unfocused). Read the question and then add a justification to each of the assertions to turn it into an argument (a response which is specific to the question and has a clear focus).

How far can it be argued that Tudor monarchs were firmly in control? (14 marks)

Henry VII limited the power of nobles by ...

Henry VIII extended his power by ...

Elizabeth I had challenges such as ...

Complete the paragraph

Below are a sample exam-style question and the start of a paragraph written in answer to this question. The paragraph contains a point and one specific example, but lacks a concluding explanatory link back to the question. Complete the paragraph by developing the example and an explanatory link.

Explain why the power of the monarchy grew in the Tudor period. (8 marks)

The Tudor monarchs increased the power they had in Parliament. Parliament was recognised as an important tool to help the monarch rule. For example, Henry VIII made sure that he worked with his nobles to force his decisions through Parliament ... ______________

____

____

____

6.5 Civil War to Restoration

REVISED

People were **unhappy** with Charles' **style of rule**

- Charles I and his father (James I) both believed that they had been appointed by '**divine right**' (directly by God).
- Charles believed in **absolutism** (this meant that he should have total control). This led to him introducing censorship to stop criticism.
- Many of Charles' subjects thought he was arrogant because he would not tolerate any challenge (even from nobles or Parliament).

Key point

The Civil War brought permanent changes to power structures in England. (See pages 140–5 for further information on the Civil War.)

Charles' actions led the country to **civil war**

- Charles' relationship with Parliament was difficult from the outset:
  - Scottish nobles were angry that Charles tried to take back Church land that had been given to them in the sixteenth century.
  - Many people were concerned about Charles' pro-Catholic views.
  - Charles waged wars; this meant he had to raise a lot of taxes.
- In 1626, Charles dissolved Parliament. It was reconvened in 1629 but then dissolved again until 1640 (this period became known as Charles' '**Personal Rule**').
- In 1635, Charles made everyone pay '**ship money**' – this was a levy which was usually only applied to people living in or near ports, but Charles applied it in peacetime.
- In 1638, Scottish leaders refused to accept the religious changes Charles was trying to impose in Scotland – as a result, Charles marched an army north.
- Charles refused to accept the proposals in the **Grand Remonstrance** (a document created by MPs that listed over 200 criticisms and demands).
- In January 1642, Charles arrested five MPs after accusing them all of treason. Parliament gathered its forces and in August 1642, Charles declared war on Parliament.

People were **divided** about how Charles should be **treated**

- Charles was imprisoned in May 1646 after he had been captured by the Scots and handed to Parliament.
- After the **First Civil War**, people generally agreed that they did not want to get rid of Charles, but people disagreed about how to move forward: some wanted to limit Charles' power, and others did not.
- After the **Second Civil War**, the majority of people still wanted the king restored, but Oliver Cromwell and other senior commanders of the **New Model Army** pushed for a trial.
- In 1648, roughly 300 MPs who disagreed with Charles being tried were thrown out of Parliament (this left a '**Rump Parliament**' of about 200).
- Many English people were genuinely shocked when Charles was put on trial and then executed in January 1649.

The victory of the Parliamentarians brought **wholesale change** to **power structures** in England

- From 1649 to 1653, England was ruled by the Rump Parliament. During this time, the monarchy and the House of Lords were abolished.
- Cromwell dismissed the Rump in 1653 because he disagreed with their tolerance of religion and their cautious actions.
- The **Barebones Parliament** (144 men who were sympathetic to Cromwell's views) ruled temporarily but Cromwell dismissed them as he thought they were too radical.
- From 1653 to 1658, Cromwell ruled as **lord protector** (this period was known as the **Protectorate**).
- Parliament was reformed and **constituencies** were resized to make them more representative.

- Parliament and the lord protector shared control of the army.
- During the Protectorate, Cromwell divided England into regions – each region was ruled by a **major-general** whose role it was to enforce **Puritanism**.
- In 1657, Cromwell accepted the **Humble Petition and Advice** which saw the abolition of the major-generals, a reduction in the army, and more governmental control over taxes.
- The Humble Petition and Advice had also proposed that Cromwell become king, but he refused.

Test yourself

1. Give one reason why people were angry with Charles I.
2. What was the 'Grand Remonstrance'?
3. What was the Barebones Parliament?

The Restoration saw the **return of the monarchy**, but with **limited powers**

- Cromwell's son (Richard) ruled England from 1658 but he retired in 1659 due to lack of experience and little support from the army or Parliament.
- Parliament negotiated with Charles' son, who accepted the terms of the **Declaration of Breda** and became King Charles II in 1660.
- Charles did have control over laws passing through Parliament but his ability to raise taxes without Parliament's permission was taken away.
- Charles could not target his opponents through the use of special Parliaments and he could not claim ship money.

Practice question

Explain why people were critical of the way in which King Charles I ruled. (8 marks)

Flow charts

Below is a blank flow diagram into which you must add four key events that led to the English Civil War breaking out in 1642. The first one has been completed for you. A list of events that you could have chosen can be found opposite.

People became angrier about Charles' pro-Catholic views				

Eliminate irrelevance

Below are a sample exam-style question and a paragraph written in answer to this question. Read the paragraph and identify parts of the paragraph that are not directly relevant to the question. Draw a line through the information that is irrelevant and justify your deletions in the margin.

How significant a change was the Restoration of the monarchy for England? (14 marks)

Charles I was executed in 1649 after he had been put on trial. Cromwell was then put in charge of the country. There were a series of Parliaments that ruled the country and Cromwell was even offered the Crown but he refused. Charles II's return to the throne was a significant change because the country had previously been ruled by Parliaments without a king. However, this change was not hugely significant as only eleven years previously a king had ruled England and therefore it was a return to how power in England used to be distributed. Some people disagreed with Charles II at first – some of his own supporters disagreed with him pardoning the people responsible for the execution of his father. Charles II had to rule in a different way to his father. People did not want the king to gain too much power again and so his power was limited. Charles could veto any law, but he could not raise taxes by himself and had to ask Parliament for permission to do so. The Cavalier Parliament also stopped Charles from attacking his opponents through special courts. These were significant changes because it was the king having rights like this that caused the Civil War in the first place, but events such as the signing of the Magna Carta show that, for a long time, there had been a gradual shift in power. On the whole, Charles II was a successful monarch and many people liked him.

6.6 The Glorious Revolution

REVISED

The **nobles lost faith** in James II and invited William of Orange to invade England

- James II was not trusted by the people and he was not well liked.
- Early in James' reign he faced a rebellion from Charles II's illegitimate son, the Duke of Monmouth.
- James was married to a Catholic and people were worried about the future of England when his wife gave birth to a son.
- Some of James' actions made people think he favoured Catholicism:
  - he converted to Catholicism
  - he gave government posts to Catholics
  - his wife was Catholic
  - he passed pro-Catholic laws, for example, in 1686 James proclaimed that Anglican ministers could not preach anti-Catholic sermons.
- Some leading nobles asked James' Protestant daughter, Mary, to take James' place. They wanted her to rule with her husband William of Orange – the ruler of the Netherlands.
- William and Mary's forces landed in 1688 and James fled to France. This was the **Glorious Revolution**, and William became King William III.

Key point

The Glorious Revolution changed the balance of power in England.

The Glorious Revolution brought **changes** for **England's relationship with Scotland, France and Ireland**

- Scotland became more **independent**.
- In 1690, William agreed to Scottish MPs having full control of the Church, the right to appoint chief ministers, and the abolition of bishops.
- James II had fled to France and so the relationship between France and England worsened. The French supplied James with troops to invade Britain – this rebellion was quashed in 1690.
- James II and the rebels had used Ireland as a base. As a result, Ireland was put under the control of Protestant landholders.

The Glorious Revolution brought **more freedom for Protestants** and **more restrictions on Catholics**

- The **Bill of Rights** decreed that a Catholic could not become king or queen in England, Scotland or Ireland.
- The **Toleration Act** was passed in 1689 – this made it legal for Protestants to belong to Churches other than the Church of England.
- There were some restrictions on non-Anglicans. For example, they could not serve in the army or in government.

The Glorious Revolution **limited** the **power** of the **monarchy** to an **extent**

- William and Mary had to agree to a new **constitution**.
- At their coronation, William and Mary had to swear an oath which stated they would rule England 'according to the laws passed in Parliament'.
- The Bill of Rights placed some restrictions on the monarchy:
  - The monarch could not keep a large army in peacetime (as James II had done), nor could they suspend laws.
  - The monarch could collect taxes but only do for a four-year period – to guarantee that the monarch would continue to work with Parliament.
  - Parliament had to meet at least once a year and MPs were given freedom of speech in Parliament.
- The monarch was still responsible for making important decisions such as whether or not the country should go to war, and they would still be in charge of appointing people to important positions.
- The position of monarch was still regarded with awe and reverence by the majority and these limits were only in case of emergencies.

After 1688, Parliament had an increased role in running the country

- William brought Britain into his war with France, which continued for another 25 years.
- The **Bank of England** was established in 1694 – this was partly to provide loans to fund William's wars.
- William began to work more closely with Parliament, partly because he needed to fund his wars through taxes and he needed Parliament's approval for this.
- Parliament began to meet more regularly, and a clear division of MPs into two groups (**Whigs** and **Tories**) developed.
- This period saw the beginnings of **parliamentary democracy** with ministers, rather than the monarchy, responsible for much of the running of the country.
- In 1701, Parliament passed the **Act of Settlement**. This offered the crown to the **Hanoverians** (a royal household of German descent – the House of Hanover).
- When William died childless in 1702 the throne went to Mary's younger sister, Anne.
- None of Anne's children survived and so the throne passed to the House of Hanover in 1714.
- England and Scotland were united in 1707 by the **Act of Union**. This was not supported by all Scots.

Checklist

Below is a list of events that may have taken place in the lead-up to the Glorious Revolution. Tick or highlight those events which you know *did* take place.

- James married a Protestant.
- James forbade Anglican ministers from preaching anti-Catholic sermons.
- James banned Protestants from England.
- James' wife gave birth to a Catholic son.
- English nobles asked William and Mary to come and take over the English throne.

Test yourself

1. Give two reasons for James II's unpopularity.
2. Who was William of Orange?
3. Give one of the terms of the Bill of Rights.

Practice question

'Between c.1000 and 1707 the power of the monarch gradually decreased.' How far do you agree with this statement? (24 marks)

Stretch and challenge

Go back through this spread and find five things that changed in England after the Glorious Revolution. Use these changes to create a five-question quiz on the impact of the Glorious Revolution.

Spot the mistake

Below are a sample exam-style question and a paragraph written in answer to this question. Why does this paragraph not get into Level 4? Once you have identified the mistake, rewrite the paragraph so that it displays the qualities of Level 4. The mark scheme on pages 180–2 will help you.

How significant a change was the Glorious Revolution for Britain? (14 marks)

The Glorious Revolution was significant because it brought about changes to Parliament. As a result of the Glorious Revolution, Britain gained a Bill of Rights which protected the rights of Parliament. The Bill of Rights also ensured that a Protestant monarch would take the throne of England.

6.7 Parliament and the people, c.1800–1918

REVISED

The political system was **not very representative** in 1800

Key point

After many struggles, different groups saw increased representation and democratic rights between 1800 and 1918.

Many constituencies were not representative

- The numbers of voters in constituencies varied
- In some larger towns or cities, a great number of voters would only return one MP
- Some constituencies were known as '**rotten boroughs**' – these were constituencies that could have had as few as one or two voters
- Oxford and Cambridge universities returned two MPs each – this was an outdated law

- There was no **secret ballot**, this meant that people had to vote in public, which encouraged corruption.
- Some candidates would offer to pay bribes in return for votes; others would host parties the night before an election to win support.
- Two revolutions in the wider world led to further scrutiny of the British system:
  - in 1776, Britain's American colonies declared their independence from Britain
  - the 1789 **French Revolution** scared lots of British aristocrats; they thought a similar type of revolution might happen in Britain.
- Thomas Paine's book ***The Rights of Man*** argued that the British political system was corrupt – 200,000 copies of the book sold before it was banned.

The **Great Reform Act** brought some **political change**

- The **franchise** (right to vote) was extended by the 1832 **Great Reform Act**, but the changes largely favoured middle-class voters.
- The same number of seats was retained (658) but the distribution of seats changed:
  - 56 boroughs (such as rotten boroughs) of less than 2000 voters were **disenfranchised** (no longer had the right to return an MP)
  - 31 small boroughs lost one of their two MPs
  - 22 new two-member boroughs were created, for example Manchester, Leeds, Birmingham.
- After the Great Reform Act one in seven English males could vote.

Some **working-class activists** felt **betrayed** by the **Great Reform Act**

- The Great Reform Act did not bring wholesale political change and although the electorate had increased, corruption still existed; for example, there was still no secret ballot.
- There was a uniform property qualification of £10 in boroughs which meant you had to be paying £10 in rates to be able to vote.
- The Great Reform Act led to the rise of **Chartism** – this was a political movement with six demands:
  - universal **suffrage**
  - payment for MPs
  - no property qualification to become an MP
  - annual Parliaments
  - secret ballot
  - equal representation.
- Activists (such as the Liberal Party) continued to put pressure on the political system – this resulted in the Second (1867) and Third (1884) Reform Acts:
  - the **Second Reform Act** doubled the electorate to 40 per cent of the male population: all male urban householders and lodgers (mostly working class) paying £10 rent a year could vote
  - the **Third Reform Act** added 2.6 million voters to the electorate, increasing it from 3.1 million to 5.7 million, and qualifications to vote were the same in all constituencies.
- After campaigning, the **Secret Ballot Act** was made law in 1872.

Trade unions and the Labour Party wanted further political reform

- A total of 40 per cent of men and 100 per cent of women did not have the right to vote after the Third Reform Act.
- '**New Unions**' emerged in the 1870s and 1880s that aimed to protect workers' rights.
- The **Trades Union Congress (TUC)** was formed in 1868 and almost all trade unions (workers who group together to protect their rights) were affiliated to this by the 1890s.
- The government did not respond kindly to the new unions and took measures to make strike action very difficult. (For example, unions could be ordered to pay companies compensation for money lost during strike action.)
- The TUC decided to support a new political party – the **Labour Party** (formed in 1900) – which was an amalgamation of smaller working-class activist groups.
- By 1910, the Labour Party had 42 MPs in Parliament.
- The rise in popularity of the Labour Party put pressure on the Liberals and Conservatives to pass welfare reforms in the early twentieth century.

Women achieved the vote as a result of campaigning and war work

- None of the Reform Acts enfranchised (gave the vote to) women.
- There were two main groups that campaigned for the right to vote: the **NUWSS (Suffragists)** and the **WSPU (Suffragettes)**.

NUWSS (Suffragists)	WSPU (Suffragettes)
Formed in 1897	Formed in 1903
Led by Millicent Fawcett	Led by Emmeline Pankhurst
Used peaceful methods to protest	Used more violent methods than the Suffragists, such as protests hunger strikes, and members would sometimes damage public property or attack politicians
Had 50,000 fee-paying members and many volunteers	Had 2000 members at its peak
Tried to put pressure on Parliament but did not gain any concessions	Their actions raised the profile of female suffrage

- Some people were opposed to giving women the vote due to the violent actions of the Suffragettes.
- Women also contributed to the war effort by doing a range of jobs such as working in munitions factories, or working as part of the **Land Army** (this involved doing jobs such as farming). This gained the respect of a lot of people.
- The **Representation of the People Act** was passed in January 1918. This gave the vote to some women (and all men over the age of 21).

Test yourself

1. What was a 'rotten borough'?
2. What was made law in 1872?
3. How many people were fee-paying members of the NUWSS?

Practice question

Explain why, after the Great Reform Act, there were still criticisms of the systems to elect MPs to Parliament. (8 marks)

Change over timeline

Use the information in this section to create a timeline which shows the views in response to the question:

'Between 1800 and 1918, the British political system became more democratic.' How far do you agree with this statement?

Annotate on to your timeline why trends change at given points and use the key dates given as the major points to plot events. You can add more if you would like to.

Extent of democracy

5	
4	
3	
2	
1	
0	1800 · 1872 · 1884 · 1910 · 1918

— Extent of democracy

6.8 Parliament and the people, c.1914–c.1980

REVISED

The government had a **lot of control** over the **people** during **the First World War**

- The whole country was geared towards supporting the war effort during the First World War – this is known as **total war**.
- **Conscription** was used from January 1916 to force men to **enlist**.
- People who refused to fight were known as **conscientious objectors**. These people could be put into prison or sent to do other war work.
- The government took control of the coal industry and set up its own munitions factories.
- The government employed female workers in factories to help the war effort but they were paid less than men.

Key point

The government became more involved in the lives of the people during this period.

By the **Second World War** the government had learned important lessons

- Conscription started in 1938 before the Second World War broke out. Fewer men were needed on the ground fighting due to the nature of the conflict, but many more were needed in industrial production.
- In 1941, over half the population was employed by the government.
- A **coalition government** was formed so that people from all political parties were running the country – the Labour minister Ernest Bevin worked to involve trade unions in governmental decisions.
- More women were needed for work, to facilitate this the government introduced flexible working hours and childcare.

Propaganda and **censorship** had a role in both **world wars**

- **Propaganda** and **censorship** were used to keep public morale high.
- In 1914, the government produced lists of topics that should not be written about; there were stiff penalties for those who broke the rules.
- In April 1915, the government informed the press to publish casualty lists that were of acceptable levels, and not to print the truth.
- In January 1917, the prime minister (David Lloyd George) created the **Department of Information** – this had the sole responsibility for issuing and enforcing guidelines for censorship.
- During the Second World War, the government was given special powers by Parliament to control what people could see and hear: this included all films, photographs and written reports.
- Propaganda posters were used in both wars, but they were more subtle in the Second World War – some were even removed after people thought they were causing offence.

Test yourself

1 What were the terms of the Representation of the People Act?
2 Why was rationing introduced in the First World War?
3 Who did the government work with during the Second World War?

Rationing was used by the government in both **world wars**

The First World War:

- **Rationing** was introduced in 1918.
- **Blockades** were used by both sides to prevent supplies from reaching their destination.
- Lots of public sites were used as allotments.
- Householders were told to use their gardens to grow vegetables. Many people also kept animals that could be used as food (such as chickens).

Practice question

Describe **two** examples of how the government controlled the people during the world wars. (4 marks)

The Second World War:

- Rationing was introduced at the start of the conflict.
- The government set up 'swap shops' for clothes.
- Recycling was encouraged.
- The **black market** (illegal trade of items) flourished – this allowed people to get hold of rationed items.

The **Home Front** played an important role in both world wars

- There were some coastal raids in the First World War but the main threat to the **Home Front** was the bombing raids and the **Blitz** during the Second World War.
- In both world wars, the government encouraged people not to talk about any kind of war work for fear of spies.
- The **Home Guard** was set up in 1940 – they were a group of volunteers who acted as a reserve force.
- The government gave people the job of checking that no lights could be seen during blackouts – these people were called **Air Raid Precautions (ARP) wardens.**

The two world wars changed the relationship between Parliament and the people

1918	The 1918 Representation of the People Act gave the vote to all men over the age of 21 and some women. This was in recognition for their war work
1920s	Some people became very angry when the relationship between the government and trade unions broke down in the 1920s, as they thought that despite their contribution to war, the government would not give any concessions
1939–45	Evacuation in the Second World War revealed differences in wealth and living circumstances to many people – this put pressure on the government to provide more welfare
1945	The Labour Party won a landslide election in 1945 and implemented a welfare state as recommended by the Beveridge Report of 1942. Historians argue that they won the election due to their promises of a new start for people

Identify an argument

The three extracts below are all responses to the question 'How did the relationship between Parliament and the people change as a result of the world wars?' Each answer demonstrates one of the following:

- assertion – a general point that is unfocused
- description – some relevant factual detail that does not tackle the focus of the question
- argument – a response which is specific to the question and has a clear focus.

Decide which feature you would apply to each extract.

1. As a result of the First World War, the relationship between Parliament and the people changed because the government rewarded people for their efforts during the war. This meant that Parliament made some concessions and, for example, extended political freedom. In 1913, all men and some women got the vote due to the ways in which they supported the war effort.
2. People began to have more political freedom because of the wars.
3. All men (over the age of 21) and some women got the vote in 1918. Female activists had stopped campaigning to get the vote so that the country could concentrate on the war – some women also helped the war effort. A lot of men either fought for Britain or helped at home.

6.9 Challenges to Parliament and democracy c.1980–2014

REVISED

Key point

From c.1980 to 2014 there have been challenges to the authority of Parliament.

Margaret Thatcher decreased state regulation, and clashed with trade unions

- Thatcher wanted businesses to have more independence as she thought this would allow them to thrive.
- She cut taxes on businesses so they could have control over their own money.
- She **privatised** some of Britain's major industries such as the British Steel and utilities such as the telephone system.
- Thatcher thought that the welfare system did not inspire people to achieve things for themselves, and so her government cut back on welfare spending.
- In 1990, Thatcher introduced the **poll tax**. Some people thought it was unfair as it was the same for everyone, regardless of wealth.

Tony Blair's government borrowed heavily from Thatcherite ideas

- Blair agreed that industries should be independent from government control.
- Blair continued to privatise some major industries.
- Restrictions that the Conservatives had placed on trade unions were continued by Blair.
- Similarly to Thatcher, Blair increased the power of central government in some areas such as education (in the 1980s when Thatcher took some powers from local government these were picked up by central government).
- Blair acted in a presidential manner – Thatcher was image conscious and acted in a similar way.

Parliament was challenged by pressure groups in the 1980s

Case study 1: Campaign for Nuclear Disarmament (CND)	Case study 2: Greenpeace
• The **CND** emerged in the 1950s with the aim of removing nuclear weapons from Britain • The CND challenged Parliament's right to sanction the use of nuclear weapons • In October 1983, roughly 300,000 people attended a public meeting, and some long-term protest camps were established • There was a lot of support for the CND: – roughly 30 per cent of the population in Britain supported the CND – the CND was not tied to any specific political party so it gained the support of a large range of people • The CND did not achieve its aims, but it succeeded in raising awareness	• Greenpeace was established in 1971. The group aimed to raise awareness of environmental issues • Greenpeace campaigns included those: – against the use of nuclear power – against the use of toxic chemicals • Greenpeace also disagreed with the government supporting big businesses that have an interest in some of its campaign areas • Greenpeace remained an embarrassment to the government throughout the 1980s

From the 1980s, regions of the UK began to demand greater autonomy

Northern Ireland:

- There have been disputes about whether or not Northern Ireland should be part of the UK for a long time. The Unionists want to stay in the UK, while the Nationalists want a united Ireland
- Between 1969 and 1996, there were many violent clashes between these groups which caused the deaths of thousands of people
- Until 1972 Northern Ireland had its own Parliament
- In 1998 a settlement was reached – this saw the setting up of an **Assembly** that represents all groups in Northern Ireland

Scotland:

- In 1998, the **Scottish Parliament** was created after Scottish people voted for **devolution** of power
- In 2014, there was a **referendum** (vote) about whether or not Scotland should become an independent country – 55 per cent of people voted not to become independent
- The **referendum on membership of the European Union (EU)** has caused some tensions between England and Scotland. In 2016, England voted to leave the EU. Scotland did not vote to leave the EU; as a result some Scottish people support the idea of a second independence referendum

Wales:

- In 1997, people in Wales voted for devolution
- By 2007, Wales had its own **National Assembly** with control over education, health and law and order

In 2010 a hung Parliament led to a **coalition government**

- In 2010 there was a '**hung Parliament**' – this meant that no one party achieved an overall majority.
- The Conservatives and **Liberal Democrats** formed a coalition government in the absence of one party having a majority.
- In a coalition, power is shared, but this can mean parties have to compromise on some of their key policies. For example, the Conservatives were able to pass an act to increase tuition fees (the Liberal Democrats had previously campaigned against this).
- The Liberal Democrats wanted to change the way in which MPs are elected into Parliament – they wanted a system of **proportional representation** (where the number of MPs in Parliament would reflect actual votes). The public voted against this in a referendum in 2011.

There is some **disillusionment** with political parties **today**

- There has been a steady decline in the number of people voting in **general elections**: in the early 2000s the Hansard Society found that roughly twenty per cent of 18–24-year-olds vote in general elections.
- However, there has been a steady increase in the number of people voting since 2014 – this has been due to topical referendums, such as on Scottish independence and membership of the EU.
- The **expenses scandal** (when concerns about MPs' expenses were raised) caused a lot of disillusionment with the political system.
- There has been growing support for fringe parties (those that are small and not mainstream) such as **UKIP (UK Independence Party)**; this shows that people are not satisfied with the current system.

Test yourself

1. Give one example of something Thatcher privatised.
2. State one policy that Thatcher and Blair agreed on.
3. What was the CND, and what was its aim?

Practice question

How significant a change was Thatcher's prime ministership for Britain? (14 marks)

Delete as applicable

Below are a question and the start of a paragraph written in answer to this question (the statement given could form part of a typical question 4). Read the paragraph and decide which of the possible options (underlined) is most appropriate. Delete the least appropriate options and complete the paragraph by justifying your selection.

'Between c.1485 and 2014 the monarchy lost authority.' How far do you agree with this statement? (24 marks)

I agree to a <u>great/fair/limited extent</u> that Parliament lost power throughout this period. The Tudor dynasty represented a strong monarchy and lots was done to centralise power – Henry VIII even got rid of the threat religion posed to the Crown by breaking from Rome and declaring himself head of the Church of England. The execution of Charles I clearly showed that people were beginning to lose faith in the monarchy …

Stretch and challenge

Go back through this spread and in one colour highlight examples of Parliament having authority and showing strength, and in another colour highlight examples of Parliament being weak. Once you have done this, plot each point on a continuum to show how strong Parliament was during this period (your continuum should focus on Parliament and range from strong to weak).

6.10 Think thematic!

REVISED

There have always been **divisions** between **those in power**, and **those being ruled**

Here are some examples of divisions from across the time period:

AD790–1500

- Aethelred was seen as a weak king by his subjects as they did not think he could protect them from Viking invasions.
- When William of Normandy became King of England, there were many rebellions against Norman rule. At times, William had to resort to harsh measures to keep control.
- Under King John, divisions between the monarchy and the barons grew as the barons became resentful of John's abuses of power. This erupted into a civil war in 1215.
- In 1251, Simon de Montfort and a group of barons forced Henry to accept the Provisions of Oxford; this saw the emergence of Parliament.
- In 1381, Richard II was challenged by the Peasants' Revolt: this was triggered by high taxation for the war with France.

c.1500–c.1750

- The Wars of the Roses saw rival factions compete for power due to people's perception that Henry VI was a weak and ineffective king.
- Henry VIII was concerned about the growing independence of some of his key ministers (Wolsey and Cromwell).
- In 1569, Elizabeth I faced the Northern Rebellion (northern nobles plotted to replace Elizabeth with Mary Queen of Scots).
- During the period known as Charles I's 'Personal Rule', Charles dissolved Parliament and ruled without it.
- In the 1640s, Parliament waged war on Charles I.
- In 1688, some leading nobles asked James II's Protestant daughter, Mary, to take James' place.
- Following the Glorious Revolution, Mary and William were forced to accept the Bill of Rights which saw the powers of the monarchy restricted.

c.1750–c.2010

- In the 1830s, there was a lot of public pressure on the government to reform the electoral system. The system was reformed in 1832 by the Great Reform Act, but further pressure was applied by those who did not think the reforms were extensive enough.
- The rise in popularity of the Labour Party put pressure on the Liberals and Conservatives to pass welfare reforms in the early twentieth century.
- Women campaigned for the right to vote in the early twentieth century.
- Censorship had to be used during the world wars to keep public morale high.
- Margaret Thatcher's decision to close some coal mines was opposed by some miners; Arthur Scargill led these miners on a year-long strike (1984–85).
- The CND challenged Parliament's right to sanction the use of nuclear weapons.
- Tony Blair received a lot of criticism for his decision to go to war with Iraq.
- Regions of the UK have been calling for devolved powers since the 1980s.

Review questions

1 Look back through the divisions listed and consider the reasons for them.

2 Can you track any examples of change or continuity from c.1000 to 2014?

3 Can you use this information to suggest:

a) when English monarchs started to lose power?

b) a turning point when it became inevitable that people would be granted greater representation?

c) when Parliament became a dominant force?

The **basis** of individuals' or groups' **claims to power** has **changed** across time

In the medieval period it was generally the consensus that the monarch was appointed by God. Their right to rule was not determined by the will of the people

→

Under the Tudor monarchs, the belief of the political nation underpinned monarchs' right to rule. Monarchs governed on behalf of their people. This represented a shift in thinking from the medieval period as the Tudor monarchs recognised the necessity to rule *for* their people

→

From the nineteenth century, people began to recognise the need for a reformed system that was more representative of the people – this was driven by popular protests and demands for reform

However, there are exceptions to these generalisations, such as:

- In Anglo-Saxon England, the king was elected by the Witan. Although the Witan was composed of important nobles and churchmen (and therefore not fully representative), this process of electing a king was arguably more democratic than it was in medieval England. Therefore, it cannot be argued that England, and later Britain, became more democratic over time in a linear fashion.
- Even though Tudor monarchs demonstrated the need to work with Parliament, the reign of Charles I saw a return to the belief that the monarch was appointed by God. This resulted in the relationship between monarch and Parliament becoming very strained.
- Many argue that true democratic reform happened very (or too) slowly. The need for reform was recognised by some in the early nineteenth century but it took a long time for change to happen.

The **way** in which individuals or groups have **maintained** their position and power has changed

During the medieval period (c.790–c.1500), force was used to stop challenges to power

- During the Normans' consolidation of power William confiscated the land of those who rebelled
- After the Peasants' Revolt, Richard ordered the deaths of 5000 rebels

→

From c.1500 to c.1750 there are still examples of individuals and groups using force to keep power, but other methods were also used

- Henry VIII got nobles on side through offering promotions or land
- After the Glorious Revolution, William and Mary agreed to a new constitution

→

From c.1750 to 2010 there was an increase in concessions:

- In the nineteenth century, various laws made Parliament more representative
- In the 1990s, Wales, Northern Ireland and Scotland were given greater political freedom

Review questions

Look at the three boxes above. Each of the statements is a generalisation. See if you can find information to challenge the statements and add this to your diagram. Then use the boxes provided to make a new generalisation that incorporates all of the evidence provided.

7 Migration to Britain c.1000 to c.2010

7.1 The Middle Ages, c.1000–c.1500

REVISED

England in 1000 was already a country of **immigrants**

- From the earliest times, people **migrated** (moved from one country to another) to trade, invade and settle.
- England in the early eleventh century was a place of many languages and cultures ruled by Anglo-Saxons and Danes whose peoples had settled from northern Europe and Scandinavia.
- There was also cultural migration – of arts, sciences and ideas – from Islamic north Africa and western Asia as well as the rest of Europe.

Key point

Immigrants from all over Europe settled and worked throughout England in the Middle Ages and had a large impact on the social, political, economic and cultural life of the country.

The **Norman invasion** had a huge impact on England

- In 1066, William, Duke of Normandy, invaded England. After defeating the army of King Harold near Hastings he took control of England.
- William seized land from English lords and gave it to Norman nobles. He replaced Anglo-Danish bishops with Normans.
- Following the **Domesday survey**, William abolished slavery.
- The Normans introduced a new language – Old French.

There were several **rebellions** against Norman rule

- William dealt with rebellion very harshly, imposing collective punishments and laying waste to part of northern England.

Jews were first **invited**, then **persecuted**, then **expelled**

Invited: Jewish immigrants arrived in the 1070s, invited by William. He wanted them to help administer his kingdom and to lend money for the building of castles and cathedrals. The Catholic Church did not allow Christians to lend money with interest

→ **Settled:** There were Jewish settlements all over England. Some were rich moneylenders but many were poor, following various occupations as artisans and traders. They enjoyed royal protection (meaning they could seek safety in royal castles in time of trouble) but were heavily taxed

→ **Persecuted:** In the twelfth and thirteenth centuries, at the time of the Crusades, **anti-Semitic** attacks on Jews increased. **'Blood libels'** in Norwich and Lincoln, as well as massacres of Jews in London and York, made Jewish communities more and more unsafe. New laws restricted their freedom

→ **Expelled:** After the Pope allowed Italian bankers to charge interest on loans in 1265, Jews lost royal protection. Edward I's Statute of Jewry in 1275 made it illegal for Jews to charge interest and most became extremely poor. Many were forced to clip coins and some were hanged for this. In 1290 all Jews were expelled

Immigrants were **living** and **working** throughout medieval England

- Immigrants were living in towns and villages all over England. We know this from records of a tax on foreigners called the alien subsidies, and from **letters of denization**.
- They came from all over the British Isles and Europe including Ireland, Scotland and the Low Countries (now Belgium and the Netherlands). Most were servants and labourers but immigrants had many occupations. Some came as **refugees** from war but most were seeking work.
- Immigrants from the Low Countries had a big effect on England. Flemish weavers passed on their skills and helped to change England's economy to one based on **manufacturing** (making) cloth rather than just producing wool. Dutch women introduced the brewing of beer using hops.

Test yourself

1 List three groups of immigrants who came to Britain during the Middle Ages and for each one state their main reason for coming.
2 To what extent were they welcomed?
3 How did immigrants affect England's economy in the Middle Ages?

- German Hanseatic merchants from northern Europe and banking families from Lombardy in northern Italy helped to develop London's trading and financial centre. The Steelyard on the Thames in London became a major business centre.
- There was often tension between monarchs who wanted immigrants to come to boost the economy and **craft guilds** who felt they were taking English jobs.
- There were cases of violence against immigrants – especially during the Great Revolt in 1381 when many were murdered – but it seems that most settled happily and were accepted in communities.

Practice question

1 Describe two ways in which Jews were persecuted in early medieval England. (4 marks)

2 Explain why monarchs such as Edward III were keen to invite Flemish and Dutch immigrants to England. (8 marks)

Turning assertion into argument

Below are a sample exam-style question and a series of assertions. Read the question and then add a justification to each of the assertions to turn it into an argument.

How important was the economic impact of immigrants to England between 1000 and 1500? (14 marks)

Jewish settlers had a significant economic impact because …

Flemish and Dutch craftspeople changed England's economy because …

German and Italian merchants and bankers affected the economy because …

Support or challenge?

Below is a sample exam-style question which asks how far you agree with a specific statement. Below this are a series of general statements which are relevant to the question. Using your own knowledge and the information on the opposite page, decide whether each factor agrees or disagrees with the stated view. As an additional challenge, you might want to think if any factors belong to both.

'Immigrants were generally accepted and well treated in medieval England.' How far do you agree with this statement? (24 marks)

- People resisted Norman rule.
- Jewish settlers were under royal protection from the 1070s onwards.
- Many Jews were executed for coin clipping.
- Several monarchs welcomed Flemish weavers.
- Craft guilds objected to immigrants undercutting their members' pay.
- Many Flemish immigrants were murdered during the 1381 Great Revolt.
- Records show that people born in other countries were living all over England.

7.2 European immigration, c.1500–1730

REVISED

Following the Reformation, large numbers of **Protestant refugees** settled in England

Reformation: After England became a **Protestant** country, Protestants suffering persecution in **Catholic**-ruled countries saw it as a place of safety →

Walloons: Walloons opposed to Spanish Catholic rule came from the Low Countries in the 1560s →

Huguenots: After 10,000 **Huguenot** Protestants were massacred in France, many escaped to England in the 1570s, often after dangerous journeys →

Huguenots again: In the 1680s, Huguenots faced persecution (extremely bad treatment) under King Louis XIV of France and many more fled to England →

Law: In 1709, the **Foreign Protestants Naturalisation Act** allowed all European Protestants to come to live in England →

Palatines: As a result, many German Palatine Protestants suffering under Catholic landlords came seeking safety

The **reception** and treatment of immigrants **varied** widely

- In 1517, violent riots in London – known as **'Evil May Day'** – were aimed at rich foreigners but many poorer immigrants were also attacked. King Henry VIII's government used extreme force to put down the riot and thirteen rioters were hanged in public.
- Romani Gypsies living in Tudor England were persecuted by governments who tried to expel them, make their lifestyle punishable by death and transport them into slavery. Their community managed to survive.
- The government welcomed Walloons and Huguenots and allowed them to worship freely. Many settled and became fully integrated into all sectors of English society including the armed forces. However, there were frequent attacks on refugees by people who believed they were getting special favours.
- Palatines were welcomed at first but when it became clear that most were poor and unskilled and needed state support, the mood turned against them. They were placed in refugee camps and many were deported to Ireland or North America. In 1712, the Foreign Protestants Naturalisation Act was repealed.

Key point

After England became a Protestant country it was a place of safety for many Protestant refugees but treatment of migrants varied widely.

European immigrants had a significant **economic effect**

- Huguenots and Walloons brought many important skills to England, transforming the trade in silk cloth and helping to start the cutlery industry. They invested skills and money into the English economy.
- Many Huguenots had business skills that helped the English **capitalist** trading economy (based on private businesses, banking, investment and profit) to grow. They played an important role in the setting up of the Bank of England and London becoming a world financial centre.

Jews returned to England for a **variety of reasons**

- In 1656, the Lord Protector Oliver Cromwell allowed a small number of European Jews to settle again in England and practise their religion.
- There were various reasons for this, including:
  - he felt that they could help the economy
  - he wanted to protect them from being massacred
  - he believed – based on the Bible – that having Jews in England would help the 'Second Coming' of Jesus.

Checklist

Below is a list of events that may have taken place in England between 1500 and 1750. Tick or highlight those events which you know *did* take place.

- On 'Evil May Day' in 1517, King Henry VIII did nothing to prevent thirteen foreigners being murdered by rioters.
- Laws passed by Tudor monarchs aimed to get rid of all Romani Gypsies living in England.
- By the time of Queen Elizabeth I, England had become a Protestant country.
- Protestant Huguenots were persecuted in France in the 1570s and again in the 1680s.
- When the Bank of England was started in 1694, several Huguenot refugees helped to finance it.
- The 1707 Foreign Protestants Naturalisation Act allowed all Protestants except the Palatines to come to settle in England.
- Many Palatines who did make it to England were deported to Ireland.
- In 1712, the law was changed so that England was no longer open to any Protestants who wanted to come to settle.
- Oliver Cromwell did not want Jews to settle in England because he believed that this went against the teachings of the Bible.

Do/don't list

This is an example of question 2 from the thematic study paper:

Explain why some immigrant groups were treated differently from others in the period c.1500 to c.1750.

(8 marks)

Below is a list of ideas that you might consider when writing the answer to this question. In the boxes marked 'Do' and 'Don't', write yourself instructions for how you should approach this question.

- Include at least two paragraphs.
- Include a brief conclusion which clearly indicates the main factor in your answer.
- Give a narrative account of key events.
- If you can't remember the facts, guess.
- When using evidence, follow it with an explanation of how that event led to the outcome.
- Link your ideas back to the question.
- Use second-order concepts like 'change', that is, how *this thing* led to *that thing*.
- Write one big paragraph with everything you can remember.

Do	Don't

Stretch and challenge

At the start of this period the French economy was far stronger than the English economy, but by the end of the period this had reversed and England was outperforming France. Why do you think historians believe migration was one of the causes of this change?

Practice question

How significant was the Reformation for immigration to England between 1500 and the early eighteenth century?

(14 marks)

Test yourself

1 Why did large numbers of people migrate from Europe to England in this period?

2 Why were groups of European immigrants treated very differently between 1500 and 1750?

7.3 African and Asian immigration, c.1500–1730

REVISED

There were **Africans** living and working in Tudor England and they may have been well **integrated**

- We know from parish and court records that a small number of black people lived free, integrated lives, mixing with the settled community.
- They had a range of occupations, mostly as part of the working poor. One – John Blanke – was a trumpeter in the Royal Court.
- Some may have been **Muslims** from Spain while others came from north and west Africa.
- They appear to have been treated equally under the law and to have experienced a mixture of positive and negative attitudes.

Key point

African people lived successfully in Tudor England but racial attitudes changed with the start of the trade in enslaved Africans and English expansion in Asia through the East India Company.

The growth of **international trade** led to the arrival of people from south Asia, Africa and the Caribbean

- The **East India Company** grew in influence and power. Increasing numbers of trading posts were created and eventually it also had its own army.
- Some officials working with the East India Company brought young Indians to England as child servants and nannies (known as **ayahs**).
- As the trade in enslaved Africans grew, African child servants were also brought to England, both directly from Africa and from enslavement on plantations in the Caribbean. Some were bought and sold and some ran away to escape cruel treatment.
- It was fashionable for rich people to show off their black servants, who often appeared in paintings.
- A few Africans and Indians managed to gain wealth and status and live freely in a range of occupations.

With the development of **ideas about race**, the status of black people in Britain began to change

- During this period, Britain became the main European power trading in enslaved Africans.
- In 1660, Charles II granted a charter to set up a trading company to Africa, which later became the Royal African Company. This gave the company a monopoly on trade with west Africa.
- Africans were transported to work on **plantations** of tobacco or sugar in North America and the Caribbean.
- The idea that people of darker skin were inferior to white people began to take hold.
- Racist attitudes became increasingly common, making the lives of black people in Britain more precarious.
- It is hard to really know about the lives of black people because of the lack of evidence, especially in their own words. However, recent studies of parish and court records are helping historians to know more.

Delete as applicable

Below are a sample exam-style question and a paragraph written in answer to this question. Read the paragraph and decide which of the possible options (underlined) is most appropriate. Delete the least appropriate options and complete the paragraph by justifying your selection.

'Black people had hard lives in Tudor England.' How far do you agree with this statement? (24 marks)

I agree to a great/fair/limited extent that black people had hard lives in Tudor England. The small amount of evidence of black lives suggests that most were part of the working poor and therefore shared the hard lives of most people in this period. There were some negative attitudes to black people and there may have been attempts to expel them. British privateers were beginning to get involved in the Atlantic slave trade. However, there is considerable evidence that Africans who settled in England were free and treated equally, such as ...

Stretch and challenge

Black people seem to have been accepted in Tudor England, but Romani Gypsies were under severe attack. Some historians suggest it was far easier to be an African Muslim than an English Catholic. Why do you think they were treated so differently?

Practice question

Explain how English involvement in the world beyond Europe affected immigration in the late seventeenth and early eighteenth centuries. (8 marks)

Test yourself

1 What sources help us find out about black lives in England between 1500 and 1750?

2 List two examples of increasing trade affecting immigration to England.

7.4 African and Asian immigration, c.1730–1900

REVISED

The position of black people in England was deeply affected by **the trade in enslaved Africans**

- Millions of people were transported from Africa across the Atlantic Ocean to the Americas in a mass forced movement organised by British businesses and government.
- British law allowed slavery in the colonies but was unclear about the status of black people in Britain. Although slavery was **unlawful** (no law permitted it on British shores) it was not clearly **illegal** (no law banned it either).
- Some black people living in England, especially those brought by their owners from the Americas, were treated with similar cruelty to that suffered on the plantations and held as slaves. There were cases of enslaved Africans being sold in Bristol and Liverpool.
- Most black residents were part of the working poor and probably had the same kind of freedom as white domestic servants. A few black people achieved status in a range of occupations.
- After American independence, enslaved Africans who were freed when they fought for Britain in the **American War of Independence** were unable to stay in the USA. Some came to Britain but ended up in poverty on the streets of London. The **Committee for the Relief of the Black Poor** organised a scheme that took many to settle in west Africa.

Key point

African and Asian migration was mainly a result of the growth of the British Empire, and many who came as seamen or domestic servants then settled in Britain.

Many black people were involved in **political movements** against enslavement

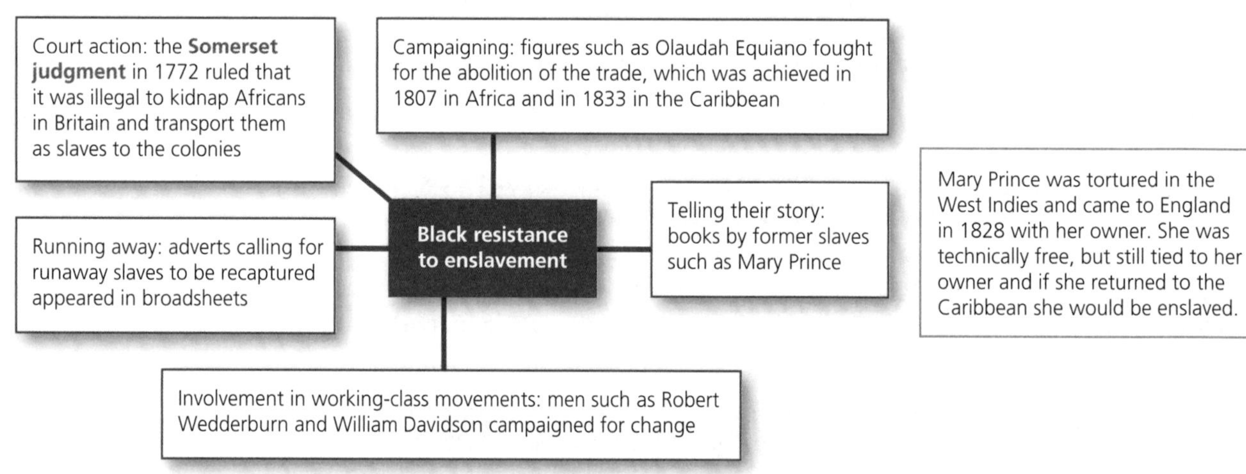

Court action: the **Somerset judgment** in 1772 ruled that it was illegal to kidnap Africans in Britain and transport them as slaves to the colonies
Campaigning: figures such as Olaudah Equiano fought for the abolition of the trade, which was achieved in 1807 in Africa and in 1833 in the Caribbean
Black resistance to enslavement
Running away: adverts calling for runaway slaves to be recaptured appeared in broadsheets
Telling their story: books by former slaves such as Mary Prince
Mary Prince was tortured in the West Indies and came to England in 1828 with her owner. She was technically free, but still tied to her owner and if she returned to the Caribbean she would be enslaved.
Involvement in working-class movements: men such as Robert Wedderburn and William Davidson campaigned for change

Asian and African merchant seamen began to settle and transform port communities

- Asian **Lascars** and African seamen were hired to work on merchant ships run by the East India Company and later by private shipping lines in the Suez Canal. The merchant shipping trade was essential to Britain's growth and wealth.
- These 'coloured seamen' were taken on as indentured labourers – a form of fixed-term enslavement.
- On board ship, Lascars suffered worse conditions and lower pay than white seamen, who saw them as a threat to their jobs and pay.
- On arrival in Britain, Lascars were often abandoned and unable to return home. They stayed in boarding houses and segregated hostels run by the company or people within their own communities.
- They often faced poverty and racism from employers and the seamen's union.
- Laws discriminating against Lascars included the 1823 Merchant Shipping Act, which stopped them having rights allowed to white seamen and prevented them from settling in Britain; and the 1894 Merchant Shipping Act, which made owners round up Lascars and remove them by force.

By the end of the nineteenth century, Africans and Asians were **living** and **working** at **all levels** of society

- Black people filled a range of occupations at different levels throughout society including in the armed forces. In spite of the spread of racist ideas, the number of mixed marriages grew and they appear to have been accepted by working people.
- Some black people were active in working-class movements for justice and equality.
- Several black people achieved public status.
- Many wealthy Indians also settled in Britain, some of them becoming public celebrities such as Maharajah Duleep Singh, the cricketer Prince Ranjitsinhji and Cornelia Sorabji, the first woman to achieve a law degree at a British university.
- Most people of African and Asian origin lived ordinary lives as part of the working poor, with many working as domestic servants or seamen.

Developing the detail

Below are a sample exam-style question and a paragraph written in answer to this question. The paragraph contains a limited amount of detail. Annotate the paragraph to add additional detail to the answer.

Explain how Lascar seamen were discriminated against in the nineteenth century. (8 marks)

Indian, Malay and Chinese merchant seamen suffered discrimination in many ways. They were often treated badly on board ship, working under worse conditions than white seamen. The law made it hard for them to settle, although many had been abandoned in British ports against their will. Many were forced into poverty. The areas where they lived gained negative reputations.

Stretch and challenge

It is far easier to trace black British people who were living here in the eighteenth century than those living here in the nineteenth century, although we think far more were here in the nineteenth century. Why is it harder to find out about them?

(Hints: owners kept records of their slaves. Slaves lost their African names and were given English names.)

Practice question

Explain how significant migrant merchant seamen were for industrial Britain's economy. (14 marks)

Test yourself

1. How did the growth of the British Empire affect immigration between 1730 and 1900?
2. What do we know of the experiences of Africans and Asians living in Britain?
3. How were immigrants' lives affected by the law and how were they involved in action for change?

7.5 European migrants in the industrial age, c.1730–1900

REVISED

Huge numbers of migrants from Ireland and Scotland helped boost Britain's industrial economy

- In 1750, the population of Britain was 11 million and 80 per cent of people lived in the countryside. By 1900, it was 42 million and 70 per cent lived in cities.
- London, Liverpool, Cardiff, Glasgow and Hull became the busiest ports in the world.
- Poverty, evictions and famine forced large numbers of people from Ireland, Scotland, and rural England, to migrate to northern English industrial cities looking for work. Their work helped to power Britain's manufacturing economy.
- As the urban population grew, families were crowded into homes with poor sanitation and cramped conditions, working long hours for low pay.
- Many Irish men worked as **navvies**, building canals and railways across the country, creating the transport network.
- Mass migration, especially from Ireland, resulted in tensions over work, housing and religion that were sometimes violent. Extreme anti-Irish and anti-Catholic feeling was common.

Key point

Migrants escaping poverty and persecution came in large numbers to fill the many jobs created by Britain's industrial expansion.

Test yourself

1 Why did so many people migrate to England from the rest of the British Isles and from Europe between 1750 and 1900?
2 What impact did these immigrants have on life in Britain?
3 How did changes in the law affect immigrants?

- Irish migrants settled all over the country in all walks of life, integrating into society. Some became famous as great achievers.

Immigrants from the rest of Europe had a significant impact on British life

- Poverty forced large numbers of people from southern Italy to migrate to Britain in search of work and a better life. They settled in distinct communities, often involved in the food business.
- Migrants from Germany had a wide range of occupations, from bakers to engineers. Germans were responsible for starting up some of the UK's most successful companies and banks.
- In the 1880s, Jews from Eastern Europe started arriving, seeking asylum from anti-Semitic **pogroms** (violent riots). They settled in the East End of London and other cities, often working in the clothing trade.
- Italian, German, Jewish and other settlers had a huge impact on every aspect of British culture, including food, entertainment, business, media, science and politics.
- Movements for social change were often led by people whose families had arrived as immigrants. Leaders of the **Chartists** included Irish activist Feargus O'Connor and William Cuffay, whose father had been enslaved in the Caribbean. Many **political refugees** from Europe and North America came and settled in Britain, where some – such as Karl Marx – were politically active.

Changing laws affected the citizenship status of foreign-born immigrants

- During the eighteenth and nineteenth centuries, restrictions on British Jews eased and they gained greater rights.
- The 1870 **Naturalisation Act** made it possible for Parliament, and not the monarch, to grant citizenship to foreigners. However, it also made it possible to remove citizenship from British women who married foreign men.
- By the end of the nineteenth century, anti-immigrant feeling, especially against Jewish refugees and Asian seamen, was growing. There was mounting pressure for a law to restrict immigration.

Eliminate irrelevance

Below are a sample exam-style question and a paragraph written in answer to this question. Read the paragraph and identify parts of the paragraph that are not directly relevant to the question. Draw a line through the information that is irrelevant and justify your deletions in the margin.

How significant was migration from Europe between 1750 and 1900 for British society? (14 marks)

During the nineteenth century, many people migrated to Britain from mainland Europe, especially from Italy and Germany. Italians settled in distinct communities in cities such as London, Manchester and Glasgow while Jews were concentrated in east London and other cities such as Leeds and Manchester. Over time, European migrants had a significant effect on the way the British eat: we owe pasta and ice cream to the Italians, breakfast sausages to the Germans and fish and chips to the Jewish refugees. European migrants also had an important effect on British business success. Many major companies such as General Electric and Harland & Wolff were started by German immigrants. Towards the end of the century, Jewish refugees from Russia, Poland and Ukraine also arrived in large numbers. Many Jews were involved in the textile business working as tailors and seamstresses, and some major high street stores such as Burtons and Marks & Spencer were started by Jewish refugees. The Jewish textile trade made it possible for the first time for most working-class Britons to afford new clothes. Immigrants therefore created key profit-making businesses that were major employers and important for the prosperity of British people, contributing to the rise in living standards by the end of the century. Immigrants therefore had a significant influence on the daily lives of people in Britain.

Complete the paragraph

Below are a sample exam-style question and a paragraph written in answer to this question. The paragraph contains a point and specific examples, but lacks a concluding explanatory link back to the question. Complete the paragraph adding this link in the space provided.

Explain why many people migrated from Ireland to England during the nineteenth century. (8 marks)

Poverty was the main reason for nineteenth-century Irish migration. Thousands of families suffered from poor harvests, bad treatment by landowners, lack of employment and, in the 1840s, the potato famine. Meanwhile, England's factory system was booming, with many jobs available in the northern mills where there was a labour shortage. England also needed workers to dig canals and railways. Therefore, ... ____________________

____

____

____

Stretch and challenge

Why do you think the nineteenth century was a period of no immigration controls, in contrast to the following century? And why were attitudes to immigration becoming more negative towards the end of the nineteenth century?

Practice question

'Between 1500 and 1900 the reasons why people migrated to Britain changed considerably.'
How far do you agree with this statement?
(24 marks)

7.6 The era of the First World War, 1900–1920s

REVISED

Anti-foreigner pressure led to tighter **controls on immigration**

- This was a period of low immigration to and high **emigration** (people leaving) from the UK.
- There were high levels of unemployment, poverty and industrial unrest, which led to anti-immigrant feeling.
- Some of this feeling was particularly directed against Lascar seamen and East European Jews.
- Anti-foreigner feeling was partly as a result of some well-publicised terrorist incidents such as the **Sidney Street Siege** of 1911.
- Pressure on the government – including marches and petitions – from some politicians and sections of the press, led to the 1905 **Aliens Act** which imposed immigration controls. Only foreigners who already had work or could support themselves could enter the country. However, the law still allowed refugees fleeing for safety.
- As a result of this law, Britain no longer had an 'open door'.

Key point

This was a period of sometimes violent anti-immigrant feeling and the first strict immigration controls, but also saw the arrival of the UK's largest ever group of refugees.

During the First World War, **Belgian refugees** were welcomed while **'enemy aliens'** were **interned**

- When war broke out in 1914, Britain accepted large numbers of Belgian refugees.
- The 1914 **British Nationality and Status of Aliens Act** made 'aliens' register with the police, restricted where they could live and made it easier to deport them.
- Anti-German feeling was strong during the First World War, leading to attacks on German businesses. It also led to the internment of German and Austrian residents, who were imprisoned in camps away from their homes.
- During the war, millions of people from countries across the British Empire fought for Britain. Thousands of Lascars, many of whom were killed, served on the convoy ships bringing food to the UK.

Tensions in the ports led to **'race riots'** after the war

- After the war, tensions over jobs erupted in port cities between unemployed ex-servicemen returning from war service and migrant seamen who had been employed on the merchant ships.
- Violently racist attacks against black people took place in 1919 in Liverpool, Glasgow, South Shields and Cardiff. Migrant seamen and their families fought back to defend their communities.

Test yourself

1. How and why did the laws on immigration change in the years before the First World War?
2. How and why did different attitudes to different groups of immigrants develop during the war?
3. What caused the explosion of violence in the port cities in 1919?

Checklist

Below is a list of events that may have taken place between 1900 and 1919. Tick or highlight those events which you know *did* take place.

- The 1905 Aliens Act stopped immigrants coming into the UK if they did not already have work or the means to support themselves.
- The 1905 Act also closed the door to refugees.
- The Sidney Street Siege of 1911 was one of several incidents that fuelled growing anti-foreigner feeling.
- About a quarter of a million Belgian refugees were welcomed into Britain early in the First World War.
- Millions of people from across the Empire joined the British war effort.
- During the First World War mobs attacked some German businesses.
- The British government decided not to intern British residents of German and Austrian origin.
- After the war there were riots in several port cities, with violent attacks aimed at migrant seamen and their families.
- During this period the number of people coming to settle in the UK was far higher than the number leaving to find a life overseas.

Which is best?

Below are two examples of answers to an 8-mark question for this paper. Read both, compare to the mark scheme on pages 180–2 and give both a mark out of 8. On a separate piece of paper, explain why the one you have chosen is best.

Explain why the authorities brought in the 1905 Aliens Act. **(8 marks)**

a) At the end of the nineteenth century, feeling was growing against various groups of immigrants. Trade unions felt that Lascar seamen and Jewish sweatshop workers were undercutting their members' wages. Popular media spread negative ideas about places like Chinatown and the Jewish East End of London, portraying them as dangerous and sinister, in openly racist and anti-Semitic language. The government was also concerned that some refugees were involved in political activity. Marches and petitions were organised calling for immigration controls. The Aliens Act was the first law to restrict immigration to Britain.

b) At the end of the nineteenth century, feeling was growing against various groups of immigrants. The government was under pressure to control immigration from several directions. Trade unions felt that Lascar seamen and Jewish sweatshop workers were undercutting their members' wages. Popular media spread negative ideas about places like Chinatown and the Jewish East End of London, portraying them as dangerous and sinister, in openly racist and anti-Semitic language. Many politicians supported the British Brothers' League, who organised marches and petitions calling for a change in the law. Pressure from politicians, press and unions stirring up anti-immigrant feeling, as well as government concern that some political refugees were involved in violent activity, led to the Aliens Act, which was the first law to restrict immigration to Britain.

Stretch and challenge

1919 was a time of extreme racial tension erupting into violence. What were the factors leading to this? How similar were they to the causes of other violent eruptions such as the attacks on foreigners during the 1381 Great Revolt, 'Evil May Day' in 1517, anti-Irish riots in the nineteenth century and the 'uprisings' in various cities in the early 1980s?

Practice question

How significant were the 1919 riots in port cities such as Cardiff, Liverpool and South Shields?

(14 marks)

7.7 The era of the Second World War, 1920s–1948

REVISED

Immigrant communities experienced a **'colour bar'**

- The 1925 **Coloured Alien Seamen Order** restricted the rights of African, Asian and Caribbean seamen. Because of the lower wages paid to the Lascars, there was conflict between colonial seamen and the seamen's union, especially at times of high unemployment.
- Black community and anticolonial organisations such as the **League of Coloured Peoples** offered support and campaigned against the '**colour bar**'.
- At the start of the Second World War, Bengali Lascars organised a strike against unequal pay on ships across the world. On some ships they won their demands, while on others the strikers were arrested.

Key point

The period between the world wars continued to be a time of low immigration, but Jewish children were accepted as refugees on the *Kindertransport* and Polish families were allowed to settle after the war.

The rise of fascism and **anti-Semitism** led to conflicts in Britain and the arrival of child refugees

- The **British Union of Fascists**, known as '**Blackshirts**', tried to march through east London in 1936. They were prevented by a mass anti-fascist protest in solidarity with the area's Jewish residents, remembered as the **Battle of Cable Street**.
- Government restrictions on numbers meant that only small numbers of Jewish refugees from Nazi Germany, Austria and Czechoslovakia were allowed into the UK. However, they – especially the 10,000 Jewish children on the ***Kindertransport*** – were received warmly.

Internment of **'enemy aliens'** happened, with mixed results

- Many German and Italian 'enemy aliens' were **interned** in camps. Sometimes Jewish refugees from Nazi Germany were interned alongside supporters of Hitler.
- After one ship carrying internees, the *Anandora Star*, was sunk by a German torpedo, most internees were freed.

People from many countries fought on **Britain's side** and some were able to **stay** in Britain afterwards

- During the war, millions of people from the empire again fought for Britain.
- Thousands of Lascars served on the merchant convoys, bringing food and vital supplies.
- People from countries occupied by Germany – including Poles, Czechs and French – escaped to Britain and joined the Allied forces.
- All the Polish army's members were given the option of remaining in England after the war – many chose to stay.
- At first, the families of Polish serviceman who had served with Britain in the armed forces were not allowed to join them. When it was clear that they could not return to a Poland dominated by the Soviet Union, the 1947 **Polish Resettlement Act** allowed them to come and settle. At first, trade unions wanted to ban Polish workers but attitudes eventually relaxed.

Event overview grid

Complete a one-sentence summary of the events listed in the grid below.

Event	Summary
The 1925 Coloured Alien Seamen Order	
The 1936 Battle of Cable Street	
The *Kindertransport*	
The 1939 Lascar Seamen's Strike	
Treatment of 'enemy aliens' during the Second World War	
The 1947 Polish Resettlement Act	
Ways in which the UK was welcoming to immigrants	
Ways in which the UK was unwelcoming to immigrants	
Ways in which migrants themselves took action to improve their lives	

Stretch and challenge

Compare the treatment of enemy aliens in the two world wars. Why did internment only happen some time after the war started in both cases? To what extent did the government's actions in the Second World War show that it had learned from the experience of the First?

Practice question

1 Describe **two** ways in which African, Caribbean or Asian people resisted the colour bar between the two world wars. (4 marks)

2 Explain why many Polish families were able to settle in Britain after the Second World War. (8 marks)

Test yourself

1 How welcoming to immigrants was Britain between 1900 and 1945?
2 In what ways were minority groups involved in action for change?
3 How did the Second World War affect immigration to Britain?

7.8 Commonwealth immigration after the Second World War

REVISED

Immigrants from the **'New Commonwealth'** came to Britain for work

- After the Second World War, the British government invited people from the Caribbean, south Asia and Africa to come to work in essential services and industries. The 1948 **British Nationality Act** stated that people in the **Commonwealth** (Britain's former colonies) had the right to hold British passports and work in the UK, where there was a labour shortage.
- Women and men from the Caribbean came to work in the UK, with the promise of jobs in the National Health Service and the transport system. They are often referred to as the ***Windrush*** generation after the name of one of the ships they arrived on. They experienced **racial discrimination** (unfair treatment according to skin colour) in housing and employment, and there were violent attacks against immigrants.
- Men from India and Pakistan came in the 1950s and 1960s, mainly to work in factories. Most expected to earn money for a few years but did not plan to stay.
- There was also significant migration from other parts of the Commonwealth, especially Africa and Cyprus, by people seeking work.

Key point

Caribbean, Asian and African immigrants came to fill the labour shortage after the Second World War. There were times of racial tension and stricter immigration controls, but over time race relations and society changed immeasurably.

The 1960s to 1980s saw tension between **anti-immigrant** and **anti-racist** political forces

- As numbers from the Caribbean, Asia and Africa grew, minority communities developed in areas of many major cities
- Migrant workers sought to protect their rights in various ways including strikes. In Bristol a bus boycott in 1963 ended the bus company's colour bar
- In the 1960s, racial tension grew, stirred up especially by Enoch Powell's 1968 anti-immigration speech
- In 1968 and 1972, Asians who had been expelled from east African countries arrived as refugees
- Racist attacks increased. The rise of the racist **National Front** in the 1970s also led to several anti-racist organisations being set up. Rock Against Racism used music to bring young white and black people together
- In the late 1970s, young people from black and minority ethnic communities formed youth organisations to respond to racist murders
- There was increased tension over the policing of black people. In the early 1980s, as social conditions and relations with the police worsened, riots erupted in several cities
- The 1999 the **Stephen Lawrence Inquiry** reported that the Metropolitan Police was **'institutionally racist'** in the way they had handled the inquiry into nineteen-year-old Lawrence's murder by a racist gang. In other words, they operated in a way that resulted in black people experiencing discrimination

Successive laws were passed both to restrict immigration and to improve **race relations**

- The 1962 **Commonwealth Immigration Act** ruled that only those issued with vouchers would be able to come to work in the UK. This also applied to those who travelled and wanted to return.
- As a result, many men decided to bring their families before the Act went into effect, and to settle permanently.

Test yourself

1. What was the main change made by the 1948 British Nationality Act?
2. What were the aims of the Race Relations Acts in the 1960s and 1970s?
3. What was the conclusion of the Stephen Lawrence Inquiry in 1999?

- A series of further laws tightened immigration controls. These included the 1968 **Commonwealth Immigrants Act** which banned entry to anyone without a father or grandfather born in the UK.
- During the 1960s and 1970s, a series of **Race Relations Acts** promoted good race relations and made racial discrimination illegal.

Practice question

'Between 1750 and 2010 Britain was always a difficult place for immigrants.' How far do you agree with this statement? (24 marks)

Commonwealth migration had a significant effect on British society

- Immigrant workers helped to rebuild the UK after the devastation of wartime bombing. They helped to keep the health and transport systems going and provided much-needed labour in factories. They played an important part in the economic boom of the 1950s and 1960s.
- Commonwealth immigrants and their descendants have brought massive social and cultural change in a wide range of fields including business, food, fashion, music, literature, sport and entertainment.

Identify an argument

Below are a series of definitions, a sample exam-style question and two sample conclusions. One of the conclusions achieves a high level because it contains an argument. The other achieves a lower level because it contains only description and assertion. Identify which is which. The mark scheme on pages 180–2 will help you.

- Description: a detailed account.
- Assertion: a statement of fact or an opinion which is not supported by a reason.
- Explanation: a statement which explains or justifies something.
- Argument: an assertion justified with a reason.

'The hopes of the *Windrush* generation were not realised.' How far do you agree with this statement?

(24 marks)

On the one hand, the Windrush *generation experienced racial discrimination in housing and employment, as well as racist violence. Their children, too, had to act against the National Front, racist policing and educational and social disadvantage in the 1970s and 1980s. It is still the case that a disproportionate percentage of black men are imprisoned, unemployed or underachieving in education. These factors all support the statement that hopes were not realised. On the other hand, many of that generation settled and achieved prosperity. Anti-racist action was successful in changing attitudes and by the end of the twentieth century, black people were prominent in many areas of society. Black and white people lived happily in mixed communities (and often mixed relationships), and a comfortable black middle class was growing. These factors contradict the statement. So, while institutional racism still impacts on black British people, many of the hopes of the* Windrush *generation have been realised. For these reasons I agree partly, but not fully, with the statement.*

The Windrush *generation experienced racial discrimination in housing and employment, as well as racist violence. Many of that generation settled and achieved prosperity. Many of their children's generation had to act against the National Front, racist policing and educational and social disadvantage. By the end of the twentieth century, black people were prominent in many areas of society. Black and white people lived happily in mixed communities (and often mixed relationships), and a comfortable black middle class was growing. A disproportionate percentage of black men are still imprisoned, unemployed or underachieving in education. I partly agree with the statement.*

7.9 Immigration as a political issue, c.1990–c.2010

REVISED

Unprecedented numbers of **migrants** from the **European Union** came to work in the UK

- A European Union (EU) agreement meant that workers could move without restriction between EU countries. Migrant workers from countries in the EU came to find employment.
- From 1993 onwards, for the first time, more people came into the UK each year than left, making **net migration** higher and higher.
- In 2004, when the EU expanded to include many Eastern European countries such as Poland, the British government decided to allow immediate freedom of entry. People came in large numbers and the UK's population increased faster than ever before.

Key point

From the 1990s, there have been high immigration levels due to European freedom of movement, and increasing numbers of refugees. This, in turn, has seen an increase in anti-immigration sentiment, and laws passed to limit numbers.

The rapid global increase in **refugees** led to many more trying to seek **asylum** in the UK

- In 1948, the British government signed the **United Nations Declaration of Human Rights**, which states that 'everyone has the right to seek and to enjoy in other countries **asylum** from persecution'. For the next half century there was a steady flow of refugees escaping war or political persecution.

Test yourself

1 What is 'net migration'?
2 How has net migration to Britain changed since 1993?
3 What was the effect of the 1985 Schengen Agreement?

Causes of the sharp rise in numbers of asylum seekers

- Some were fleeing violent civil unrest (for example, from Somalia, Syria, Congo, Libya) or foreign invasion (for example, from Afghanistan, Iraq)
- Under the 1985 **Schengen Agreement**, there were open borders and no passport control between most European countries. This made travel easy across the continent to northern France
- Some people chose to come to the UK because they could speak English, they already had family here, they had colonial links to Britain or because it was seen as a safe and stable country
- There were also **economic migrants** from many other parts of the world, forced to move by poverty often brought about by environmental crisis
- The collapse of communism in Eastern Europe made it easier to travel to Europe from western Asia

Several laws tightened **controls on asylum seekers**

- Government efforts to deter further immigration led to the increasingly restrictive and harsh treatment of asylum seekers and immigrants.
- A series of asylum and immigration laws made it harder to gain **refugee status**. Many asylum seekers were held in detention centres. In some of these camps, there were protests about conditions.
- Tighter restrictions on the lives of those seeking asylum took away their right to work and replaced benefits with government-issued vouchers.
- Many refugees ended up in a makeshift camp on the French coast at **Sangatte**, hoping to cross to the UK. This was closed in 2001 and immediately replaced by **'the Jungle'** – an encampment of people hoping to reach the UK, which was closed down in 2017.

Practice question

'Immigrants to Britain since 1500 have brought more benefits than problems.' How far do you agree with this statement? (24 marks)

Since 2000 **immigration** has become a major **political issue**

- Following the **7/7 terrorist bombings** in London in 2005, there was a sharp rise in **Islamophobic** incidents in the UK.
- After the 2008 **banking crisis**, anti-immigration feeling grew.
- Immigration became a major political issue, linked to arguments about whether the UK should leave or stay in the EU.
  - Some – especially the UK Independence Party which gained 4 million votes in the 2015 general election – argued that UK services (housing, education, health) could not cope with the population increase and that immigration was pushing down wages.
  - On the other hand, others argued that EU immigrants were boosting the economy by filling vacancies and creating more jobs.
- In a 2016 **referendum** on leaving or remaining in the EU, 52 per cent voted that the UK should leave, following a **Brexit** campaign during which immigration was a major issue.

Which is best?

Below are two examples of answers to an 8-mark question for this paper. Read both, compare to the mark scheme on pages 180–2 and give both a mark out of 8. Underneath, explain why the one you have chosen is best.

Explain how membership of the European Union affected immigration to the UK. (8 marks)

a) Under European Union rules, citizens of member states have the right to move freely between countries to work and settle. This caused immigration numbers from EU nations to rise sharply and every year since the early 1990s has seen far more people coming in than leaving. This put strains on community life in many smaller towns that were experiencing high levels of immigration for the first time. After the banking crisis of 2008, when the government cut public spending and froze wages, immigration was blamed in much of the popular press for overstretched health and education services and the fact that many people were on low-wage zero-hours contracts. These factors affected attitudes and support grew for tighter immigration controls. Immigration was a main factor in the 2016 referendum vote to leave the EU. EU membership therefore caused a rapid rise in immigrant numbers and, when there was a financial crisis, a rise in anti-immigrant feeling which played a big part in the vote to leave the EU.	**b)** Under European Union rules, citizens of member states have the right to move freely between countries to work and settle. Immigration numbers from EU nations rose sharply and every year since the early 1990s has seen far more people coming in than leaving. Many smaller towns were experiencing high levels of immigration for the first time. After the banking crisis of 2008, many blamed immigration for overstretched health and education services and the fact that many people were on low-wage zero-hours contracts. Partly stirred up by the popular press, support grew for tighter immigration controls. In the 2015 General Election the UK Independence Party gained 4 million votes. Immigration was a main factor in the 2016 referendum vote to leave the EU..

7.10 Think thematic!

REVISED

People's **reasons for migration** have been similar in all periods

- Internal migration, emigration and immigration have been constant factors in the history of these islands from the earliest times. This country has always been shaped by migration.

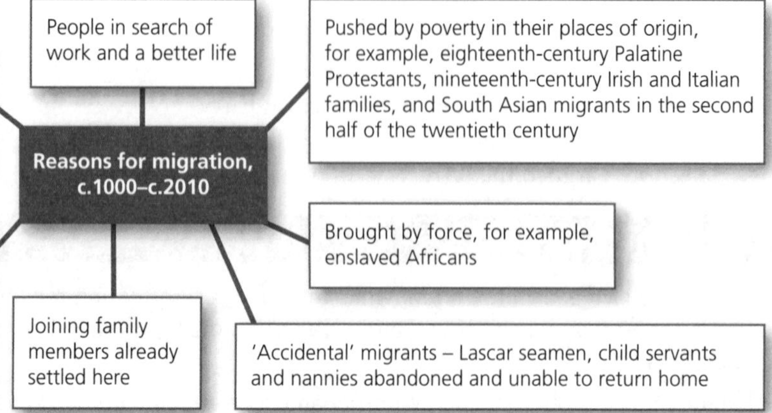

Reasons for migration, c.1000–c.2010
People invited by governments to help boost the economy or fill a labour shortage, for example, eleventh-century Jewish moneylenders, fourteenth-century Flemish weavers and Caribbean immigrants after the Second World War
People in search of work and a better life
Pushed by poverty in their places of origin, for example, eighteenth-century Palatine Protestants, nineteenth-century Irish and Italian families, and South Asian migrants in the second half of the twentieth century
Brought by force, for example, enslaved Africans
Refugees in search of safety, for example, Huguenots in the sixteenth and seventeenth centuries, Eastern European Jews in the late nineteenth century, Belgians during the First World War and asylum seekers from western Asia and Africa in the early twenty-first century
Joining family members already settled here
'Accidental' migrants – Lascar seamen, child servants and nannies abandoned and unable to return home

Within each period, immigrants have had very **different experiences**

- In every period, immigrants have settled, established livelihoods, intermixed and become part of their local communities.
- Many have felt welcomed and fully included in a society which has always been culturally diverse and usually able to absorb new cultural groups peacefully.
- In every period, however, there has also been hostility to immigrants. At times of social upheaval or economic crisis immigrants have been targeted.
- The reasons for different treatment have varied. It was often easier for wealthy migrants than poorer ones, and for skilled migrants than unskilled ones.
- An atmosphere of bigotry and fear was at times stirred up by religious leaders, politicians or the press and directed at particular groups.
- Examples of this include the blood libel accusations against medieval Jews and the 1968 'Rivers of Blood' speech by Enoch Powell.

Within each period, **government and popular responses** to immigrants have varied, but the factors affecting these have been similar across periods

- Migrant workers have often been preferred by employers who paid them less than native workers. Some workers, in turn, felt that migrants were undercutting their wages, taking their jobs and putting pressure on public services.
- Governments have often encouraged immigration as a means of boosting or changing the country's economy. This at times put them in conflict with guilds and trade unions who saw cheap migrant labour as a threat.
- Strong governments at times of economic health have tended to open the doors to immigrants. Weak governments at times of crisis often targeted 'aliens' and made the lives of immigrants more difficult.
- There were earlier laws against particular groups such as Jews, Gypsies and Catholics, as well as taxes on foreign-born people, but it was only in the twentieth century that governments passed a series of laws restricting and controlling immigration.

Continued migration has affected what is seen as **British 'identity'**

- The 'English' in about 1000 were in fact a mixture of Angles, Saxons, Jutes, Danes, Celts, Normans and others.
- The 'British' in 2010 included Irish, Scottish, Welsh, English and the descendants of all the many African, Asian, American, Australasian and European migrants.
- What we define as British identity – customs, clothes, food, language – is continually changing as each migrant group leaves its impact.
- British identity is made up of all its varied cultures and is continually in flux.

Britain's migration story reflects its **relationship with the wider world**, changing both

- Between 1000 and 1500, the Norman Conquest brought a migrant ruling class and England's first Jewish community.
- During the Hundred Years' War migrants from the Low Countries helped boost England's manufacturing economy.
- Between 1500 and 1750, the Reformation and England's changing relationship with Spain and France resulted in the arrival of Africans and later of Walloon and Huguenot refugees. Some of these people helped finance the start of Britain's capitalist trading economy.
- The early years of the East India Company and the trade in enslaved Africans resulted in the arrival of servants, many of them children.
- Between 1750 and 1900, the slave trade and the British Empire led to increasing numbers of African and Asian immigrants.
- The factories of the Industrial Revolution attracted poor families from Ireland, Scotland and Italy as well as richer entrepreneurs from Germany.
- The industrial system also provided work in sweatshops for Jewish refugees who in turn helped boost the rise of retail business.
- After 1900, both world wars resulted in immigration – Belgian refugees, Jews escaping the Nazis, Poles and people from the New Commonwealth answering Britain's labour shortage. Membership of the EU led to the sharpest ever rise in immigrants and eventually to the referendum vote to leave the EU.

Essay style

Below is a sample exam-style question. Use your own knowledge and the information on the opposite page to produce a plan for this question using the template below. Your extended essay should contain at least three paragraphs. Once you have planned your essay, write the introduction and conclusion for the essay. The introduction should list the points to be discussed in the essay. The conclusion should summarise the key points and justify which point was the most important.

'Between c.1000 and c.1750, immigrants settled in England successfully.' How far do you agree with this statement? **(24 marks)**

Introduction	Answer the question	State your overall belief, for example: It is clear that most immigrants were [successful/unsuccessful] in settling during this period because ... On the other hand, however ...
Paragraph 1: Public attitudes to foreigners	State	Throughout this period, there is evidence that attitudes to foreigners were mainly [positive/negative] although there were also cases of [negative/positive] attitudes
	Prove	[Give detailed pieces of evidence]
	Explain	[Explain how your evidence shows negative/positive attitudes]
	Answer	[State explicitly how this factor leads you to agreement or disagreement with the statement]
Conclusion	Answer the question	[Refer back to the points you have covered and state the overall reason why you agree or disagree]

Section 3 British depth studies

What the British depth study is about and how it will be examined

Overview of the British depth study

This section focuses on your understanding of the impact of a specific significant historical event and how it affected the lives of ordinary people.

We are looking in particular at the changes that took place, and their impact on the people of Britain in each case.

Depth studies require you to:

- Understand the significance of the change taking place, and how it affected: politics, the economy, society and religion.
- We must consider how different groups in society were affected by these major events, and the lasting changes which occurred as a result.
- This is a **primary source** paper, so you need to make sure you practise using the sources and think about how we **compare** sources.
- In order to help with this, you must make sure that you know how people viewed these events as they were taking place: this is the **contemporary view**. To do this you will:
  - Engage with how different groups of people were affected by state policies.
  - Consider the reasons for, and nature of, support and/or opposition to the state from different groups.
  - Consider the influence of international affairs on a domestic situation (this will require you to consider aspects of the period study).
  - Engage with primary source material.

Main question types in the British depth study

This is Section A of Paper 2. It is worth 35 marks in total. You will be asked the following types of question.

1 **Explain why/how ...** *(10 marks)*

This is very similar to the 10-mark question in Paper 1.

A full-mark answer would explain more than one feature in relation to the question with a good amount of supporting detail.

The focus is not on the number of examples explained. You should concentrate on producing an explanation which is focused on the second-order concept identified by the question (for example, cause, consequence, change).

2 **Source question: 'How far do the sources convince you that this view is correct'** *(20 marks + 5 SPaG)*

You will not have seen the sources before and will have to assess each one to write your answer.

You need to read and examine each source carefully. You need to establish the **extent** to which they lead you to agree with the viewpoint or not. A simple 'yes they convince me' or 'no they do not' will not earn high marks.

You need a clear argument, and in each paragraph you should consider the source, demonstrating that you understand what the source is saying, and how it succeeds/fails to convince you of the view in the question.

Remember, it is asking you whether the **sources** convince you, not your own knowledge. You must use your own knowledge only to help your understanding of the sources.

'Second-order concepts' needed for the British depth study

'Second-order concepts' are a way to organise 'big ideas' in history.

Here are the second-order concepts **most** relevant to the British depth studies.

Consequence – You may be asked to consider the impact of an action or event, and who and what was **affected** by it. You may also want to consider whether some consequences were more **significant** than others. Useful words: 'resulted', 'ensued', 'arose'

Similarity and difference – This is about **how far** experiences are shared in the same place and at the same time: did **everyone** experience something in the same way? The answer to this question is never going to be a straightforward 'yes' and therefore you will be looking at the **diversity** of people's experiences in a given historical situation

THE BRITISH DEPTH STUDY

Significance – 'Significant' is not the same as 'important'. There are different ways in which you can judge the historical significance of an event: it may have many consequences; it may have **parallels** with another period; it may have been something which many people have chosen to remember. You demonstrate your understanding of significance by using criteria

Key skills: analysing primary sources

There are primary sources in both Paper 1 and Paper 3, but it is the British depth study that most tests these skills.

Content – What is the source actually saying? This can seem obvious, but it is the easiest thing to forget. And remember, you should always aim to use **details** from the source in your answer

Nature – This is more than just **type** of source. Something being a diary or a cartoon only takes you so far. Nature is a quality judgement. For example: is the source meant to be taken seriously? A lot of primary sources do not necessarily mean what they say: they use **satire**. Some may be deliberately dishonest

EVALUATING PRIMARY SOURCES

Origin – Who created this source? What do you know about the author. Are they likely to be reliable? However, you still need to look carefully at a source. Just because you don't trust the author, what they say may still be correct. Conversely, a reliable author does not automatically make a reliable source

Typicality – 'Is this what you would expect this person/this type of person to produce?' If so, you can discuss why, and if not, you can explain why not

Purpose – Why it was written. Was this source meant to change people's minds? Was it meant for public viewing? If so, there is a good chance that it was designed to **persuade** people. Be careful though. This does not automatically make it wrong or dishonest

How we help you develop your exam skills

- The revision tasks help you to build understanding and skills step by step.
- The **practice questions** give you exam-style questions.
- There are annotated model answers for every practice question online at **www.hoddereducation.co.uk/myrevisionnotes** or use this QR code to find them instantly.

8 Personal Rule to Restoration 1629–1660

8.1 The end of Charles I's Personal Rule

REVISED

Charles and Parliament had different ideas about their roles

- Charles I and his father (James I) both believed that they had been appointed by '**divine right**' (directly by God).
- Charles believed in **absolutism** (this meant that he should have total control).
- After **Magna Carta** in 1215, Parliament believed that the monarch had to obey the law, just like everyone else.
- In reality, the relationship between king and Parliament needed to be one of compromise: Parliament could approve the king's taxes, but the king needed to listen to the concerns of the political nation expressed in Parliament.

Key point

Charles had a rocky relationship with Parliament.

Test yourself

1 How did William Laud deal with Puritans?
2 List three criticisms the Long Parliament made about Charles' style of rule.
3 What was ship money?

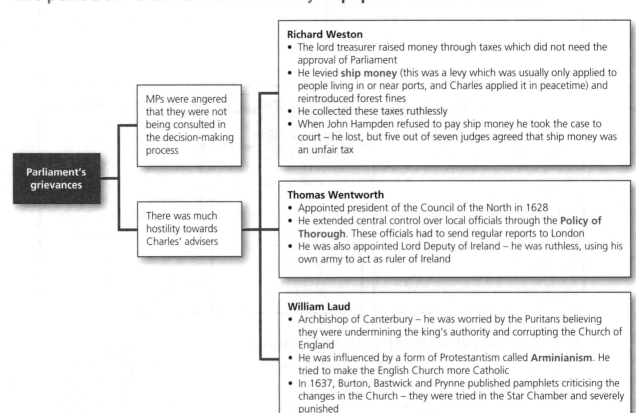

When Parliament disagreed with Charles, a period of Personal Rule began

- Charles was not Catholic, but was accused of being sympathetic to Catholics – he suspended the **Recusancy Laws** and his wife was Catholic.
- A costly war with Spain began to fail.
- When Parliament criticised Charles' actions he suspended Parliament and 1629–40 was known as a period of Personal Rule.

The period of Personal Rule was very unpopular with Parliament

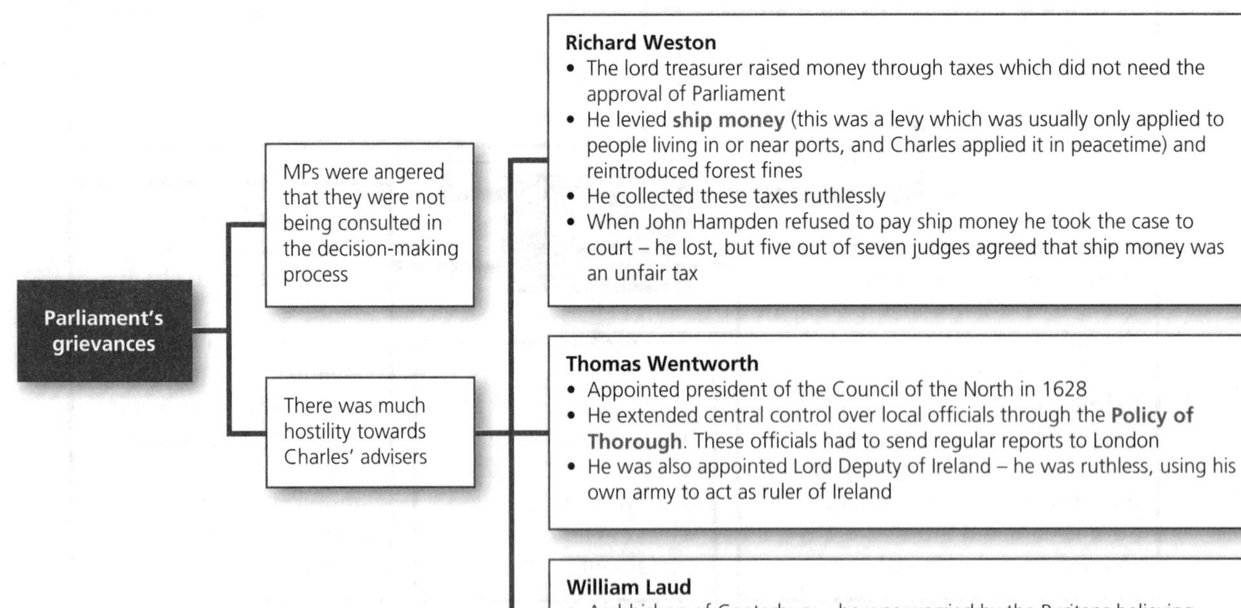

Parliament's grievances
MPs were angered that they were not being consulted in the decision-making process
There was much hostility towards Charles' advisers
Richard Weston
• The lord treasurer raised money through taxes which did not need the approval of Parliament
• He levied ship money (this was a levy which was usually only applied to people living in or near ports, and Charles applied it in peacetime) and reintroduced forest fines
• He collected these taxes ruthlessly
• When John Hampden refused to pay ship money he took the case to court – he lost, but five out of seven judges agreed that ship money was an unfair tax
Thomas Wentworth
• Appointed president of the Council of the North in 1628
• He extended central control over local officials through the Policy of Thorough. These officials had to send regular reports to London
• He was also appointed Lord Deputy of Ireland – he was ruthless, using his own army to act as ruler of Ireland
William Laud
• Archbishop of Canterbury – he was worried by the Puritans believing they were undermining the king's authority and corrupting the Church of England
• He was influenced by a form of Protestantism called Arminianism. He tried to make the English Church more Catholic
• In 1637, Burton, Bastwick and Prynne published pamphlets criticising the changes in the Church – they were tried in the Star Chamber and severely punished

Charles was forced to recall Parliament in 1640 and make concessions

- In 1640, Charles was forced to recall Parliament to gain funding for a conflict with Scotland. However, Parliament refused to grant taxes until Charles had listened to its grievances.
- Parliament was successful in getting Charles to make some concessions:
  - Laud was impeached and imprisoned in the Tower of London
  - the Hampden case judges were impeached
  - the Triennial Act agreed that Parliament would meet at least every three years
  - Strafford was executed
  - the Own Consent Act was passed, which meant Parliament had to agree to being dissolved
  - in July 1641, the Royal Prerogative Courts – where Charles had tried many opponents – were abolished
  - in August 1641, ship money and knighthood fines were declared illegal
  - Charles also appointed several leading parliamentarians to important government positions.

Practice question

Study Sources A–C. 'The poor relationship between Charles I and Parliament in the period 1629–1642 was caused by Charles' beliefs about his role.' How far do Sources A–C convince you that this statement is correct? Use the sources and your knowledge to explain your answer. (20 marks)

SOURCE A *Petition signed by twelve members of the House of Lords (1640).*

That your majesty's sacred person is exposed to hazard and danger in the present expedition against the Scottish army, and by occasion of this war your revenue is much wasted, your subjects burdened with coat-and-conduct money, billeting of soldiers, and other military charges, and divers rapines and disorders committed in several parts in this your realm, by the soldiers raised for that service, and your whole kingdom become full of fear and discontents.

SOURCE B *Statement sent by Charles I to Parliament (1626).*

I must let you know that I will not let any of my ministers be questioned by you ... hasten my supply [taxes] or it will be worse for yourselves; for if any ill happen, I think I shall be the last to feel it.

SOURCE C *A 1641 woodcut shows the godliness of the Puritan (left), as opposed to the superstitions preached by Laud and his fellow bishops.*

Checklist

Decide whether or not each statement below is correct and put a tick next to them. Consider what evidence you can use to support your decision.

- Charles was an absolutist monarch.
- Charles ruled without Parliament from 1625 to 1640.
- Charles held no religious beliefs.
- Charles recalled Parliament in 1640.
- Only a few MPs made challenges to Charles' methods of rule.
- Laud reformed religion in England and Scotland.
- Laud introduced ship money.
- Wentworth did not go through the normal courts when punishing people.

Stretch and challenge

Go back through this spread and create a list of anything that was causing tension between Charles and Parliament. Then rank each item to show which caused the most to least tension.

8.2 Events leading to civil war

REVISED

After the king's concessions it became clear that **Parliament** was **not united**

- Charles had dismantled the key elements of his Personal Rule and still needed his money for the conflict in Scotland.
- It became clear that Parliament was divided between:
  - moderate MPs (such as Viscount Falkland and Sir Edward Hyde) who thought Charles had made enough concessions and should be granted the money
  - radical MPs (such as John Pym) who thought it was the right time to demand more of the king.

Key point

Fallouts between Charles and Parliament led to Civil War.

Test yourself

1 Who was John Pym, and why did he oppose Charles?
2 What was the Grand Remonstrance?
3 Why did Charles reject the 'Nineteen Propositions'?

Charles faced problems that **challenged** his **authority**

- In October 1641, Charles faced rebellions from Catholics in Ireland – this posed a huge problem for Charles as he needed parliamentary approval for money to quash the rebellions.
- John Pym introduced a document called the **Grand Remonstrance**, which contained a summary of the grievances with Personal Rule, and a list of recommendations including:
  - Parliament to control the king's ministers
  - bishops and Catholic lords to be banned from the House of Lords
  - fundamental reform of the Catholic Church to make it more Puritan.
- The Grand Remonstrance was very controversial and was just passed by 159 votes to 148. It deepened the divide in Parliament – Charles refused it and many moderate MPs supported him.

The **Grand Remonstrance** led to the **attempt on five members** in 1642

- By late 1641, Charles was angry that extreme MPs were calling for further reforms.
- John Pym – who was talking with the Scots, and had the support of the **London mobs** – continued to push for further reforms.
- In a final attempt to reach a compromise, Charles offered Pym the position of **chancellor of the exchequer**. Pym refused and Charles sent armed men into Parliament to publicly arrest five MPs (including Pym) on a charge of high treason.
- In this action, Charles broke parliamentary privilege by disturbing a debate and by using armed men against MPs.
- After the city authorities refused to surrender the five MPs, Charles left London (as did many **Royalist MPs**) and Parliament raised its own armed forces.

The failure of the **Nineteen Propositions** ultimately led to **civil war**

- Fearing Charles would use force, the **Militia Ordinance** was passed in 1642, which put Parliament in charge of the appointment of the militia. This meant Parliament controlled armed forces.
- On 1 June 1642, Parliament presented Charles with a peace deal with some harsh demands, known as the '**Nineteen Propositions**'. These demands included that:
  - Parliament should be in control of the army
  - Parliament should approve the appointment of ministers
  - Parliament should discuss and approve all government policy
  - the Church should be reformed along Puritan lines.
- Charles rejected the Nineteen Propositions – this marked the start of the **Civil War**.

Checklist

Below is a list of events that may have taken place in the lead-up to the English Civil War. Tick or highlight those events which you know *did* take place.

- The Grand Remonstrance proposed the expulsion of all bishops from Parliament.
- Charles arrested 100 MPs.
- Edward Hyde and some moderate MPs thought that the king's power was being restricted too much.
- John Pym was the chancellor of the exchequer.
- Charles rejected Parliament's 'Nineteen Propositions'.

Support or challenge?

Decide if each piece of information listed below supports or challenges the statement 'Charles was responsible for the outbreak of the English Civil War'. Put a tick or a cross in the appropriate box to demonstrate your thinking.

Information	Supports	Challenges
Some people argue that MPs such as John Pym had unrealistic expectations of how far the power of the king should be limited		
A group of moderate MPs remained loyal to Charles and thought his powers should not be so severely limited		
The Grand Remonstrance limited the power of the monarch greatly, but was passed by a majority of MPs		
Charles used military force to try to arrest MPs		
Parliament took control of armed forces without the consent of the monarch		
Charles refused to accept the 'Nineteen Propositions'		

Stretch and challenge

1 Who do you think was responsible for the outbreak of the Civil War? Look back through this spread and find:

a) evidence that Charles was to blame for the outbreak of war

b) evidence that Parliament was to blame for the outbreak of war.

After you have done this, rate each piece of evidence out of 10 to show how much tension the action concerned would have caused (10 = lots of tension).

2 Henry Slingsby was an MP from Yorkshire. He sat in the House of Commons at various times. In 1643 he was commissioned as a colonel in the Royalist army.

Read Source D and consider how useful the source is for telling us who was to blame for the outbreak of the English Civil War.

SOURCE D *Diary entry of Yorkshire MP Henry Slingsby, 1642.*

We have lived a long time ... without war ... We have had peace when all the world has been in arms ... It is I say a thing most horrible that we should engage ourself in war with another ... with our own venom ... we will destroy ourself.

Practice question

Explain why the English Civil War broke out in 1642. (10 marks)

8.3 Attempts to reach an agreement between Charles and Parliament, 1646–47

REVISED

The Civil War was a **brutal** conflict

- The Civil War ended in 1646 with the imprisonment of Charles I.
- The country had been divided between Royalists and Parliamentarians, the fighting had been bloody and the casualty level was high.
- People wanted an end to the conflict.

Key point

At the end of the Civil War people wanted a return to the monarchy, but it proved difficult to reach a settlement between the factions.

The war had challenged the **social order**

- The authority of the king had been challenged.
- New social and religious groups emerged with different ideas about society, such as:
  - The Levellers: they believed that society should be 'levelled' – that all men should have the right to vote, and that property should be equally distributed.
  - The Diggers: they believed that all land and property should be shared equally. They set up small communities to work the land and share the produce.
  - The Quakers: they thought that people could be close to God through Bible study (a church was not necessary).
- But people wanted peace, and were happy to still accept the trusted form of government – the monarchy.
- The **New Model Army** had emerged as a well-organised fighting force led by Cromwell. But people were concerned at its expense and power.

Test yourself

1 What did the Diggers believe?
2 Which two groups were MPs in Parliament divided into?
3 Who offered the Newcastle Propositions to Charles in 1646?

Negotiations between Charles and Parliament **failed** after the First Civil War

- Parliament was divided into the **Presbyterians** and **Independents**:

	The Presbyterians	The Independents
Led by:	Denzil Holles	Oliver Cromwell and other key MPs
Aimed to:	Reach a settlement with Charles	Force Charles to concede to their demands
View on Charles:	Charles should play a key role in discussions and he should be reinstated with few or no limits on his power	Were not interested in allowing Charles to have many concessions. They were sympathetic to the New Model Army and were willing to use force
View on religion:	The Church of England should be reformed to make it more similar to the Scottish Presbyterian Church. Felt threatened by Puritans and radical religious sects	Everyone should be free to worship as they wished – as long as it was Protestant

- The New Model Army refused to disband after the conflict and also wanted a say in the negotiations. Many of these army members were Levellers with radical ideas.
- The Scots had been promised by Parliament that Presbyterianism would be introduced as payment for their support in the Civil War.
- These divisions slowed Parliament's efforts to make a settlement with Charles. He listened to all sides, but refused to make any decisions in order to delay.

Charles refused both Parliament's and the army's separate peace settlements

Parliament offered: the Newcastle Propositions, 1646	The army offered: the Heads of Proposal, 1647
Parliament to be called at least every three years	Parliament to be called at least every two years
Parliament to nominate commanders of the army	Parliament to control army for ten years
Church of England to be reformed under Presbyterian lines	No Presbyterian reform of the Church
Anti-Catholic laws to be enforced	Anti-Catholic laws to be abolished, and new ones formed
58 leading Royalists to be punished	Seven leading Royalists to be punished

Event overview grid

Complete a one-sentence summary of the events/key people listed in the grid below.

The Levellers	
The Quakers	
The Presbyterians	
The Independents	
Denzil Holles	
Oliver Cromwell	
The Newcastle Propositions	
The Heads of Proposals	

Practice question

Study Sources E–G. 'Parliament was to blame for the failure of attempts to reach a settlement with Charles by 1647.' How far do Sources E–G convince you that this statement is correct? Use the sources and your knowledge to explain your answer. (20 marks)

SOURCE E *An extract from the Newcastle Propositions, sent to Charles I in 1646.*

10. That an Act be passed in Parliament, whereby the practices of Catholics against the State may be prevented, and the laws against them duly executed, and a stricter course taken to prevent the saying or hearing of Mass in the Court or any other part of this kingdom.

SOURCE F *Thomas Rainborough was one of the leaders of the Leveller soldiers. He opposed all attempts at compromise with Charles I.*

For really I think that the poorest he that is in England hath a life to live, as the greatest he; and therefore truly, sir, I think it's clear, that every man that is to live under a government ought first by his own consent to put himself under that government; and I do think that the poorest man in England is not at all bound in a strict sense to that government that he hath not had a voice to put himself under. ...

SOURCE G *An extract from 'The Engagement', 1647. The Scots agreed to provide military support to Charles if he supported the establishment of Presbyterianism in England.*

... an army shall be sent from Scotland into England, for preservation and establishment of religion, for defence of His Majesty's person and authority, and restoring him to his government, to the just rights of the Crown. ...

8.4 The execution of Charles I

REVISED

The outbreak of the Second Civil War demonstrated that it would be **difficult** to reach a **compromise**

- The **Second Civil War** started when Charles escaped to Scotland and got Scottish military support when offering to trial Presbyterianism in England.
- Charles lost the trust of some MPs after he sought the support of Scotland.
- The outbreak of the Second Civil War demonstrated that Parliament needed a permanent army and so the prospect of a settlement agreed on by both sides seemed unlikely.
- The New Model Army crushed the Scots and Charles in the Second Civil War.

Key point

The failure to reach agreement led to the Second Civil War and Parliament's victory made it adamant that the king had to be removed from power.

Regicide became more **likely** during the course of the Second Civil War

- After Parliament's victory at the **Battle of Preston** in August 1648, settlement terms were discussed but some of the Parliamentarians' attitudes towards settlement had hardened.
- Some radical MPs and members of the New Model Army thought that Parliamentarian victories were God's will, and so they should not negotiate with Charles.
- In December 1648, Colonel Pride (of the New Model Army) arrested all MPs who had voted to continue negotiations with Charles. This was known as **Pride's Purge**.
- In January 1649, the remaining MPs (who became known as the '**Rump Parliament**') voted for a 'High Court' to be established to try Charles.

Charles' **execution** was **not welcomed** by all

- Charles was executed on 30 January 1649, and in May 1649 England was declared a **Commonwealth**, but many people were not happy to see the end of monarchy in England.
- Some people argued that Parliament was trying to force Charles to make concessions by putting him on trial, and that execution was not intended.
- Many English people were shocked by the execution of Charles – it was reported that there were no cheers when Charles was executed, and some people began to refer to him as the 'martyr-king'.
- Some people who were called to sit as judges in Charles' trial refused to take part.

Test yourself

1 Give one reason why the Second Civil War started.

2 What was Pride's Purge?

3 What was the Rump Parliament of 1649?

Practice question

Explain why Charles and Parliament had not come to an agreement by 1647. (10 marks)

Complete the mind map

Below is an incomplete mind map. Your task is to complete the mind map by filling in the missing boxes. You could challenge yourself by annotating links between topics.

Why was Charles executed?

Charles' refusal to cooperate		
Charles refused to accept both settlement terms and Parliament's charges when he was on trial		

Identify an argument

The three extracts below are all responses to the question: 'Why couldn't Parliament and the king reach a settlement?' They demonstrate one of the following:

- assertion – a general point that is unfocused
- description – some relevant factual detail that does not tackle the focus of the question
- argument – a response which is specific to the question and has a clear focus.

Decide which feature you would apply to each extract.

- Charles did not agree on any of the terms offered to him by Parliament or the army. He bought time by refusing to agree with either side. For example, he did not accept the army's Heads of Proposal even though its terms were better than those offered by Parliament.
- Parliament and the king could not reach a settlement because those offering peace terms to Charles were divided; this meant the terms they offered were different. Charles took his time and played each side off against each other which slowed negotiations and this became a reason for their failure.
- Charles was an arrogant ruler.

Stretch and challenge

1 Create a graph to show when you think it became inevitable that Charles was going to be executed. Go back through the spread and plot each key event (*x*-axis – Chronology; *y*-axis – Likelihood that Charles would be executed). Highlight what you believe to be the turning point and write a short paragraph explaining your choice.

2 What do you think the image reveals about what the English people thought about the execution of Charles I? Do you think it is useful for telling us that Charles' execution was not supported?

A German copper engraving of the execution of Charles I.

8.5 The relationship between the Rump Parliament and Cromwell, 1649–53

REVISED

The **Rump Parliament** faced many **challenges**

Taxes	Lack of loyalty	Scotland and Ireland	Radical groups	No religious reforms
People were opposed to the high taxes needed to maintain the Rump's army. The fact that the Rump had taken England to war with the Dutch provoked further taxes. This was one of the reasons Parliament had originally opposed Charles	Some people thought that the Commonwealth lacked legitimacy and integrity, and as a result some refused to swear an **Oath of Loyalty**. Some people believed that members of the Rump did not have a right to sit in Parliament. The last elections had been in 1641 and many people wanted fresh elections	There was potential for Scotland to support Charles' son to come to the throne of England, and rebellions in Ireland were still threatening English rule	Some of the groups that had emerged during the Civil War continued to grow – this worried the Rump and the gentry	Many people had been opposed to Charles because they wanted a reformed Church of England – despite some feeble Presbyterian reforms, this did not happen. Therefore religious divisions remained

Cromwell won the **respect** of the Rump and of the army

Cromwell dealt effectively with each of the challenges:

Ireland

- Cromwell led an army into Ireland in 1649 to deal with the historic issues with rebellious Catholics; he crushed all resistance.
- Cromwell received a lot of criticism for his actions in Ireland – the towns of Drogheda and Wexford were besieged after they refused to surrender and 4600 men, women and children were killed (this broke the rules of war which stated they should only be sacked).

Scotland

- After the execution of Charles I, Scotland immediately declared Charles' son, Charles, King of England.
- Cromwell invaded in 1650 and was victorious at the **Battle of Dunbar**.
- In 1651, the Scots invaded England under the leadership of the future Charles II.

Key point

Oliver Cromwell took control from the Rump Parliament.

- The Scots were defeated again at Dunbar in 1651, which saw the end of the **Third Civil War** – following this, Charles II fled to France.

Radical groups

- In 1649, the leaders of the Levellers were arrested and imprisoned. The Levellers continued to rebel (for example, about having to fight in Ireland). By late 1649 the movement was no longer regarded as a threat – key leaders had been executed, and others had stopped rebelling.
- In the 1650s, the Quakers were growing in strength and important preachers were arrested or imprisoned temporarily. By 1660 the government had destroyed the movement.

Cromwell was not satisfied by the religious reforms of the Rump

- In February 1641, the Rump created a council of state with 41 members who were elected annually.
- The council put forward laws that the Rump would then discuss and vote on.
- Some of the measures they passed included:
  - March 1649: monarchy and the House of Lords officially abolished.
  - April 1649: sale of royal lands to help to pay wages owed to the army.
  - May 1649: England declared to be a Commonwealth ruled by Parliament.
  - September 1650: compulsory church attendance abolished.
  - December 1650: the use of English rather than Latin in courts of law.
  - October 1651: the Navigation Act introduced, which helped British merchants and increased their trade and also ensured Britain had plenty of experienced sailors in case of a war.
- Cromwell was unhappy that the Rump seemed to be passing laws to protect its own power, rather than laws for the good of the country.
- Cromwell had hoped for religious reforms so that people could practise freely. This aim was feared by much of the gentry.
- A deal was made with the Rump that it would dissolve Parliament and hold fresh elections so Cromwell and his troops could select people who were willing to introduce religious reforms.

Cromwell dissolved the Rump by force

On 20 April 1653, Cromwell stormed into Parliament and dissolved the Rump after it reneged on its deal to hold fresh elections, supervised by the army

Cromwell formed the **Nominated Assembly** but the religious extremists in this government proved to be too radical and had many disagreements with the moderates

On 12 December 1653, the moderates met (without the radicals) and voted to dissolve themselves

Cromwell personally took control and the period 1653–58 became known as the '**Protectorate**'; Cromwell was given the title 'lord protector'

Test yourself

1. List three weaknesses of the Rump Parliament.
2. How did Cromwell deal with the threat presented by the Levellers?
3. What was the Nominated Assembly?

Stretch and challenge

Look back to the challenges facing the Rump table – there is a blank box at the bottom of each column which you should use to rank the weaknesses to show which was the most threatening to the Rump (1 = most threatening).

Flow charts

Below is a blank flow diagram into which you must put four key events that led to Cromwell becoming lord protector. The first one has been completed for you. A list of events that you could have chosen can be found above.

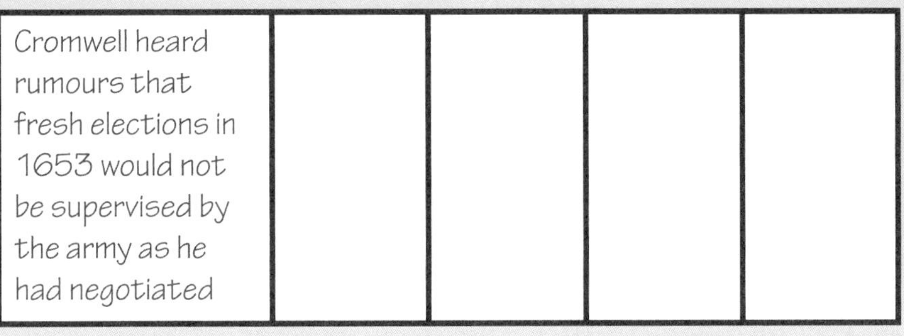

Cromwell heard rumours that fresh elections in 1653 would not be supervised by the army as he had negotiated				

Practice question

Explain why Cromwell dissolved the Rump.
(10 marks)

8.6 The relationship between the Rump Parliament and Cromwell, 1653–58

REVISED

Cromwell had conflicting **aims**

- Cromwell had two aims:
  - to build a 'godly' society based on religious freedom – this was supported by the army and Puritans
  - to heal the country after the Civil Wars and to establish order – this was supported by the gentry, but the gentry believed in a strong Church and were against the power of the army.
- When the Nominated Assembly (Barebones Parliament) was created, Cromwell hoped that its members, some of whom were chosen by Cromwell and others who were moderates, would achieve his aims.

Key point

Cromwell found it difficult to achieve his aims.

The **Instrument of Government** was a failed attempt to set up a new constitution

- The Barebones Parliament established after the Rump was dissolved did not last long as the moderates within it were alarmed at the ideas of the radicals.
- The **Instrument of Government** was then drawn up to try to make a workable constitution:
  - Cromwell was created head of state as lord protector – his power was limited as Parliament had to be called at least once every three years.
  - A standing army was established; this was paid for by regular taxes.
  - Parliament had to sit for at least five months before it could be dissolved.
  - It provided a religious settlement – Protestant Christianity would be the national faith, but religious freedom would be tolerated.
- MPs (such as Haselrig and Bradshaw) rejected the Instrument of Government, declaring it illegal as it gave too much power to Cromwell.
- Cromwell dissolved his First Protectorate Parliament on 22 January 1655 after repeated attempts from MPs to rewrite the Instrument of Government.

The rule of the **major-generals** was unpopular and short lived

Cromwell realised that the Royalist threat was not dead, so he used the **major-generals** to impose control.

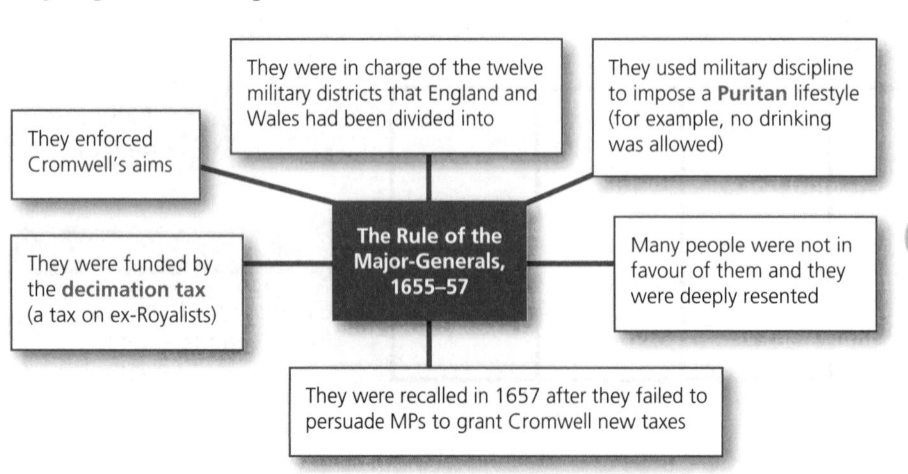

The Rule of the Major-Generals, 1655–57
They were in charge of the twelve military districts that England and Wales had been divided into
They used military discipline to impose a **Puritan** lifestyle (for example, no drinking was allowed)
They enforced Cromwell's aims
They were funded by the **decimation tax** (a tax on ex-Royalists)
Many people were not in favour of them and they were deeply resented
They were recalled in 1657 after they failed to persuade MPs to grant Cromwell new taxes

Test yourself

1. Who were the major-generals?
2. What was the decimation tax?
3. Why did Cromwell reject the Humble Petition and Advice?

Cromwell **refused** to take the position of monarch

- In 1657, a group of moderate MPs presented the **Humble Petition and Advice** to Cromwell.
- Had Cromwell accepted, he would have been made king (it included other terms to appease Parliament such as the reduction of the army to save money).
- Members of the army encouraged Cromwell to reject the proposal as it would go against his principles.
- On 8 May 1657, Cromwell rejected the Humble Petition and Advice, but accepted a revised version that allowed him to remain lord protector.
- When the **Second Protectorate** Parliament began in 1658, Cromwell was heavily criticised for assuming the role of king in all but name.
- The army were also unhappy and Cromwell had to dissolve Parliament once more.

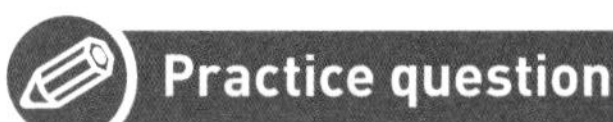

Practice question

Explain why there were challenges to Cromwell's new methods of rule.
(10 marks)

Stretch and challenge

1 'The failure of the Protectorate was inevitable.' How far do you agree with this statement? Write an extended paragraph explaining your views. You may want to consider the following:
- Was the Protectorate inherently weak?
- Did Oliver Cromwell set the Protectorate up to fail?

2 Read Source H. How useful is this source for telling us about the threats facing Cromwell's Protectorate?

SOURCE H *An extract from a document appointing Colonel William Boteler as a major-general.*

... and do by these presents give full power and authority unto you to take into your charge, and to train, exercise, command, and keep in good discipline the said Militia Forces, and such others, as shall be raised or assigned to you within the said Counties; And also to conduct and lead them against all and singular enemies, rebels, traitors, and other offenders and their adherents against Us, and this Commonwealth. And with the said traitors, enemies, and rebels to fight, and them to invade, resist, repress and subdue, slay, kill and put to execution of death by all ways and means according to your good discretion.

Developing the detail

Below you can find a summary of the Protectorate under Oliver Cromwell. Annotate the paragraph to add supporting evidence. If you get stuck, try to find evidence for the sections of text that are underlined.

Cromwell wanted change in England – he did not agree with the way in which the Rump Parliament had ruled. Cromwell made some changes so that England was more religious. He also changed the way in which parts of England were controlled. During his term as lord protector, Cromwell faced some challenges.

Support or challenge?

'The Barebones Parliament was doomed to fail.' How far do you agree with this statement?

Here are a series of statements which you could use to answer the question above. Using your own knowledge, and the information on these two pages, decide if each factor 'agrees' or 'disagrees' with the stated view. As an additional challenge you might want to consider if it could be argued that any factors do both.

Actions/events in the lead-up to the dissolution of the Barebones Parliament:

- Cromwell was created head of state as lord protector.
- Radicals voiced ideas which the moderates disagreed with.
- Cromwell's power was limited by the Instrument of Government.
- There were deep divisions within the Barebones Parliament.
- Cromwell tried to get MPs to agree by presenting a different version of the Instrument of Government.
- The Instrument of Government presented a religious settlement.

8.7 Attempts to reach a settlement, September 1658–April 1660, and Restoration

REVISED

Richard Cromwell's failure left the country in an unstable position

- Cromwell nominated his son, Richard, to take over as lord protector.
- Richard gave up his leadership in 1659 for many reasons:
  - he did not have a strong enough relationship with the **army** to control it
  - he had grown up as a member of the **gentry** and so he did not appeal to people in the same way his father had done
  - he faced pressure from army officers and republican **MPs** who wanted England to be run according to their individual aims.
- People then became worried about the stability of the country as power shifted between the army and the Rump Parliament.
- Some began to look to the restoration of the monarchy as a solution to the country's instability.

Key point

The return of a monarch, with few limits on his power, was very popular in 1660 in Britain.

There was popular support for the return of a king

- Despite everything that had happened, the restoration of the monarchy was a popular move for several reasons:
  - the unpopularity of the **regicide**
  - the desire for stability
  - the unpopularity of the republic
  - the fear of radical groups
  - the way in which Charles II had waited and that he offered no reprisals.

General Monck insisted the old MPs who supported Charles were readmitted, and advised Charles II.

Charles' proposed Declaration of Breda calmed fears of a return of an absolutist monarchy

- On 4 April 1660, Charles presented the **Declaration of Breda** as a solution to the country's problems.
- Charles' proposal was officially accepted by MPs on 2 May 1660 but some adaptions were made in the final **Restoration Settlement** to give Parliament more powers.
- There were some fears that the return of a king would be accompanied by absolutism but Charles promised to:
  - share power with Parliament
  - maintain religious freedom
  - pardon all regicides
  - maintain stability.

The monarchy lost some power in the Restoration Settlement

- In 1641, Charles I's power had been limited by the Grand Remonstrance and some of these limitations remained in force.
- England under Charles II was very different to what it had been under his father – although many powers were restored, the king could no longer rule without Parliament.

Test yourself

1. List three reasons for people supporting the return of a king.
2. What was the Declaration of Breda?
3. List two terms of the Restoration Settlement that had not been part of the Grand Remonstrance.

Features of the Restoration Settlement that were not part of the Grand Remonstrance	Features of the Restoration settlement that *had* been part of the Grand Remonstrance
• King could appoint ministers and advisers • King was the sole commander of the army and navy • King was not forced to hold new elections • Parliament granted the king the right to raise tonnage and poundage • King was allowed to raise revenue from Crown lands • A strict approach to religion was taken – the 'Clarendon Codes' saw that Puritanism was discouraged and that radical sects were banned • Book of Common Prayer was reintroduced • Culture was embraced and the Royal Society was created	• Special courts were abolished • Parliament had to be called once every three years • The king had to have Parliamentary approval before raising a tax • Ship money remained illegal

Turning assertion into argument

The statements below are **assertions** (general points that are unfocused): they all relate to the exam-style question. You task is to turn each assertion into an **argument** (a response which is specific to the question and has a clear focus). You should do this by adding a second sentence which adds more detail to the assertion so that it becomes focused and has more substance.

Explain why the monarchy was restored. **(10 marks)**

People were happy with instability, for example ...

Many people never agreed with the execution of Charles, some thought ...

The Protectorate showed signs of weakness such as ...

Stretch and challenge

Refresh your understanding of the Grand Remonstrance. Once you have done this, you should consider how similar the monarchy was in 1660 to what it had been at the start of Charles' reign. Create a continuum with 'very similar' and 'very different' at each end, and try to add ten examples to your continuum.

Practice question

Study Sources I–K. 'The Protectorate failed because there was popular support for the return of a king.' How far do Sources I–K convince you that this statement is correct? Use the sources and your knowledge to explain your answer. (20 marks)

SOURCE I *John Lilburne, who was one of the leaders of the Levellers, wrote a pamphlet attacking the execution of Charles I (1649).*

I refused to be one of his [Charles I's] judges ... they were no better than murderers in taking away the King's life even though he was guilty of the crimes he was charged with ... it is murder because it was done by a hand that had no authority to do it.

SOURCE J *The entry of Charles II of England into London on 29 May 1660. Coloured engraving after a contemporary Dutch engraving.*

SOURCE K *An extract from the Declaration of Breda, 1860.*

He will, in compassion to us and our subjects, after so long misery and sufferings, remit and put us into a quiet and peaceable possession of that our right, with as little blood and damage to our people as is possible; nor do we desire more to enjoy what is ours, than that all our subjects may enjoy what by law is theirs, by a full and entire administration of justice throughout the land, and by extending our mercy where it is wanted and deserved.

9 The English Reformation c.1520–c.1550

9.1 The role and importance of the Church in the sixteenth century

REVISED

The **Church** was an incredibly **powerful** organisation that fulfilled a huge range of **roles** in society

- The **Church** was an incredibly powerful institution which dominated life in England. In 1520, the Church was making approximately £400,000 annually, compared to £40,000 a year being earned by the Crown.
- There were 45,000 clergy in England at this time, out of a population of around two and a half million. They were led by the Pope in Rome, and then by a hierarchy of cardinals, archbishops and bishops.
- At this time, the King of England did not have direct control over the Church.
- Many churchmen were very influential members of government. For example, all bishops and archbishops sat in the House of Lords.
- The Church was extremely important in maintaining the king's power, as it supported the idea of the **Great Chain of Being** – the idea that the monarch had been placed on the throne by God.

Key point

The Catholic Church dominated the medieval world – its power and wealth exceeded that of the monarch.

The **Church** had a huge amount of power because it was incredibly **wealthy**

- Worshippers in the Catholic Church wanted to ensure they went to **Heaven** after death, rather than **Hell**. This could be achieved, it was believed, by making very generous donations to the Church either in life or in your will. **Indulgences** (paying for people to pray for you) were also common.
- Parishioners also had to pay a tax to the Church known as a **tithe**.
- The Church was an extraordinarily wealthy body, able to pay for lavish churches and monasteries: most medieval churches were built of stone and are still standing, whereas the wooden houses near them are long gone.
- The Church also gave a great deal of money to the poor and needy.

People were **devoted** to their religion and particularly to their **local church**

- Most of the English population were rural **peasants** who would never leave the vicinity of their village. Their connection to the rest of the world came through their parish priest, who was usually a local man who had been educated while being ordained.
- Priests were tasked with leading their congregation in prayer and in teaching the lessons of the Bible. In the Catholic Church, the Bible was written, read and spoken in Latin, so it was the priest who needed to explain the text.
- There were many elements of Catholic faith, therefore, which revolved around the priest giving religion to people through ceremony and ritual, such as the **Eucharist**, where worshippers ceremonially drink wine and eat bread which represents the blood and body of Christ.
- Most importantly, religion made a generally very difficult life for the peasants considerably more bearable – there were various holy days to celebrate, and it gave people the promise of seeing loved ones again in Heaven and spending eternity in bliss.

Test yourself

1. What was the annual income of the English Church in the early sixteenth century?
2. Into what did Catholics believe the afterlife was divided?
3. What was the name of the idea that meant the king was 'meant' to be on the throne?

People were also deeply **superstitious**, and had many **rituals** and **beliefs**

- The Catholic afterlife was split into three: Heaven, Hell and **Purgatory**, which lay in between the two. Many Catholics believed that prayer and a sinless life would result in a shorter stay in Purgatory.
- Communities lavished a great deal of their wealth, devotion and energy on ensuring that their church was well decorated, maintained and furnished. It would always be the most dominant building in the local area.
- There were a huge number of festivals, **holy days** (where we get the word 'holiday') and traditions which people enjoyed and found a great comfort. A lot of these traditions were ancient and really important to ordinary peasants.
- The English peasantry understood their world in terms of God rather than science. If they had a bad harvest, if someone was ill or if they had a run of bad luck, it was down to God's will.

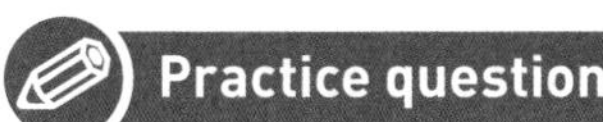

Practice question

Explain how important the Church was to the people of England in the early sixteenth century. (10 marks)

Stretch and challenge

It is really important to understand the nature of everything that the Church did for people. Create a mind map which shows all of the elements of the people and the Church.

Considering usefulness

Below is a source on church life in sixteenth-century England. Look at the source, and consider how useful it is based on the criteria of: content, provenance and context. Rate each one for usefulness out of 10 and then explain why you think this source is useful to a historian or not.

SOURCE A *From Ethan H. Shagan,* Popular Politics and the English Reformation, *2003.*

On Palm Sunday, ... , John Vasye, parson of Lytchett Maltravers in Dorset, was listening to confessions when a number of parishioners burst in, threw Vesye out of the church, and took from him both his chalice and his keys. Afterwards the parishioners, 'without authority ... assigned another priest to sing in the same church, without license [or permission of the local squire]'.

Content	Provenance	Context

Complete the paragraph

Below are a sample exam-style question and a paragraph written in answer to this question. The paragraph contains a point and specific examples, but lacks a concluding explanatory link back to the question. Complete the paragraph adding this link in the space provided.

Explain why the Church was such an important part of people's lives in the early sixteenth century. (10 marks)

Because people were not very educated, and because they had no other source of support, most peasants relied on the Church for many things. For example, if they were unwell they would visit ...

9.2 Critics of the Church

REVISED

Lollards and Humanists both argued for a Bible in English

- The **Lollards** were a group of fourteenth-century reformers who believed that the priesthood was not necessary, and that people should read the Bible in English.
- If people were discovered believing in these ideas, they would be tried for **heresy** – 73 such people were executed under King Henry VII between 1485 and 1509.
- In the late fifteenth century, a similar group called the **Humanists** emerged from the beginning of the **Renaissance**.
- They also argued that the Bible should be in English to allow more people to have 'direct' access to God, so that Christianity could be about studying the word of God rather than ceremony.

Key point

Although the majority of people still supported the Church, there were growing calls for reform in the 1530s.

Luther and Zwingli's criticisms of the Church sparked the Reformation

- Luther and Zwingli were two Church reformers from central Europe, known as Protestants. They both had a great deal of complaints about Catholicism and called for many reforms:
  - they wanted the Bible in the language of the people
  - they wanted people to pray only to God, not to saints
  - they believed that Purgatory did not exist.
- Luther also criticised the Church for practices such as the selling of indulgences and relics by priests and other churchmen for personal wealth.
- This sense of corruption and misuse of power was notable, and these arguments started to spread across Europe, despite the danger that criticising the Church could put people in.

The Reformation developed in England from both outside and inside the Church

- In England, there was a stronger uptake of Protestant ideas than on the Continent. Not just London, but larger towns like Norwich and Bristol started to see people preaching Protestant views. The criticisms came from two sources:
  - **Laymen** (people who were not churchmen) criticised the amount of land, wealth and power of the Church. One of the most notable lay reformers was Simon Fish, who publicised a widely read pamphlet.
  - **Clerical** (within the **clergy**) criticism was somewhat different, aimed more at the spiritual problems in Catholicism: William Tynedale was a priest who made the demand that priests be trained and educated properly.
- Cambridge became the centre of the development of Protestant ideas. Men such as Miles Coverdale, Hugh Latimer and Thomas Cranmer developed the idea of **Evangelism**. The authorities kept a close eye on them.

There were other **criticisms** of the Church, and some people who tried to **defend** it

- There further criticisms which covered a range of other issues: Thomas Wolsey was the son of a butcher from Ipswich, but thanks to the Church hierarchy he was able to become one of the most powerful people in England and the man who ran the country for Henry VIII.
- **Pluralism** was the practice of people holding more than one office – it meant that someone like Wolsey was able to hold several titles and positions at once and therefore earn a huge amount of money and influence.
- There was also a serious concern about the morals of the Church – priests were supposed to be **celibate** (abstain from sexual relations) but, for example, in London it was discovered that there was a brothel set up for priests.
- In response, Wolsey had theologians write books and speak out in defence of Catholicism, and he also had the works of Luther burned in public. Another person defending Catholicism was Thomas More, who wrote a response to Simon Fish's work, and who later replaced Wolsey as chancellor.

Test yourself

1. Who were the first notable critics of the Catholic Church?
2. What did Luther and other Protestants want to make the main aspect of belief?
3. Who was the Englishman who tried to defend the Church?

Considering usefulness

Below is a source on the Christian faith from 1520. Look at the source, and consider how useful it is based on the criteria of: content, provenance and context. Rate each one for usefulness out of 10 and then explain why you think this source is useful to a historian or not.

SOURCE B *Martin Luther, writing about his views on Christian faith, 1520.*

One man builds a chapel, another donates this, still another one that. However, they refuse to face the true issue, that is, they will not give their inmost self to God and thus become his kingdom. They perform many outward works which glitter very nicely, but inwardly they remain full of malice, anger, hatred, pride, impatience, unchastity, etc. It is against them that Christ spoke when he was asked when the kingdom of God was coming, 'The kingdom of God does not come with outward signs or appearances; for behold, the kingdom of God is within you'.

Content	Provenance	Context

Practice question

Explain the main criticisms of the Catholic Church as made by Protestants. (10 marks)

Stretch and challenge

Create a diagram which shows the aspects of the Catholic Church which the Protestants disliked, and the reasons for their views.

9.3 Henry VIII breaks with Rome

REVISED

Henry VIII **unsuccessfully** attempted to persuade the Pope to grant him a **divorce**

- The most important role for a medieval monarch was to secure their **succession** by producing a legitimate male heir. The 'King's Great Problem' for Henry VIII was that by 1529, he had been married to Catherine of Aragon for twenty years and still did not have a son.
- Henry's solution to this problem was to seek a new wife. His initial hope was that he could seek an **annulment** (legally stating that a marriage is 'null and void') because previously Catherine was married to Henry's brother, Arthur.
- Henry had to appeal directly to Pope Clement VIII, as divorce was not (and still is not) permitted in the Catholic Church. Catherine was devastated and fought against it, but to no avail.
- The problem for Henry was that Clement needed the support of the Spanish, and the Spanish king was Catherine's cousin. As such, he was very unlikely to grant Henry's wish. Henry was furious, and his anger led to the imprisonment of Wolsey, who died in prison.

Key point

To secure his divorce, Henry VIII took control of the Church of England, and with the influence of Cromwell and Anne Boleyn, carried out reforms.

Thomas **Cromwell** encouraged Henry to **break with Rome** in 1532

- Another reason why Wolsey fell was that he became an enemy of Anne Boleyn and her **faction** at **court**. Henry had fallen in love with Boleyn, possibly as a result of her seducing him. She influenced him to become more anti-clerical in his views.
- As a result, Wolsey's successor as Henry's chief minister, Thomas Cromwell, guided the king to accuse the clergy of **Praemunire**, which made it treasonous to obey the Pope over the king.
- Anne Boleyn fell pregnant, so Cromwell and his assistant, Audley, drafted laws which divorced Henry from Catherine, and made their recent secret marriage legal.
- Despite the threat of **excommunication**, Henry and his advisers pushed ahead to sever links with Rome, just in case his new child was declared **illegitimate** (born outside marriage).

Henry became Supreme Head of the Church, in part due to the influence of Cromwell and **Anne Boleyn**

- In 1534, Henry was declared **Supreme Head of the Church**. This allowed him to change the Church to reflect the anti-clerical and reformist views of Anne Boleyn and Cromwell.
- It is uncertain if Henry himself truly agreed with the reforms, or if he just enjoyed having the power and wealth of the Church at his disposal.
- It seems unlikely that Henry had truly changed his mind fully from 1521, when he had written a tract attacking the critics of the Catholic Church.
- In reality, Henry had one desire – a legitimate son – and this seemed like the only way to achieve it. At no point while he was king did he ever accept that things would not go his way, and people such as Wolsey, Cromwell and even Anne Boleyn paid with their lives when they failed him.

Test yourself

1 How did Henry want his marriage to Catherine to be ended?
2 What was Praemunire?
3 What title did King Henry take in 1534?

Stretch and challenge

There are a lot of notable figures in this section. Create a list of all the main people involved, and for each summarise their role in the break with Rome in a sentence.

There was only **minimal opposition** to the changes to the Church by 1535

- There was very little opposition to the break with Rome among the peasantry, largely because (at least at first) it had very little effect on their lives or worship.
- At court there was some opposition from nobles who sympathised with the former queen.
- Cromwell discovered that Bishop John Fisher had been secretly in contact with the **Holy Roman Emperor** Charles V, to try to get his help in overthrowing Henry. Thomas More publicly refused to take the **Oath of Succession**. Both were beheaded.
- Elizabeth Barton was a nun who gained a following as an outspoken critic of the annulment and of Henry's supremacy. She was eventually arrested and she and five supporters were executed. There were many monks and nuns who did the same and suffered the same fate.

Which is best?

Below are two examples of answers to a 10-mark question for this paper. Read both, compare to the mark scheme on pages 180–2 and give both a mark out of 10. On a separate piece of paper, explain why the one you have chosen is best.

Explain why Henry chose to break with Rome in 1534. **(10 marks)**

a) *Henry really wanted to have a son. This was so that when he died, he would have a son to take over from him. To do this, he needed a divorce from his wife who was now too old to have children, so he could marry Anne Boleyn. The Pope would not give him a divorce so he decided to break with Rome, which would mean that he would have to take charge. Once he was in charge, he was able to give himself a divorce.*

b) *By 1529, Henry VIII was very concerned about his succession. Catherine of Aragon had not produced a son, while at the same time, Henry had fallen in love with the much younger Anne Boleyn. Henry attempted to persuade Pope Clement VII to grant him an annulment, but was unsuccessful. He was persuaded by the Protestant-leaning Anne, and his chief minister Thomas Cromwell, to break the Church away from Rome. This process was given added urgency when Anne fell pregnant in 1533.*

Practice question

Study Sources C–E. 'There was a great deal of resistance to the idea of Henry VIII becoming Head of the Church.' How far do Sources C–E convince you that this statement is correct? Use the sources and your knowledge to explain your answer. (20 marks)

SOURCE C *Thomas More, expressing his sentiments about the Oath of Succession in 1534.*

But as for myself in good faith my conscience so moved me in the matter, that though I would not deny to swear to the succession, yet unto the oath that there was offered me I could not swear, without condemning my soul to perpetual damnation.

SOURCE D *Thomas Cranmer's orders for preaching, 1534.*

Neither with nor against purgatory, honouring of saints, that priests may have wives; that faith only justified; to go on pilgrimages, to forge miracles ... considering that thereupon no edification [improvement] can ensue in the people, but rather occasions of talk and rumour, to their great hurt and damage.

SOURCE E *A scathing letter from Cromwell to Michael Throgmorton, who had shown some loyalty to Reginald Pole. Cromwell threatens both Throgmorton and his servant with death, 1537.*

I thought that the singular goodness of the kings highness showed unto you, and the great and singular clemency showed to that detestable traitor your master, in promising him not only forgiveness but also forgetting of his most shameful ingratitude, unnaturalness, conspiracy against his honour, of whom he hath received no more.

9.4 The suppression of the monasteries

REVISED

Henry VIII made significant **changes** to the **Church** between 1534 and 1535

- Henry VIII and Thomas Cromwell took their roles as leaders of the English Church very seriously – we know that Henry VIII was deeply religious, and it is likely that Cromwell was too.
- Cromwell created a series of laws to take legal and spiritual control of the new English Church:
  - the **Treason Act** made it illegal to speak out against the king or queen
  - the bishops could be given new laws and made to carry them out
  - monastic orders had to swear a new **Oath of Allegiance**.
- Cromwell (in his new role of **Vicegerent**) set about reforming Church taxes by evaluating the wealth of the entire English Church with a new commission called **Valor Ecclesiasticus**.
- Many historians have suggested that this was simply an excuse to seize the wealth of the Church. Others argue that although that was a strong motivation, both Henry and Cromwell did seem to believe in the necessity of reform.

Key point

The Dissolution of the Monasteries was carried out quickly and easily by Cromwell and Henry VIII.

The **Visitations** were an evaluation of the wealth of every monastery in the country

- Cromwell appointed six commissioners to examine every monastery in England. These men had the task of accounting for the value and worth of everything within a given monastery, and reporting back to Cromwell. It was an enormous task.
- The commissioners' aim was to consider whether each monastery was doing its job properly: in other words, were the monks sufficiently pious and was the monastery charitable?
- The report was extremely critical of the monasteries. They said that there was evidence of laziness, ungodliness and even sexual corruption. They also criticised many churches for encouraging **superstition**.
- The report did have its positive elements, praising a monastery in Durham, but it seems fairly clear that from the beginning the commissioners had been instructed to find faults where possible.

Practice question

Explain why the Dissolution of the Monasteries had such a negative impact on the English peasantry. (10 marks)

Stretch and challenge

Create a set of cards for the different reasons Henry chose to dissolve the monasteries. Use these as templates to help you with exemplar questions.

The results of the Visitations led to the **Dissolution of the Monasteries**

- The fundamental principle that was allowing Henry and Cromwell to attack (and ultimately destroy) the monasteries was the fact that Protestant and reformist beliefs did not allow for the existence of Purgatory. Since monasteries existed to allow monks to pray for the souls of people in Purgatory, it meant that Protestants and reformists did not believe in the need for monasteries.
- Smaller monasteries were targeted first with the **Dissolution of the Lesser Monasteries Act** (1536), which dissolved 243 out of 419 monasteries that were deemed not to be doing a good job. All the wealth went to the Crown.
- Unlike the break with Rome, this directly affected ordinary people and was deeply unpopular, leading in part to the **Pilgrimage of Grace** (see page 160). Visitations then started to take in the larger monasteries.

Test yourself

1. What was the name of the commission that evaluated the wealth of the English Church?
2. What kind of monasteries were targeted first?
3. What were those who voluntarily surrendered really looking for?

- Some **abbots** offered to voluntarily 'surrender' their monasteries in exchange for their monks and nuns being offered generous pensions.
- In 1539, the **second Dissolution Act** was passed and within a year all of the small monasteries were closed.
- This was followed by the closure of the friaries. The majority of the friars were given permission to become **secular** (church) priests instead.

The dissolution saw the **destruction** of many buildings and had a huge impact on the **peasantry**

- The biggest indication that the dissolution was not only spiritually motivated is the fact that everything that was of any value was stripped from the monasteries: lead from the roofs, anything inside which could be sold, even the buildings themselves were often sold off and used for other things.
- There was no concern for the intrinsic value of what was taken: ancient relics and precious items were melted down for the raw materials (gold, silver, and so on); the libraries of the monasteries were destroyed, losing thousands of precious books.
- The monasteries had been the centre of their communities: they provided housing, education and poor relief, and looked after roads and their local area. They were also big customers for fisheries and farmers, and employed servants, craftsmen and labourers.
- There were a number of actions to save buildings: wealthy people bought monastic buildings and donated them to the community. But many members of the gentry were able to buy land at much lower than market value, for their own profit.

Flow chart

Below is a blank flow diagram into which you must put the five key events involved in the Dissolution of the Monasteries. The first one has been completed for you. A list of events that you could have chosen can be found opposite.

The break with Rome

Which is best?

Below are two examples of a paragraph that might be written to answer part of a 10-mark question for this paper. Read both, compare to the mark scheme (pages 180–2) and give both a mark out of 10. Underneath, explain why the one you have chosen is best.

Explain the impact of visitations on the monasteries in England. **(10 marks)**

a) *The Visitations were a way for the Crown to evaluate what wealth the Church had so that they could take it for themselves. King Henry VIII wanted to take all of the wealth for himself, and he needed to know how much each monastery was worth. This was also because he was a Protestant who did not believe in monasteries.*	**b)** *Thomas Cromwell began a series of Visitations with a small team of men in order to effectively audit the monasteries with a view to seize the money, goods and lands of the Church for the Crown. This was devastating to local communities as they had relied for centuries on the monasteries to provide aid for the poor, education and care for the sick. Without the monasteries, all of these things were taken away.*

9.5 Responses to the Dissolution of the Monasteries

REVISED

The **Act of Ten Articles** led to the **Lincolnshire Rising**, which was put down with the threat of execution

- As we have seen, most people were not affected by the break with Rome. In contrast, the destruction of the smaller local monasteries led to an outpouring of grief and rage that led to the greatest rebellion of the entire Tudor dynasty.
- Following the Dissolution of the Monasteries, a group of senior, radical bishops (**Convocation**), met to agree on the fundamental beliefs of the Church. These were published as the **Ten Articles**, and banned the use of images, the cult of saints and chantries.
- The **Lincolnshire Rising**: on 2 October 1536, the people of Louth found that a registrar was on his way to examine their church. The spire was only twenty years old and rumours had spread that Louth would lose money, possessions and even the church.

Key point

The Pilgrimage of Grace was a large protest against Church reform, but Henry VIII was never really threatened, and dealt with the leaders of the rebellion brutally.

- This led 3000 men to gather to march on Lincoln. They wanted the church to be left as it was. The local noble, Lord Hussey, fled.
- Henry VIII sent the Duke of Suffolk to supress the rising, which he did by threatening that every rebel who did not stand down would be charged with treason and executed.
- When the rebels heard this, the uprising quickly came to an end.

The **Pilgrimage of Grace** involved nearly 40,000 people

- Just a few days after Lincolnshire, a much bigger rising took place that spread across much of the north of England, from Northumberland to Cheshire.
- The rebels had two key concerns:

The rebels' two key concerns

Economic problems: the fundamental problem in the north of England was economic. **Enclosure** was an issue that was starting to affect a lot of peasants across the region, and the closure of the monasteries was only going to make this worse

Changes to the Church: people were deeply upset at the idea of the Church's wealth (which was really wealth that had been donated by the people) being taken by the Crown

- Additionally, rumours spread about what Henry was intending to do, such as increasing taxes and perhaps even destroying churches altogether.

Robert Aske was **betrayed** by Henry and **executed**

- The rebels quickly came under the leadership of a lawyer named Robert Aske. Unlike a lot of rebel leaders, Aske was organised, and demanded organisation from the rebels, making them swear oaths to encourage orderly and reasonable behaviour.

On 16 October 1536, 10,000 rebels marched on York. They issued a proclamation of their peaceful intentions. Hull fell three days later.

The rebels restored abbeys as they marched.

By late October, the rebellion involved nine well-armed companies, totalling 30,000 men

→ Henry and Cromwell were slow to respond. Eventually a delegate named Bowes was sent to meet Henry at Windsor, where Henry agreed to pardon all but ten of the leaders and to listen to the peasants' grievances

→ The rebels' demands, the **Pontefract Articles**, were then drawn up.

Henry invited Aske to spend Christmas in London, after promising he would air the Articles in Parliament. Aske then told a gathering of 3000 rebels that Henry could be trusted and that they should disband

→ Henry's offer to listen to the rebels' demands was a lie. He was playing for time to gather his forces and calm the rebels. He had 216 rebels arrested, including Aske, who was hanged, drawn and quartered in front of hundreds of his former supporters in York in July 1537

No monasteries survived in England after 1558

- There were sixteen major rebellions against Tudor monarchs, and the Pilgrimage of Grace was certainly the largest. Despite this, it had no impact on delaying the **Reformation** in England and in fact may have encouraged it.
- Several monks and nuns were hanged for their part in the Pilgrimage of Grace. The abbots of Colchester, Reading and Glastonbury were **hanged, drawn and quartered** for their refusal to voluntarily surrender their abbeys.
- This harsh treatment, plus that of Aske, led to relatively little in the way of resistance from this point onwards. Tudor propaganda in turn made it hard to tell whether people agreed or were just too scared to disagree.
- Only one monastic order survived the dissolution in England: the Dartford Priory in Kent. Two other orders, the Carthusian monks and the Bridgettine nuns, chose **exile** instead.

Test yourself

1. Where did the Lincolnshire Rising begin?
2. List two concerns of the rebels who joined the Pilgrimage of Grace.
3. Who was the leader of the Pilgrimage of Grace?

Developing the detail

Below are a sample exam-style question and a paragraph written in answer to this question. The paragraph contains a limited amount of detail. Annotate the paragraph to add additional detail to the answer.

Explain why the Pilgrimage of Grace took place. **(10 marks)**

After a previous uprising, the Pilgrimage of Grace began in the summer of 1536. The people of northern England had some economic concerns, but the main thing that they were concerned about was the changes that were being made to the Church. The rebels hoped that by marching through the north, they would make the king reconsider what he was doing, particularly to the monasteries.

Practice question

Study Sources F–H. 'The Pilgrimage of Grace was mainly a response to King Henry's desire to seize control of the English Church.' How far do Sources F–H convince you that this statement is correct? Use the sources and your knowledge to explain your answer. (20 marks)

SOURCE F *Robert Aske, in a speech about the Pilgrimage of Grace delivered in York, October 1536.*

We have taken [this pilgrimage] for the preservation of Christ's church, of this realm of England, the king our sovereign lord, the nobility and commons of the same ... the monasteries ... in the north parts [they] gave great alms to poor men and laudably served God ... and therefore the suppression of the monasteries diminishes the service of Almighty God.

SOURCE G *The indictment of John Bulmer, April 1537.*

John Bulmer ... with other traitors, at Sherburn, Yorkshire, conspire to deprive the king of his title of Supreme Head of the English Church, and to compel him to hold a certain Parliament and Convocation of the clergy of the realm, and did commit diverse insurrections ... at Pontefract, diverse days and times before the said 10th of October.

SOURCE H *A letter from Henry VIII to the Earl of Derby, October 1536.*

We lately commanded you to make ready your forces and go to the earl of Shrewsbury, our lieutenant to suppress the rebellion in the North; but having since heard of an insurrection attempted about the abbey of Salley in Lancashire, where the abbot and monks have been restored by the traitors, we now desire you immediately to repress it, to apprehend the captains and either have them immediately executed as traitors or sent up to us. We leave it, however, to your discretion to go elsewhere in case of greater emergency. You are to take the said abbot and monks forth with violence and have them hanged without delay in their monks' apparel, and see that no town or village begin to assemble.

9.6 Reforming the churches

REVISED

Henry's Church **reforms** became more **moderate** once Anne Boleyn's influence was removed

- The principal forces persuading Henry to take a strongly Protestant line were Anne Boleyn and Thomas Cromwell. When Anne was executed (falling foul of Henry's temper) this took away one of those voices and reform slowed.
- The **Act of Ten Articles** had been highly reformist, but its replacement, the **Act of Six Articles** was much more moderate in character, guaranteeing several things like private masses, which reformers had campaigned against.
- Cromwell was the most powerful reformer at court, but without his ally, Anne Boleyn, he was vulnerable, and he was brought down and executed by those people who persuaded Henry to go back to a more moderate line.
- Although the English Bible was not withdrawn, Henry did ban all peasants and all women below the gentry from reading it. He did not go all the way back to Catholicism, however, and allowed reformers like Thomas Cranmer to stay at court.

Key point

After initial reforms, Henry favourited moderate action for the rest of his reign, but Edward VI passed more radical reforms.

Under **Edward VI**, reform came back and was even stronger

- With the death of Henry VIII in 1547, his nine-year-old son, Edward VI, became king. Until he was an adult, a **minority council** was led by Edward's uncle, the Duke of Somerset. Most were committed Protestants, and they brought in several further Protestant changes, despite their lack of support outside London.
- The **Chantries Act** of 1547 closed down 2347 chantries across the kingdom. These were places of education and support, as well as worship.
- The **Royal Proclamations** of 1548 replaced the Act of Six Articles, and ordered the removal of altars, icons and images from churches; it also ended a wide range of holy days.
- In 1549, a new **Book of Common Prayer** was issued. It was in English, not Latin, and although it was relatively moderate in its character, it was still widely unpopular and in part led to the **Western Rebellion**.
- The rebellion was unsuccessful, but it did lead to Somerset's fall.
- His replacement was the Duke of Northumberland, who pushed England even further towards Protestantism with an even more radical Prayer Book in 1552, and the **Second Act of Uniformity**, which made attendance at church on Sunday compulsory.

Test yourself

1 The Act of Ten Articles was replaced by what?
2 Which book helped cause the Western Rebellion?
3 What was the fine for the failure to use an English Bible?

The **threat** of punishment and the use of **propaganda** were used to successfully pass the reforms

- These reforms were enforced firmly. It is important to remember that everyone at this time was religious, and by and large was willing to die for their beliefs.
- Under Henry VIII, the Treason Act gave the Crown wide-ranging powers to prosecute **heretics**. It also put a great deal of pressure on the clergy to report anyone who spoke out against the Reformation.
- During Edward VI's reign there was a relatively moderate approach taken under the leadership of Somerset. Under Northumberland, however, the 1552 Act of Uniformity made the failure to use the new Prayer Book heresy, which was punishable by death.
- Finally, propaganda had a big impact on many people: proclamations, sermons, books and speeches were all used to persuade the people that the Reformation was the right thing for them.

Further reforms were **visible** within the churches, but there were no further major **rebellions**

- The early changes to the Church had little impact on ordinary people. Bigger effects took place from 1538 onwards.
- One example was that candles from anywhere in a church, other than on the altar, had to be extinguished. This was extremely significant as it was a very visual sign of change at a time when few people could read.
- This was followed by the removal of icons, paintings, stained glass and other expensive items.
- In many more remote areas, churches attempted to continue with as much Catholic practice as they could get away with, although the imposition of a £2 fine for not using English Bibles encouraged their uptake.
- The Crown was now taking most of the income that once went to the Church, the difference being that now it very, very rarely ended up in the hands of the people. Ultimately though, the Reformation met little serious resistance.

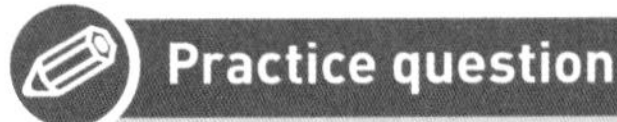

Practice question

Explain how Protestant reforms changed the English Church under the rule of Edward VI.

(10 marks)

Spot the mistake

Below are a sample exam-style question and a paragraph written in answer to this question. Why does this paragraph not get into Level 5? Once you have identified the mistake, rewrite the paragraph so that it displays the qualities of Level 5. The mark scheme on pages 180–2 will help you.

Explain how England became more Protestant under Edward VI. (10 marks)

Because Edward VI was a minor, the Duke of Somerset led a minority council which took control of the country. He was a Protestant, so he brought in a new English Bible in 1549, and then ordered the dissolution of the friaries.

Complete the mind map

Use the information on these two pages to complete to the mind map below.

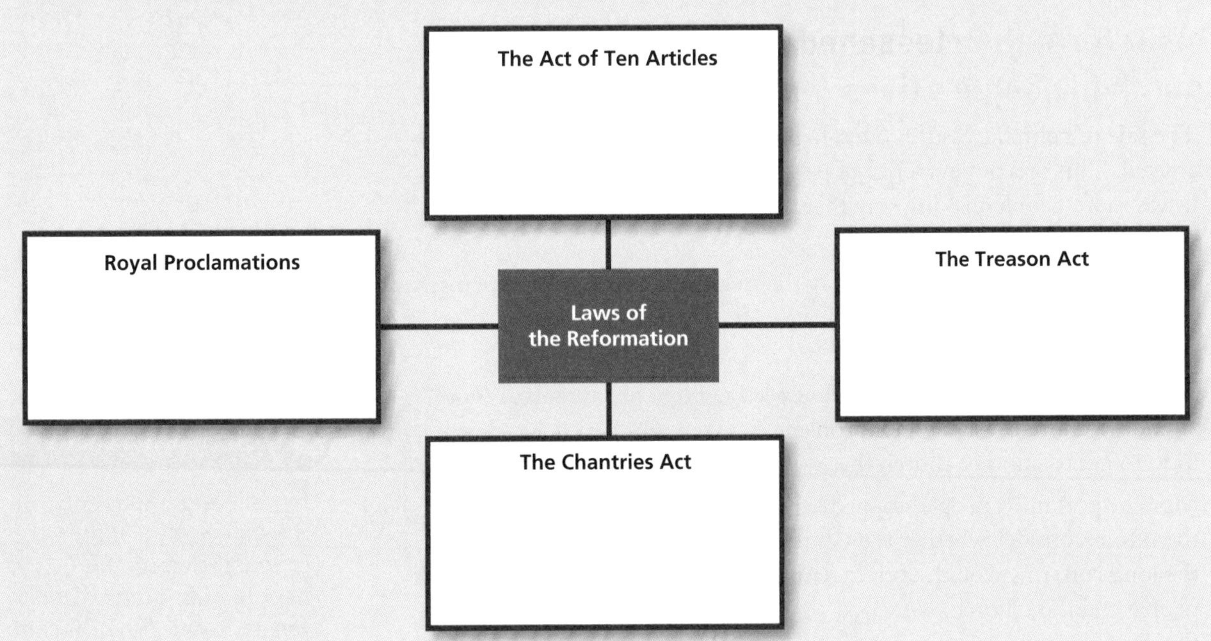

9.7 Reaction of the people to the Reformation

REVISED

The **Prayer Book Rising** was a demonstration of people's anger against the Reformation

- The introduction of the new Prayer Book in 1549 caused a great deal of resentment across the country. In the south-west, it coincided with the introduction of a **sheep tax** which severely affected many peasants and landowners.
- These factors led to the **Prayer Book Rebellion** directed by a Cornish landowner named Humphrey Arundell. The rebels demanded a return to practices that had been accepted under Henry VIII. Around 2000 people marched to Exeter on 10 July 1549 and laid siege to the city.
- Lord Russell, with an 8000-strong royal army, suppressed the rebels. They broke the siege and pursued the rebels back into Cornwall. Around 4000 people were killed in the fighting.
- The death toll, plus the violent death of leaders like Robert Welshe, meant that very few people were willing to consider resisting again.

Key point

The changes brought about by the Reformation led to a change in people's relationships with the Church.

People were mainly interested in how the Reformation affected their **day-to-day lives**

- For ordinary people, the biggest impacts were those which changed religious practices they had taken comfort in for their whole lives.
- Among ordinary peasants, fewer than twenty per cent of people were genuinely **evangelical**. This mattered little to the nobility and monarchy.
- The main tool used to try to convert people to evangelical and Protestant ideas was to preach in public. Hugh Latimer did so in Bristol and Matthew Price in the Severn Valley. This did have some effect where a few communities stripped their church before being forced to.
- The dissolution of the chantries removed the last form of monastery, which prayed for people's souls after death. These had been of great comfort to people who had lost loved ones. As a result, people stopped leaving their money to the Church and instead left their money to charities.

Test yourself

1 Which city did the Western Rebellion lay siege to?

2 How did churches avoid their wealth being stolen by the Crown?

The Reformation **lessened** the importance of the Church in people's lives

- The sale of church treasures often happened before the commissioners arrived. This was not evidence of people accepting the reformers' ideas, it was more people making sure that the wealth of their church was not simply stolen by the Crown.
- Elsewhere, people simply took away the treasures of the church themselves. There are still valuable items that have become family heirlooms which were once the property of the Church.
- The Second Act of Uniformity acknowledged that **absenteeism** (not attending church) was a major problem. People would even travel miles, on foot, to get to another church that was using the old prayer book.
- More importantly, people stopped leaving money to the Church. This forced them to reconsider whether the Church could help them in the afterlife. In the long run, this would severely damage the relationship between the people and the Church.

Stretch and challenge

Explain the impact of the dissolution of the monasteries on the people of England. (Don't forget to refer to different levels of society.)

Most, but not all of the **nobility** were inclined to **support** Protestantism

- The Crown relied on the **nobility** (lords, earls and so on) and the **gentry** (for example, Sir Francis Drake) to run the country in their various localities. They took their orders from the Crown and then controlled their regions accordingly.
- Unlike the peasantry, the nobility and gentry were educated. The nature of Protestantism was such that the more people read and discussed, generally they became open to its ideas (think of the impact of Anne Boleyn on Henry VIII).
- There were some exceptions, for example, John Scudamore was an MP who was able to buy up a great deal of land and even Dore Abbey, but who remained Catholic in his heart.
- The Throckmorton family were different. George Throckmorton stood up to speak out against the annulment and later the break with Rome. This said, he was loyal and even raised troops to help defeat the Pilgrimage of Grace.

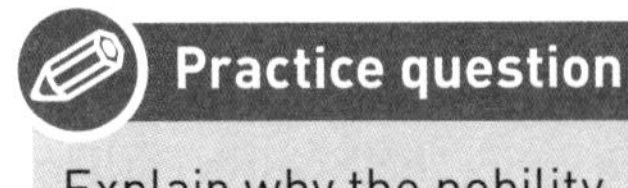

Practice question

Explain why the nobility generally favoured Protestantism.

(10 marks)

Eliminate irrelevance

Below are a sample exam-style question and a paragraph written in answer to this question. Read the paragraph and identify parts of the paragraph that are not directly relevant to the question. Draw a line through the information that is irrelevant and justify your deletions in the margin.

Explain how religious reforms under Somerset led to the Prayer Book Rebellion. (10 marks)

The Prayer Book Rebellion took place in 1549 and was partly caused by religion. In the south-west of England, people tended to be very old-fashioned in their views, and therefore resisted the attempts of the government to make the Church more Protestant. The rebellion also took place because Lord Somerset had imposed a new sheep tax which hit the livelihoods of the Cornish and Devonian people very hard. The rebels were also very angry about how the clergy in the south-west were being treated by these reforms. Eventually, the rebellion was put down by a rebellion led by Lord Russell.

Doing reliability well

Below are a series of attributions from various sources. Consider the attribution and make a comment about its reliability after having rated it. Consider the following concepts and try to use them in your evaluation of the attribution:

- **Vested interest**: the source is written so that the writer can protect their power or their financial interests.
- **Second-hand report**: the writer of the source is not an eyewitness, but is relying on someone else's account.
- **Expertise**: the source is written on a subject on which the author (for example a historian) is an expert.
- **Political bias**: a source is written by a politician and it reflects their political views.
- **Reputation**: a source is written to protect the writer's reputation.

Source	Rating	Reason for rating
Anne Askew, a Protestant poet, produced an account of her torture in the Tower of London in June 1546. It was smuggled out to her friends	/10	
A sixteenth-century painting entitled 'Coronation of King Edward the Sixth, Popery banished True Religion Restored'	/10	
Yorkshire clergyman Michael Sherbrook, explaining why he took part in plundering one of the dissolved monasteries	/10	

10 The Impact of Empire on Britain 1688–c.1730

10.1 Ireland, 1688–c.1730

REVISED

The 'Glorious Revolution' led to war in Ireland

- By 1688, Ireland had already been colonised by the English for centuries. Although most Irish people were **Catholics**, **Protestants** had settled in **plantations** (Irish land they took over) on much of the island, especially in the north. Tension between them was great.
- In 1688, the English Parliament invited William of Orange to come and become King William III, forcing Catholic King James II to flee. English politicians called this the '**Glorious Revolution**'.
- Most Irish Catholics were **Jacobites** (supporters of James) while most Irish Protestants were **Williamites**.
- Conflict between Williamites and Jacobites was part of a wider European war – the **Nine Years' War**. James had the support of the French King Louis XIV, William's enemy.

Key point

War between Williamites and Jacobites led to English control of Ireland with power in the hands of the Protestant minority.

The Williamites defeated the Jacobites

Rebellion: in 1689 James landed in Ireland with a French army and was joined by Irish Catholic troops led by the Earl of Tyrconnell

→ **Siege:** at first the Jacobites were successful. They swept through Ireland and laid siege to Derry. William sent troops and ships and broke the siege in July, freeing the Protestant inhabitants

→ **Confusion:** William's army landed near Belfast but was struck down by disease. At the **Battle of the Boyne** in 1690, there was no clear winner, but James left Ireland causing the Jacobites to lose heart and William entered Dublin in triumph

→ **Showdown:** the final battle was at Aughrim in 1691. Two international armies faced each other and the Williamites won

→ **Settlement:** the war ended with the **Treaty of Limerick** in 1691, which allowed many Jacobite soldiers to leave for France

As a result of the war, power in Ireland rested with a Protestant ruling class

- Following the Treaty many Catholic landowners lost their land and Catholics lost their army and their say in government. England now ruled Ireland.
- Harsh **penal laws** took away the rights of Irish Catholics to carry weapons, to study overseas, to inherit property, to hold public positions or to vote.
- Wealthy Protestants, known as the **Ascendancy**, became very powerful and dominated the government of Ireland. However, many poorer Protestants, as well as Catholics, resented British and Ascendancy rule.
- The Protestant Ascendancy viewed its relationship with England as two parallel kingdoms. In England, however, Ireland was clearly seen as a **colony**.

Flow chart

Below is a blank flow diagram into which you must put five key events that led to English control of Ireland. The first one has been completed for you. A list of events that you could have chosen can be found opposite.

The 'Glorious Revolution'				

Considering usefulness

Below is a source on the war between Williamites and Jacobites in Ireland. Look at the source, and consider how useful it is for a historian wanting to find out why the Jacobites lost the war. Rate its content, provenance and context for usefulness out of 10 and then explain why you think this source is useful to a historian or not.

SOURCE A *James' words to his advisers after the Battle of the Boyne.*

When the Irish soldiers faced the challenge of battle they fled from the field like cowards, allowing the enemy to seize our provisions. They could not be persuaded to come back and fight, even though our losses were only small. From now on I have decided never to lead an Irish army. I now resolve to look after myself, and so, gentlemen, must you.

Content	Provenance	Context

Stretch and challenge

These events had great significance for the future of the British Isles, right up to the present day. Look carefully through the events: what do you think was the *most important* reason why the English succeeded in gaining control of Ireland, and why?

Test yourself

1 Why did war break out in Ireland in 1689?
2 How was Ireland ruled after the war?
3 What was the impact on Ireland of British control after 1691?

Practice question

Explain why there was war in Ireland between 1689 and 1691. (10 marks)

10.2 Scotland

REVISED

A **Jacobite** rebellion against William III was defeated

- In 1688, Scotland and England were ruled under the **Union of Crowns**, with separate kingdoms and Parliaments but under one king.
- There were deep divisions between the **Highland** and **Lowland** Scots, and between Jacobites and Williamites.
- The Scottish Parliament and many Lowlanders backed William because he was a Protestant and his wife Mary – who shared the Crown – was James' daughter and therefore a **Stuart** from the Scottish royal family.
- Others – including most Highlanders – supported James because he was a Stuart and also because the Scottish Parliament had not been consulted and so William becoming king was illegal under Scottish law.
- William's forces faced **Jacobite rebellion** at the **Battles of Killiecrankie** and **Dunkeld**, which they ultimately won. William imposed military control of the Highlands, where people deeply resented William's commanders from the Campbell clan.
- William decreed that James's clan supporters would be pardoned if they swore loyalty to him by 1 January 1692. After the chief of the clan McDonald swore the oath a day later than the deadline, Williamite soldiers killed 38 of the clan in the 1692 **Massacre of Glencoe**. Forty more died of cold and hunger.

Key point

The accession of William III led to conflict in Scotland, ultimately resulting in the Act of Union in 1707, bringing prosperity to many in the Lowlands, but disaster to the Highland way of life.

The **Darien Scheme** caused economic disaster for Scotland which led to the **1707 Act of Union**

Depression: in the 1690s, Scotland's economy was in crisis, due to government neglect, poor harvests and English laws that damaged Scotland's trade

→ **Solution?** Large numbers of Scottish people invested in a scheme to settle and trade at Darien in Panama. The project was a disaster due to fatal mistakes, terrible conditions and undermining actions by the English government

→ **Crisis:** in the early 1700s, relations between the English and Scottish governments worsened. However, as a result of economic and political pressure and bribery, the Scottish Parliament agreed to a union with England

→ **Union:** the **Act of Union** was passed in 1707, creating the Kingdom of Great Britain. The Scottish Parliament was abolished. The act was very unpopular with many Scots

- Union with England brought economic benefits to many Scots, especially Lowlanders, as trade and business improved.
- Union was a disaster for Highlanders, bringing poverty and military occupation.

Practice question

Explain why the Scottish Parliament voted for union with England in 1707. (10 marks)

The **1715 Jacobite rebellion** against George I failed

- After a German nobleman became the **Hanoverian** King George I, Jacobites rose up in an attempt to try to put the son of James II, known as the 'Old Pretender', on the throne.
- The Jacobite forces, led by the Earl of Mar, were defeated.

Stretch and challenge

Look at the reasons why the Scottish Parliament voted for the Act of Union, and then at the resulting effects on Scotland. Was union with England the right decision for Scotland at that time, and why?

Test yourself

1 Why did Jacobite rebellions in Scotland fail?
2 Why did the Scottish Parliament agree to the Act of Union in 1707?
3 How did union with England affect people in Scotland?

Event overview grid

Complete a one-sentence summary of the events listed in the grid below.

Event	Summary
Scottish reactions to the 'Glorious Revolution'	
The 1689 Jacobite Rebellion	
The Massacre of Glencoe	
The Darien Scheme	
The Act of Union	
The 1715 Rebellion	

Identify an argument

Below are a series of definitions, a sample exam-style question and two sample conclusions. One of the conclusions achieves a high level because it contains an argument. The other achieves a lower level because it contains only description and assertion. Identify which is which. The mark scheme on pages 180–2 will help you.

- **description:** a detailed account
- **assertion:** a statement of fact or an opinion which is not supported by a reason
- **explanation:** a statement which explains or justifies something
- **argument:** an assertion justified with a reason.

Study Sources B and C. 'The massacre of Glencoe was planned from the very top of government.' How far do Sources B and C convince you that this statement is correct? Use the sources and your knowledge to explain your answer. **(20 marks)**

SOURCE B *John Dalrymple, Secretary of State for Scotland, 1692.*

My Lord Argyle tells me that Glencoe has not taken the oath, at which I rejoice. It is a great work of charity to be exact in the rooting out of that damnable sect, the worst in all the Highlands.

SOURCE C *An order received on 12 February 1692 by Captain Robert Campbell from Major Duncanson.*

You are hereby ordered to fall upon the rebels, the McDonalds of Glencoe, and put all to the sword under seventy ... This is by the king's special command, for the good and safety of the country, that these miscreants [criminals] be cut off root and branch.

In Source B the government minister in charge of Scotland is saying he is glad that the chief of the McDonalds was late signing the oath of allegiance to King William. This gave the government an excuse to punish his people. This suggests that the government wanted the massacre to happen, but, it does not prove that they planned it. Source C, an official order from a high officer, does say that the order comes from the king, which strongly supports the statement. However, the order is not directly from the king and Duncanson could be saying this just to persuade Campbell to carry out the killings. Taken together, the two sources – one from high up in government and the other from the army – do strongly support the statement, but not with absolute certainty.

In Source B the government minister in charge of Scotland is saying he is glad that the chief of the McDonalds was late signing the oath of allegiance to King William. This gave the government an excuse to punish his people. It shows that the government wanted this. In Source C an official order to carry out the massacre says that it is an order from the king. It suggests that the government was directly involved in planning the massacre. I therefore believe the statement is likely to be correct, but not certain.

10.3 Emigration, 1688–c.1730

REVISED

Large numbers of people **emigrated** from the British Isles to the Americas

- Poverty and lack of opportunity forced many people to leave the British Isles to start a new life in North America and the Caribbean. Many were affected by harvest failures, famine, the enclosure of land or the Ulster plantations.
- Many more people were leaving England than arriving, so net emigration (the number of emigrants minus the number of immigrants) was high.
- Most people who emigrated to the Americas had to live a number of years as someone else's property – after which they would be free.

Key point

Emigration was higher than immigration during this period – different groups found new lives for differing reasons and had varying experiences.

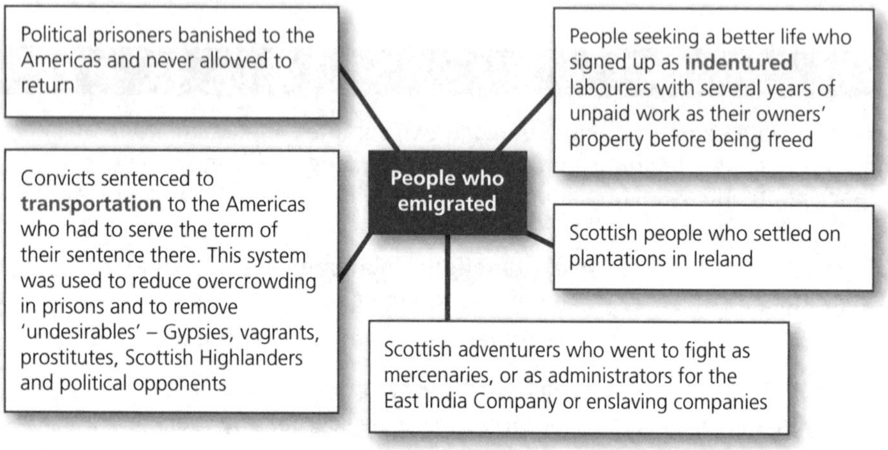

People who emigrated

- Political prisoners banished to the Americas and never allowed to return
- People seeking a better life who signed up as **indentured** labourers with several years of unpaid work as their owners' property before being freed
- Convicts sentenced to **transportation** to the Americas who had to serve the term of their sentence there. This system was used to reduce overcrowding in prisons and to remove 'undesirables' – Gypsies, vagrants, prostitutes, Scottish Highlanders and political opponents
- Scottish people who settled on plantations in Ireland
- Scottish adventurers who went to fight as mercenaries, or as administrators for the East India Company or enslaving companies

Emigrants to the Americas had a range of **experiences**

- There was a very high death rate due to poverty, disease, hard work or abuse by plantation owners and employers.
- Many of those who survived until they were freed from indenture did very well. They applied their skills to building a new life and some achieved high status.
- Some joined the armed forces used to put down attacks by Native Americans or slave uprisings.
- Some Scots found advancement in Jamaica and others were politically active there.

Test yourself

Why did so many people emigrate from the British Isles in this period?

Checklist

Below is a list of reasons why people may have emigrated from the British Isles during this period. Tick or highlight those items which you know *were* a factor at the time.

- Scottish Protestants took over Irish land after the treaty of Limerick in 1691.
- English people agreed to work as enslaved labourers in America to be sold in auction for a fixed number of years before getting freedom.
- Irish Catholics took over Scottish land after the 1691 defeat of the Jacobite uprising.
- Convicted prisoners were sent to North America as a punishment.
- Scottish Jacobite rebels were banished to the Caribbean and not allowed to return.
- Irish soldiers served in the French army.
- Vagrants and beggars were transported until the 1718 Transportation Act stopped this.
- Some Scottish emigrants worked for the East India Company.
- Prostitutes were forced to leave England.

Stretch and challenge

How accurate would it be to say that the main reason for emigration was an attack on the poor by British authorities?

Practice question

Study Sources D and E. 'Indentured service was a form of slavery.' How far do Sources D and E convince you that the statement is correct? Use the sources and your knowledge to explain your answer.
(20 marks)

SOURCE D *From the novel* Moll Flanders *by Daniel Defoe (1722).*

They were of two sorts. Either (1) such as were brought over by masters of ships to be sold as servants ... but they are more properly called slaves. Or (2) such as are transported from Newgate and other prisons, after having been found guilty of crimes punishable by death. When they come here we make no difference: the planters buy them, and they work together in the field till their time is out.

SOURCE E *From an account in the 1700s of the English sugar plantations.*

The colonies were plentifully supplied with Christian servants ... being excellent planters and soldiers ... that they neither feared the insurrection [uprising] of their Negroes, nor any invasion of a foreign enemy.

10.4 The Atlantic trade

REVISED

Britain came to dominate the **transatlantic trade in enslaved Africans**

- Britain's trade in enslaved Africans was organised from fortresses along the west African coast. British ships brought guns, cloth and iron goods in exchange for gold, ivory, hardwoods, spice and – mainly – kidnapped and enslaved African women, men and children.
- The '**triangular trade**' involved British ships bringing goods to the west African coast to trade in exchange for enslaved people who were transported across the Atlantic to the Americas to work on **plantations**. Sugar, tobacco and other raw materials grown by their labour was then shipped to Britain.
- The British trade in enslaved Africans was at first entirely controlled by the **Royal African Company** which was given a **monopoly** of the trade by the monarchy. This meant that it was the only company allowed to be involved.
- Its monopoly was removed by Parliament in 1698. Private businesses then ran the slave trade, which expanded, bringing more wealth to Britain and devastation to parts of Africa. Some African rulers and merchants, however, also profited greatly.
- As demand for slave-produced goods grew, so the demand for labour – and therefore the slave trade – grew.
- Millions of Africans were transported and enslaved under the system of **chattel slavery**, which meant that each slave and her or his children were the owner's property to be bought and sold.
- This had a devastating social, political, economic and humanitarian effect on west Africa, taking away many of the strongest and most productive people.
- The **Treaty of Utrecht** in 1713 gave Britain the contract (*asiento*) to supply slaves to the Spanish colonies in the Americas for 30 years.

Key point

Britain profited immeasurably from the Atlantic slave trade.

Test yourself

1. How did Britain gain control of the transportation and trade in enslaved Africans?
2. How did the plantation system contribute to the growing power and wealth of Britain?
3. How did enslaved people resist?

Practice question

Explain how the ending of the Royal African Company monopoly increased profits for British businesses from the triangular trade.

(10 marks)

The plantation system depended on **indentured** and **enslaved** workers

- British settlers in the Americas developed large plantations, mainly of sugar in the Caribbean and tobacco in North America.
- The plantations depended on large numbers of workers. At first, many of these were indentured labourers and convicts from England, Ireland and Scotland.
- As demand grew in Britain for sugar, tobacco and other **commodities**, the workforce consisted increasingly of Africans brought over on the slave ships. The plantation system came to depend entirely on a continual source of slave labour from Africa.

Britain profited greatly from the trade in enslaved Africans

- Britain's American colonies became whole systems called **plantocracies**, every aspect of which was controlled by plantation owners. These systems brought great wealth to plantation owners, ship owners, traders and financiers and they were backed up by military force and the law.
- The plantations had strong support in London due to: access to raw materials, new markets for British goods and work opportunities for British people, and it gave Britain an advantage over other European powers.
- Some historians think the plantocracies were inefficient and not cost effective. Others think they were highly organised businesses that paved the way for the factories of the industrial age.

Stretch and challenge

In 1745 a British writer about financial matters called Malachy Postlethwayt wrote: 'If we have no Negroes ... will this not turn many hundreds of thousands of British manufacturers a begging?' Explain what he meant and why he thought this was true.

Resistance and uprisings by the enslaved were feared and punished severely

- Slave resistance on the plantations – sometimes supported by indentured labourers – was usually punished violently. Planters continually feared uprisings and therefore divided white indentured labourers and enslaved Africans who shared a common cause.
- Some uprisings were successful, notably by the Jamaican Maroons, who used **guerrilla** tactics against the British. In 1739, the British government signed a peace treaty with them to end the First Maroon War.
- Pirate attacks, African opposition and slave uprisings on ships and plantations threatened the system.
- Some African rulers and traders collaborated with the slave trade while others opposed it.

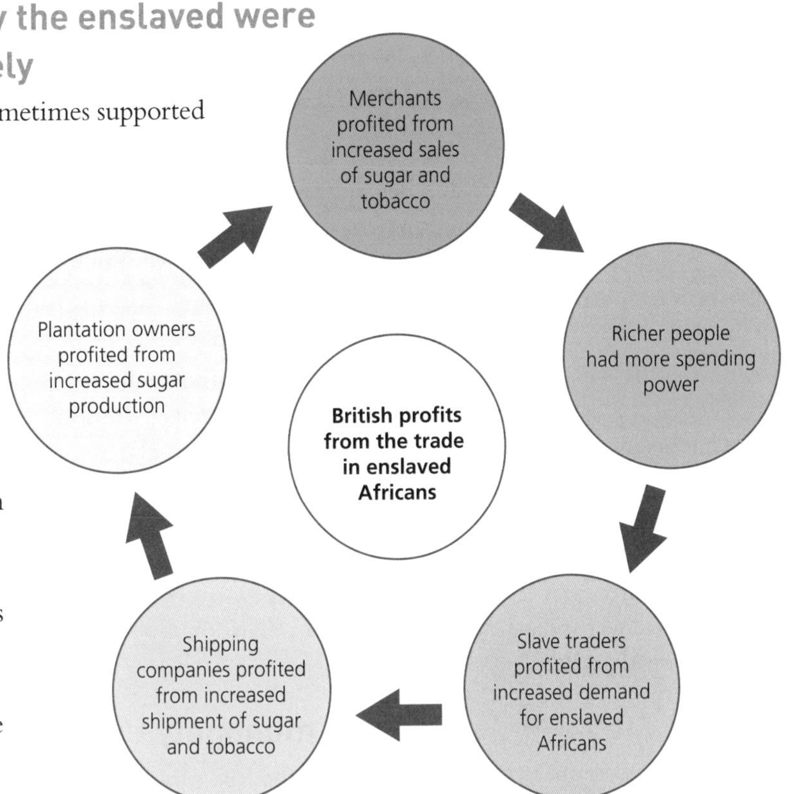

Turning assertion into argument

Below is a sample exam-style question and a series of assertions. Read the question and then add a justification to each of the assertions to turn it into an argument.

Explain how effective the plantation system was at making money. **(10 marks)**

The system was an effective way of making money because …

The system was not such an effective way of making money because …

Considering usefulness

Look at the source below, and consider how useful it is based on the criteria of content, provenance and context. Rate each one for usefulness out of 10 and then explain why you think this source is useful to a historian or not.

SOURCE F *Extract from Virginia Act for Suppressing of Outlying Slaves (1691).*

For the prevention of the abominable mixture [of Europeans and non-Europeans] ... be it enacted ... that for the time to come, whatsoever English or other white man or woman being free shall intermarry with a negroe, mulatto, or Indian man or woman, bond or free, shall within three months of such marriage be banished and removed from this dominion for ever.

Content	Provenance	Context

10.5 The role of the East India Company

REVISED

The **East India Company** increased its economic and political power

- The East India Company (EIC) began as a small-scale capitalist venture, which set up 'factories' or trading posts on the Indian coast and carried spices and textiles to Britain by ship, in return for gold and silver bullion.
- Its aim was to carry out trade between Britain and Asia, and to rival the Portuguese who were dominating trade in the area.
- After the EIC was granted a monopoly of trade with Asia by **royal charter**, it grew in power – it could mint its own money, run its own justice system and had its own army and navy. It fought the Dutch and Portuguese to take over trade in parts of India.
- In the 1680s, the EIC went to war against Dutch and French competitors and against the **Mughal** Empire that ruled India. War with the Mughal Emperor Aurangzeb ended in defeat, but under Governor Josiah Child the EIC set up a factory in Calcutta (now Kolkata) in 1690, which would grow to be its headquarters.

Key point

The East India Company survived many setbacks to become the dominant European power in India, bringing great wealth to Britain through trade.

Attempts to remove the EIC's **monopoly** failed

- Private businesses in Britain wanted to end the EIC's monopoly. Parliament set up an inquiry which revealed deep corruption in the company. Weavers in Britain also marched against the EIC in protest against the import of Indian cloth.
- The EIC was on the brink of collapse.
- When King William renewed the EIC's monopoly, Parliament reacted by setting up a new company and forcing the EIC to close. Before Parliament managed to close it down, the EIC bought shares in the new company and merged with it in 1702. The EIC survived.

The trade with India brought great wealth to Britain

The EIC was part of a global system of trade and colonialism that was driven by the desire for profit and that brought increasing wealth to its investors

→ After the merger the EIC still held its monopoly. It grew in strength and wealth, with new markets in South-East Asia, a growing opium trade with China and a *firman* (decree) from the Mughal emperor, allowing it to trade freely across India

→ By the end of the century, the EIC ruled India and controlled half the world's trade

Delete as applicable

Below are a sample exam-style question and a paragraph written in answer to this question. Read the paragraph and decide which of the possible options (underlined) is most appropriate. Delete the least appropriate options and complete the paragraph by justifying your selection.

'The East India Company's activities in India brought great benefit to Britain.' How far do Sources G–I convince you that this statement is correct? Use the sources and your knowledge to explain your answer. **(20 marks)**

SOURCE G *EIC governor, Sir Josiah Child's, instructions to set up a base in Bengal, December 1687.*

Establish ... civil and military power, and create and secure such a large revenue ... as may be the foundation of a large, well-grounded sure English dominion in India for all time to come.

SOURCE H *An extract from the Mughal emperor's* firman, *1717.*

All goods and necessities which [the company's] factors bring or carry away by land or water [are] to be free from custom duties.

SOURCE I *From a leaflet describing weavers' complaints, 1720.*

Europe like a body in a warm bath with its veins opened ... and her bullion which is the life-blood of her trade flows to India to enrich the Great Mogul's subjects.

Source G shows that Child clearly wanted to increase British power in India and make it permanent. Source H shows that the Mughal emperor allowed the British to trade freely without paying tax. However, in Source I English weavers feel that India, not Britain, is gaining from the deal. I agree to a <u>great/fair/limited</u> extent that the sources show that Britain benefited from the EIC.

Stretch and challenge

The company was in real trouble at the end of the seventeenth century but was doing very well in the early eighteenth century. What were the main reasons for this change?

Practice question

Explain how the East India Company was organised. (10 marks)

Test yourself

1 How was the East India Company organised?
2 Why did the East India Company nearly fail in the late seventeenth century?
3 How did the company recover in the early eighteenth century?

10.6 The British economy

REVISED

The **Bank of England** and the **national debt** were set up in 1694

- The government needed money for its wars. Financiers established the Bank of England, which lent money to King William at a rate of interest.
- This became the **national debt** – a loan owed by the government, rather than the monarch, and paid for by the taxpayers.

The **British economy** boomed, but there were risks

- The credit system enabled new business projects to grow. It also made it possible for the Royal Navy to be rebuilt. The combination of capital investment and military force protecting and expanding the colonies increased Britain's wealth.
- This increasing wealth helped to start the Industrial Revolution. These economic advancements saw power shifting from the monarch towards the owners of wealth and their representatives in Parliament.
- But there were risks:
  - In time of war, trade routes became dangerous and the system came under threat.
  - The **joint stock system** (with businesses owned by shareholders) always carried the danger that companies could collapse. This happened spectacularly in the case of the South Sea Bubble of 1720.

Britain became a **world power**

- The global trading system managed from London's financial markets and policed by the Royal Navy gave Britain a boost in trade and a fast growth in profits. This strengthened the development of **capitalism** – the economic system based on private businesses controlling trade and industry for profit.
- Based on enslavement and empire, this system set Britain on the path to eventual world dominance.

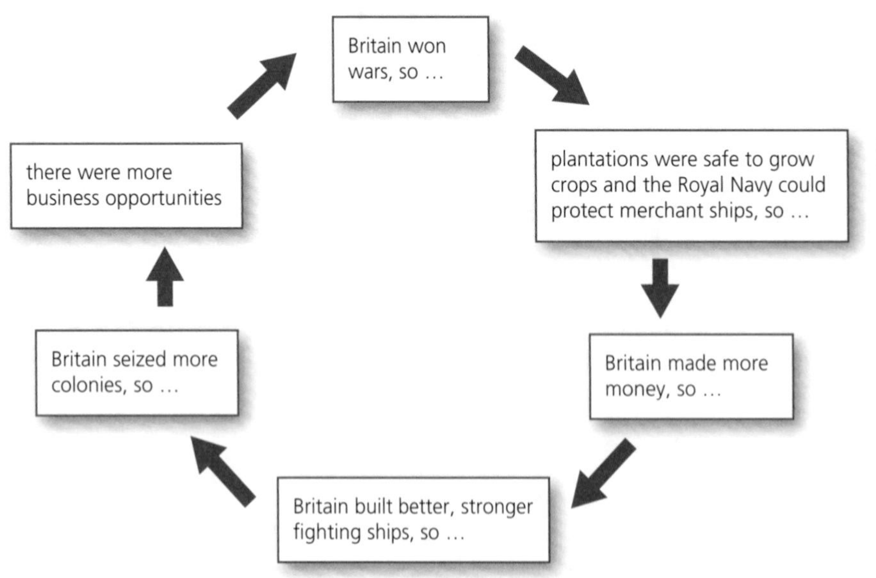
Britain won wars, so …
plantations were safe to grow crops and the Royal Navy could protect merchant ships, so …
Britain made more money, so …
Britain built better, stronger fighting ships, so …
Britain seized more colonies, so …
there were more business opportunities

Key point

The establishment of the Bank of England and the national debt, along with the economic successes of the colonies, established Britain as a world power.

There was a boom in trade

Those involved in the trade made huge profits

Capitalism developed and strengthened

This created new employment opportunities

The system was globalised and all aspects were interlinked

Test yourself

1. How did the British economy change after 1688?
2. How did the Bank of England and joint stock companies help build Britain's global power?
3. What caused the collapse of the South Sea Company and what was its impact?

Which is best?

Below are two examples of part of a longer answer to a 20-mark question for this paper. Read both, compare to the mark scheme on pages 180–2 and give both a mark out of 20. On a separate piece of paper, explain why the one you have chosen is best.

'The main cause of Britain's wealth in this period was the establishment of the Bank of England.' How far do these sources convince you that this statement is correct? Use the sources and your knowledge to explain your answer. **(20 marks)**

SOURCE J *Writer and journalist Daniel Defoe in* The Complete English Tradesman, *1725.*

Credit makes war, and makes peace; raises armies, fits out navies, fights battles, besieges towns ... and fills the Exchequer and the banks with as many millions as it pleases, upon demand.

SOURCE K *Malachy Postlethwayt, a financial writer, 1745–46.*

If we have no Negroes, we can have no sugars, tobaccos, rice, rum etc ... consequently the public revenue, arising from the importation of plantation produce, must be annihilated. And will this not turn many hundreds of thousands of British manufacturers a begging? The extensive employment of our shipping in, to, and from America ... and the daily bread of the most considerable part of our British manufacturers, are owing primarily to the labour of Negroes ... The Negro trade, therefore ... may be justly esteemed an inexhaustible fund of wealth and naval power to this nation.

a) When the Bank of England was set up in 1694 it made possible the national debt, which meant the government could borrow to fight wars. Victory in these wars extended Britain's empire, giving more and more land from which Britain could take raw materials and in which they could set up plantations.

In Source J, Defoe explains how the credit provided by the Bank made it possible for Britain to win wars and make money. His argument supports the statement that it was the Bank that enabled Britain to become rich. Source K also describes how Britain's wealth depended on plantations in its colonies. However, Postlethwayt argues that the success of British business is due to slave labour. It is true that the use of enslaved Africans as labour made profit for shipping companies, plantation owners and merchants, as well as funds for waging war. According to this source the plantocracies, rather than the Bank, were the main cause of British wealth.

In reality, Britain's global system of trade and profit relied on the plantocracy, investment by banks and military power, and all were feeding each other. As the sources show, no one factor was making Britain rich, so I agree with the statement partly, but not fully.

b) In Source J, Defoe explains how the credit provided by the Bank made it possible for Britain to win wars and make money. His argument supports the statement that it was the Bank that enabled Britain to become rich.

Source K describes how Britain's wealth depended on plantations in its colonies. However, Postlethwayt argues that the success of British business is due to slave labour. According to this source the plantocracies, rather than the Bank, were the main cause of British wealth.

I agree with the statement partly, but not fully.

Stretch and challenge

Looking back over this section and the previous ones about the Atlantic and Asian trades, how do you think these changes affected migration to Britain?

Practice question

Explain the causes and effects of the 1720 South Sea Bubble.

(10 marks)

10.7 The social and political impact of empire

REVISED

All **classes** in Britain **benefited** from the enslavement system

- All classes of people in Britain benefited from the enslavement system, which provided work for people in a wide range of occupations. Chains from the Midlands, tools made in Wales, guns from Birmingham, silks and wines from the West Country were among the products made for use on the plantations. Those who benefited included tailors, weavers, carpenters, glassmakers, brewers, potters, printers and all those involved in shipbuilding.
- Ports such as London, Liverpool and Bristol experienced fast growth and economic boom by sending out slave ships and profiting from the trade. Buildings and statues linked to enslavement still stand today.
- Many major institutions such as the British Museum and Guy's Hospital were founded by people who profited from the slave trade.

Key point

Britain's success as a world power led to large-scale changes within political and social life in Britain.

Coffee, brought from Arabia by the East India Company, transformed social and political life

- Men with power and influence discussed the issues of the day in the coffee houses, which had a great influence on political and economic decisions. Many banks and insurance companies were started in coffee houses.
- Coffee houses were popular across the classes. Some also sold alcohol and some were linked to criminal activity.
- The two-party system developed at a time when only the elite could vote. The two parties were the Whigs and the Tories. Each party had its own newspaper.
- Ideas were spread through these broadsheets, newspapers and magazines, which were read in the coffee houses.

Test yourself

1. How were the lives of people in Britain affected by the slave plantation system?
2. How did trade with Asia affect life in Britain?
3. What was the significance of the coffee houses?

Consumerism grew with the popularity of goods from Asia and the Americas

- Commodities from Asia such as textiles, tea and ceramics became highly fashionable. Asian craftspeople adapted their styles to suit Western tastes, while Western craftspeople copied Asian styles.
- Slave-grown sugar and tobacco from the Americas became widely popular and, as demand grew, supply and competition increased, forcing down prices and making them accessible to more people.

Ideas of **racial hierarchy** took hold

- The system of enslavement and expansion of empire were justified by dehumanising enslaved and colonised people. Racist ideas that white people were superior to people of colour became widespread in Europe. **Plantocracy racism** claimed there were natural differences between Africans and Europeans.
- At the same time, ideas of individual religious and political liberty for people in Britain began to develop, and a few people began to oppose enslavement.
- Life for black people in Britain was complex: some lived as free working people while others were brought as enslaved servants and were denied freedom.

Stretch and challenge

The changes described in this chapter happened as a result of the events described in Chapter 2: the Atlantic and Asian trades and the changes in Britain's economy. Can you design a poster to show how all these factors were interlinked?

Developing the detail

Below are a sample exam-style question and a paragraph written in answer to this question. The paragraph contains a limited amount of detail. Annotate the paragraph to add additional detail to the answer.

Explain how the growth of empire and trade affected the lives of people in Britain between 1688 and the 1730s. **(10 marks)**

New trade routes brought commodities from Asia that became fashionable. Ordinary people could afford products that had previously been luxuries. People of all classes in Britain benefited economically from the plantation and enslavement system. Racist ideas had a terrible effect on the lives of black people. Business expansion brought new opportunities and risks.

Practice question

Study Sources L and M. 'Access to commodities from Asia and the Americas improved the lives of people in Britain.' How far do these sources convince you that this statement is correct? Use the sources and your knowledge to explain your answer. (20 marks)

SOURCE L *Thomas Tryon, in* A Way to Health, Long Life and Happiness, *1691.*

Of late 'tis grown the fashion ... now every Plowman [farmer] has his Pipe to himself ... How much precious time do Men spend in smoking Tobacco, dosing and stupefying their Senses? And how many through such neglect of time ... have half starved their poor Families, and involved themselves in many Mischiefs and Inconveniences?

SOURCE M *Daniel Defoe, in* Everybody's Business is Nobody's Business, *1725.*

Plain country Joan is now turned into a fine London madam, can drink tea, take snuff, and carry herself as high as the best. She must have a hoop, too, as well as her mistress; and her poor scanty petticoat is changed into a good silk one, four or five yards wide at the least.

Event overview grid for the whole unit

Complete a one-sentence summary of the events listed in the grid below.

Event	Summary
Anglo-Mughal War 1686	
'Glorious Revolution' 1688	
Parliamentary inquiry into the East India Company 1688	
Treaty of Limerick 1691	
Massacre of Glencoe 1692	
Establishment of the Bank of England 1694	
Penal Laws 1695	

Event	Summary
End of the Royal African Company monopoly 1698	
Darien Scheme 1698	
The Act of Union 1707	
Treaty of Utrecht 1713	
Jacobite Rebellion 1715	
South Sea Bubble 1720	
Treaty between British forces and the Jamaican Maroons 1739	

Indicative mark scheme

This is not a **full** exam board mark scheme. This simply represents what might characterise a full marks (level 5) or average (level 3) answer. The aim is always to 'answer the question. Level 1 answers (in case you are wondering) are those where you simply list a few facts but don't really use them to answer the question at all.

Paper 1 Section A: International Relations

Question 1: Outline… [5 marks]

Level	Marks	Mark scheme summary	Guidance
3	4–5	■ Demonstrates a **range of detailed** and accurate knowledge and understanding that is fully **relevant** to the question. ■ Presented as a narrative that shows clear understanding of the **sequence** or concurrence of events.	■ Don't try to write too much. One medium-length paragraph is enough. ■ 'Outline' means to show an overview of what happened, and in what order. ■ Make sure that you are writing about the right time period.

Question 2: Explain… [10 marks]

Level	Marks	Mark scheme summary	Guidance
5	9–10	■ Clear, detailed evidence. ■ Explicit analysis directed at the question. ■ A clear judgement.	■ The aim is to 'prove your point' – for example, make your point, support it with good, precise evidence, then explain clearly how it answers the question. ■ Do this twice (once for each factor) and add a conclusion which answers the question.
3	5–6	■ Some evidence used. ■ Basic/implicit analysis.	■ Either one developed paragraph or two less developed paragraphs.

Question 3: Do you think this is a fair comment…? [25 marks]

Level	Marks	Mark scheme summary	Guidance
5	21–25	■ Clear use of evidence from the interpretation, from your own knowledge of the other interpretations and from your own knowledge. ■ Explicit comparison of the interpretation with at least **two** of the others. ■ Considers how the interpretations can be both fair and unfair. ■ A clear judgement.	■ The question asks you to consider why this interpretation is fair and unfair. ■ Even modern sources, which to our eyes are fair, might be considered unfair by previous historians. ■ Each paragraph should link to the overall fairness of the interpretation mentioned in the question. ■ Naming an historian will earn credit
3	11–15	■ Some evidence used from the interpretation. ■ Some evidence of the other views used to compare to this view. ■ Possibly only one side – it is or isn't fair. ■ Undeveloped analysis.	■ You show how some historians would have agreed or how they would have disagreed, but not both.

Question 4: Why would some historians agree/disagree…? [20 + 5 marks]

Level	Marks	Mark scheme summary	Guidance
5	21–25	■ Clear use of evidence from the interpretation, from your own knowledge of the other interpretations and from your own knowledge. ■ Explicit comparison of the interpretation with at least **two** of the others. ■ Considers how the interpretations can be both fair and unfair. ■ A clear judgement.	■ The question is asking how would consider where different historians would have agreed or disagreed. ■ The best answers are balanced – some historians would have agreed with parts of the interpretation, but not the whole thing. ■ Each paragraph should link to the overall idea of how many historians would and would not have agreed. ■ Naming an historian will earn credit.
3	11–15	■ Some evidence used from the interpretation. ■ Some evidence of the other views used to compare to this view. ■ Possibly only one side – it is or isn't fair. ■ Undeveloped analysis.	■ You show how some historians would have agreed or how they would have disagreed, but not both.

Paper 1 Section B: Non-British depth studies

Question 1: Describe… [2 marks]

Level	Mark	Mark scheme summary	Guidance
N/A	2	▪ One point which has supporting detail.	▪ Each point should describe, rather than explaining. Keep it short – two sentences per point.

Question 2: Explain… [10 marks]

(The same as the 'Explain' question for the International Relations section above.)

Question 3: Which of these two sources is more useful…? [10 marks]

Level	Mark	Mark scheme summary	Guidance
5	9–10	▪ Clear, detailed evidence from the source and own knowledge. ▪ Explicit analysis directed at the question. ▪ A clear judgement.	▪ Remember that 'useful' means 'can you, as an historian, learn anything about this issue from this source?' There will always be something that you can use. ▪ Make sure you use your own knowledge to explain why this source was like it was. ▪ Do this for each source; add a conclusion which answers the question.
3	5–6	▪ Some evidence used from source. ▪ Possibly some use of own knowledge. ▪ Basic/implicit analysis.	▪ This is a good level to aim for if you are not too sure: either a single good paragraph or two brief underdeveloped paragraph

Question 4: How far do you agree with this statement…? [18 marks]

Level	Mark	Mark scheme summary	Guidance
5	5–18	▪ Clear, detailed evidence. ▪ Explicit discussion of the whole time period of the question. ▪ Considers points that both agree and disagree with the statement. ▪ There is an argument running from the start to the end of the essay. ▪ A clear judgement at the end.	▪ The question is asking for your opinion, but you should avoid saying 'I think'. Simply state it and prove it. ▪ Have a clear overall argument in mind from the beginning, and stick to it. ▪ Remember to consider the whole of the period – there is a good chance that opinions changed significantly across the period in question.
3	7–10	▪ Some evidence used from a range of periods. ▪ Reasonable attempt to answer using a range of evidence. ▪ Possibly only one side of the argument.	▪ Many students get stuck at this level, because they tell the examiner about a number of different events, without linking it together as an argument.

Paper 2: Thematic Studies

Question 1: Describe… [4 marks]

Level	Mark	Mark scheme summary	Guidance
N/A	4	▪ Two points which has supporting detail.	▪ Each point should describe, rather than explaining. Keep it short – two sentences per point.

Question 2: Explain why… [8 marks]

Level	Mark	Mark scheme summary	Guidance
4	7–8	▪ Clear, detailed evidence. ▪ Explicit analysis directed at the question. ▪ A clear judgement.	▪ This is the same as other 'Explain' questions, but only marked out of 8 ▪ Aim to 'prove your point' – make your point, prove it with good, precise evidence, then explain clearly how it answers the question. ▪ Do this twice, add a conclusion which answers the question.
3	5–6	▪ Some evidence used. ▪ Basic/implicit analysis.	▪ This is a good level to aim for if you are not too sure: either a single good paragraph or two brief underdeveloped paragraphs.

Question 3: How significant…? [14 marks]

Level	Mark	Mark scheme summary	Guidance
4	11–14	■ A thorough explanation that shows excellent analysis to explain overall significance. ■ Very detailed own knowledge. ■ A clear judgement that evaluates significance.	■ 'Significant' means 'importance in history', not just at the time. ■ Two very well-developed or three developed points that evaluate and judge the significance of the event. ■ For each point suggests how it was and was not significant. ■ Refer directly to the 'second order concept' in the question, for example, 'change'.
3	7–10	■ An explanation that uses analysis to explain overall significance. ■ Good own knowledge. ■ A judgement of significance.	■ Students who have written good answers will get stuck here if they only show how the event was or was significant.

Question 4: How far do you agree with this statement…? [24 marks]

Level	Mark	Mark scheme summary	Guidance
5	19–24	■ Clear, detailed evidence. ■ Explicit discussion of the whole time period of the question. ■ Considers points that both agree and disagree with the statement. ■ There is an argument which runs from the start to the end of the essay. ■ A clear judgement at the end.	■ The question is asking for your opinion, but you should avoid saying 'I think'. Simply state it and prove it. ■ Have a clear overall argument in mind from the beginning, and stick to it. ■ Remember to consider the whole of the period – there is a good chance that opinions changed significantly across the period in question.
3	11–15	■ Some evidence used from a range of periods. ■ Reasonable attempt to deliver an answer that looks at a range of evidence. ■ Possibly only one side of the argument.	■ Many students get stuck at this level, because they tell the examiner about a number of different events, without linking it together as an argument.

Paper 3: British Depth Studies

Question 1: Explain… [10 marks]

(The same as the 'Explain' question for the International Relations section above.)

Question 2 Do these sources convince you that…? [20 + 5 marks]

Level	Mark	Mark scheme summary	Guidance
5	21–25	■ Clear, detailed evidence from the sources and from own knowledge. ■ Explicit analysis of the sources to answer the question. ■ Considers how each source can be both convincing and unconvincing. ■ A clear judgement.	■ The question is NOT asking if you agree, it is asking if the sources could be used to persuade someone of the viewpoint. ■ Each paragraph should link the source to the question.
3	11–15	■ Some evidence used from each source. ■ Some evidence from own knowledge. ■ Possibly only one side of the argument. ■ Basic/implicit analysis.	■ Many students get stuck at this level, because they don't look at both sides of the sources.

TIP

If you are looking for the glossary you'll find it here: www.hoddereducation.co.uk/myrevisionnotes. It defines all the key terms found in **purple** in this book.